YOU DESERVE
THE BEST

Also available from Quality Press

TQM: A Step-by-Step Guide to Implementation
Charles N. Weaver

Where Leadership Begins: Key Skills of Today's Best Managers
Michael J. Langdon

A Basic Approach to Quality Control and SPC
Peter D. Mauch

Recovering Prosperity Through Quality:
The Midland City Story
Robert A. Schwarz

The Customer Is King!
R. Lee Harris

To request a complimentary catalog of publications,
call 800-248-1946.

YOU DESERVE THE BEST

A Consumer's Guide to Product Quality and Total Customer Satisfaction

Eugene R. Carrubba
Mark E. Snyder

ASQC Quality Press
Milwaukee, Wisconsin

*You Deserve the Best: A Consumer's Guide to Product Quality
and Total Customer Satisfaction*
Eugene R. Carrubba and Mark E. Snyder

Library of Congress Cataloging-in-Publication Data

Carrubba, Eugene R.
    You deserve the best: a consumer's guide to product quality and
total customer satisfaction/Eugene R. Carrubba, Mark E. Snyder.
        p. cm.
    Includes bibliographical references and index.
    ISBN 0-87389-144-9
    1. Consumer protection—United States—Handbooks, manuals, etc.
    2. Quality of products—United States—Handbooks, manuals, etc.
    3. Consumer satisfaction—United States—Handbooks, manuals, etc.
    I. Snyder, Mark E.   II. Title.
    HC110.C63C37   1993
    381.3'.4—dc20   93-4386
                                                                 CIP

©1993 by ASQC

Information in Appendixes A through G is taken from *Consumer's Resource Handbook*,
1992, which is available from the Consumer Information Center, U.S. Office of Consumer
Affairs, Pueblo, Colo.

10 9 8 7 6 5 4 3 2 1

ISBN 0-87389-144-9

Acquisitions Editor: Susan Westergard
Production Editor: Annette Wall
Marketing Administrator: Mark Olson
Set in Garamond Book by Linda J. Shepherd. Cover design by Barbara Adams.
Printed and bound by BookCrafters, Inc.

ASQC Mission: To facilitate continuous improvement and increase customer satisfaction by
identifying, communicating, and promoting the use of quality principles, concepts, and
technologies; and thereby be recognized throughout the world as the leading authority on,
and champion for, quality.

For a free copy of the ASQC Quality Press Publications Catalog, including ASQC membership information, call 800-248-1946.

Printed in the United States of America

  Printed on acid-free recycled paper

 ASQC
Quality Press
611 East Wisconsin Avenue
Milwaukee, Wisconsin 53202

DEDICATION

This book is dedicated to you—the consumer—and to consumers everywhere!

Contents

Appendixes   Consumer Assistance Directory

Figures and Tables

Preface

Many books have been written about quality, quality control, and quality assurance and their related disciplines, such as safety and reliability. In fact, just as the concern for quality has been increasing, so has the number of books on the subject. At times, it seems the number has increased exponentially each year!

These books address product quality almost exclusively from the perspective of the manufacturer. However, what about the buyer and user of the product—the consumer? Certainly it is important for the manufacturer to do the right things to deliver quality products. But it is also important (and given today's prices, perhaps essential) for the consumer to know what to do and what to look for to ensure that he or she gets a quality product. And it shouldn't stop there. The consumer should know what to do if he or she gets stuck with a less-than-satisfactory product.

This book is the first of its kind to treat product quality from the consumer's perspective. Too often, a consumer makes a bad decision (from a quality viewpoint) that costs him or her dearly in terms of lost enjoyment, potential embarrassment, money, or worse still, personal harm. It might be the lure of the advertisement, price, appearance, or some other factor that swings the pendulum in the direction of buying a product which later proves to have less than the desired quality. Then, lack of appropriate and timely action on the part of the consumer only aggravates an already bad situation.

As a matter of fact, there are many factors to consider when pursuing a quality product. This book is aimed at helping the consumer sort through these factors in lay terms, without the statistical mumbo-jumbo that characterizes other books on quality.

Statistical methodology is extremely important to the quality practitioner. This is as it should be, since statistics is an important building block of quality. However, the consumer need not be bogged down in this level of detail, nor will the reader of our book!

Instead, the approach taken in this book is to provide the consumer with a practical, down-to-earth understanding of quality considerations so that he or she can get the best value for the money. The book is written at a level that allows it to be readily used and applied. It treats quality from the viewpoint of the consumer looking in at the manufacturer and covers what it takes to make a customer satisfied—for total customer satisfaction is, or certainly should be, the aim of product manufacturers.

The book is limited to product quality. For the most part, it excludes issues related to service quality. This exclusion is not an oversight, nor is it because service issues are viewed to be of lesser importance. Rather, the authors believe that a separate, more focused treatment of this subject would be more appropriate. Nevertheless, the reader will find that some sections of this book apply to both product and service quality.

This book is structured in four parts. Part 1 gives the reader some background into the evolution of the assurance sciences—how they started and evolved, and where they are now. It provides an historical review, followed by a discussion of the various elements of the assurance sciences and how they relate to one another. It also covers what it takes to be a world-class quality manufacturer.

Part 2 provides important insights into what manufacturers should be doing to ensure quality. It helps a consumer weed out the potentially good manufacturers from the potentially bad. The overall quality activities which take place during the design, manufacture, and test of a product are described. Part 2 concludes with a discussion of the role of customer service.

Part 3 offers a practical how-to treatment of quality from the consumer's perspective. It includes important guidelines and tools to help make the best and most intelligent decisions about the product being considered. This part begins with a discussion of the meaning and cautions related to warranties and guarantees. Insight is given into the value, choices, and decisions surrounding service contracts, and the role of independent product testing and evaluation organizations is discussed. This is followed by a general view of customer satisfaction. Part 3 ends with a step-by-step description of how to select quality products.

Part 4 gives the "get-well" approaches that can be pursued to remedy post-purchase quality problems. It acts as a safety net for the consumer stuck with a less-than-acceptable situation. This part discusses help available from consumer assistance groups and the employment of legal remedies. The book concludes with a step-by-step plan of action to increase the chances of satisfactory resolution of outstanding problems.

The book is supplemented by seven appendices that provide the reader with an expansive consumer assistance directory. Included in this directory are names, addresses, and phone numbers of corporate consumer contacts, car manufacturers, Better Business Bureaus, trade and other dispute resolution programs, state, county, and city government consumer protection offices, and selected federal agencies.

Now you know how the book is organized. What is the best way for you to use it? Let's give you a road map! Obviously, the book is laid out so that as you proceed from front to back it gets into topics which are more directly relevant to you, the consumer. The early chapters (into the first half of Part 2) provide background information. As you proceed, the text covers things that you can and should do to get the best value for your money and become a satisfied consumer.

Of course, we highly recommend that you read the whole book. A better-informed consumer will generally be a more satisfied consumer. Nevertheless, you may have specific interests and issues at heart. If you just want to learn more about quality, you should read chapters 1, 2, and 3. If you also want to know what a manufacturer ought to be doing in the quality domain from a semitechnical view, read chapters 4, 5, and 6. As you move into chapters 7 and 8, you'll start to get a two-pronged view of quality from the manufacturer's perspective as well as your own. Thus, if you want to zero in solely on a focus on quality, you should browse through chapters 7 and 8 and carefully read chapters 9, 10, and 11. If you are in the midst of trying to get a product quality problem resolved, or if you see one coming, go directly to chapters 12 and 13. Finally, if you are interested in expanding your knowledge, references to further readings appear at the end of most chapters.

In summary, this book is for the consumer. It is aimed at giving the consumer all the general knowledge needed to assure total customer satisfaction. It may not prevent a consumer from ever having a quality problem, but it will give him or her the information necessary to minimize such a problem and to know what to do if a problem cannot be resolved to his or her satisfaction. We hope that we have succeeded in achieving what we believe to be an important objective!

Acknowledgments are due to ASQC Quality Press and the McGraw-Hill Book Company, co-publishers of *Product Assurance Principles* by Eugene R. Carrubba and Ronald D. Gordon, from which chapters 1, 2, 4, 5, and 6 were extracted. In addition, acknowledgments go to the U.S. Department of Commerce, through its National Institute of Standards and Technology, for creating and making available the *Award Criteria* (1993 edition) around which chapter 3 is structured. Also, acknowledgments are appropriate to the U.S. Office of Consumer Affairs for developing and publishing its 1992 *Consumer's Resource Handbook,* upon which chapters 13 and 14 are based, and from which the appendices are reproduced in their entirety.

We further wish to acknowledge Lisa Urban for her tireless efforts in typing and retyping portions of the manuscript. Thanks go to Gary Kushner for manuscript formatting help. Finally, we want to thank our wives, Nancy Carrubba and Barbara Snyder, and children Jill and Jared for their continued patience, understanding, and support throughout this project.

Eugene R. Carrubba
Mark E. Snyder

Part 1

The Foundation of the Assurance Sciences

Part 1 gives background on the assurance sciences—how they started and evolved, and where they are now. Chapter 1 provides a historical review. Chapter 2 discusses the various elements of the assurance sciences and how thcy relate to one another. Chapter 3 examines what it means to be a world-class quality manufacturer.

Chapter 1
History

The Historical Role of the Master Craftsman

What is product integrity? In its broadest sense, it deals with the total quality aspects of a product. In the next chapter, we define product integrity in more formal terms. Still later, in Part 2, we present the techniques that the manufacturer employs, or should employ, to assure product integrity.

When did the concern for assuring product integrity begin? How did the so-called assurance sciences evolve? Where did product assurance get its roots? As we shall see, these aspects of product integrity have a curious history.

Whether we recognize it or not, we have had the goal of achieving product integrity for a long time. Maybe it wasn't recognized as such, but nevertheless it was there. You had better believe that the ancient Romans were concerned when their swords broke during battle or their chariot wheels fell off. However, they didn't say, "We have a problem in product integrity!" Conversely, the early Egyptians didn't gloat "By golly, we have shown that we can assure product integrity" as they assembled the pyramids which today stand as one of the Seven Wonders of the World. Yet these monuments of the ages are long-lasting evidence of the know-how and perseverance the Egyptians demonstrated in making durable products. One could go back through time and cite many such examples of product integrity or lack thereof.

Chapters 1, 2, 4, 5, and 6 are adapted from Eugene R. Carrubba and Ronald D. Gordon, *Product Assurance Principles: Integrating Design Assurance and Quality Assurance* (New York: McGraw-Hill and ASQC Quality Press, 1988). Copyright © 1988 by McGraw-Hill Inc. Used with permission.

In those early days, and even much later, approaches to product integrity were far from formal. For the most part they were based on the pride of the worker or the master. Sometimes the master's pride in having a good product was directly translated to his slaves in the form of threats. This might be considered a unique approach by today's standards.

The first real concern for quality began to emerge in medieval times with the guilds that appeared around the year 1000. These associations required that apprentices undergo a long training period. Those striving to become master craftsmen had to produce ample evidence of their ability. These rules were directed to some degree to product quality. In one sense, these guilds were crude versions of today's assurance-oriented professional societies, such as the American Society for Quality Control.

However, as products such as machinery became more advanced, there was a resistance on the part of the guilds, which were really geared for the self-interests of the master craftsmen. Although the master craftsman did much for product quality in those early days, he also hindered it by resisting attempts to apply innovations. Furthermore, there were struggles both within and between guilds, as well as between guilds and outsiders.

Nevertheless, the master craftsman did much to foster the early advances of product assurance. It was a way for him to promote his craft. Although he was involved in custom-made, low-volume products, the craftsman generally assured his products' quality and durability. Considering the tools, equipment, and materials he had to work with, one can marvel at some of his accomplishments. However, his products suffered from lack of standardization.

During those times, an informal view of product integrity existed. Pride was the key. The result was products that were, for the most part, good. The craftsman did it all himself. He designed, built, inspected, and tested his product until he was satisfied with it. He made sure that it was worthy of bearing his name. He had an interest in the quality of his product, even though he may not have looked at product quality quite the same way we do today. For the relatively primitive products of yesteryear, this was not a bad approach.

Then some semblance of formalization came to the problem of assuring product quality. During the making of weaponry in

France in the early 1500s, instructions were given on important measurements, and some details were even provided concerning inspection. Some of the products of these times, such as locks and clocks, required the precision that only a highly skilled craftsman could achieve. Since only a skilled craftsman could put the necessary parts together, achieving precision was an art. This resulted in the creation of many one-of-a-kind products.

Standardization started to creep forward in the 1700s and 1800s. With Eli Whitney and his musket came the first serious attempts at product assurance as we recognize it today. The basic concept applied by Whitney was interchangeability, an important principle of American manufacturing and a concept vital to the roots of the product assurance "tree." Special metalworking tools had to be developed. Material properties had to be closely examined. The ability to make precision measurements had to be advanced. Documented requirements (of elements like dimensions and tolerances) that could be monitored had to be generated. This was the formal beginning of the assurance sciences. This was also the rudimentary beginning of what we know today as quality control. Whitney and his collaborators applied such quality control techniques as

- In-process gauging
- Testing and inspection
- Defect prevention
- Inspection standards
- Quality and workmanship standards

In addition, the making of interchangeable parts in quantity laid the groundwork for acceptance sampling concepts. The assurance sciences had attained an embryonic stage.

The Industrial Revolution

Around the same time, in the early 1800s, the factory system was developing in various industries in the United States. The degree of mechanization was light; therefore, the worker's skill was still the most important factor. Product quality was tied directly to the worker or his or her immediate supervisor. However, as industry advanced during the Civil War period, so did the factory system. As more industries arose during the mid-1800s, workers left their jobs to seek better opportunities elsewhere. Newly arrived immigrants were being used to meet the growing labor demand. Long-term employees were hard to find; new and untrained workers were prevalent. Product quality suffered, mostly from lack of identification with the product.

As a way of bringing product quality under control, the responsibility for quality was wrested from the worker/supervisor and given to an independent agent (inspector). He or she was to decide whether the product was satisfactory. This approach seemed to work to a certain degree.

However, as the industrial revolution began to gain momentum in the 1900s, mass production and automation complicated the achievement of product quality. The speed of machinery (output) was replacing the skill of the craftsman (quality). With this growth came specialization of the quality control function. One group specified quality, another set the standards, still another did the inspection and test, and on it went. Everyone was involved, but no one group was responsible; product quality still suffered. To compound matters, the need for a larger volume of uniform precision parts became more obvious, and so did the need for precision measuring techniques and equipment.

Nevertheless, some order was emerging out of all this chaos. Progress was being made in the management fields. The concepts of scientific management were developed and put into practice. Quality control efforts started to become more coordinated and effective. In the early 1920s, Dr. Walter A. Shewhart of the Bell Telephone Laboratories started to apply statistical methods, such as the use of statistical quality control charts, to help control quality. The application of these techniques to mass production industries, though slowly recognized (and finally pushed by the U.S. War Department with the outbreak of World War II), did much to enhance product quality. There was some semblance of control being achieved by quality control.

Enter the Age of Complexity
And so it went, with quality control being the standard bearer of product integrity. However, products became more intricate, complicated, and sophisticated, and so did the processes necessary

to make them. It soon became apparent that it was insufficient to be concerned solely with a limited set of product quality characteristics.

Early in the 1950s, commercial airlines became seriously concerned with the problem of electron tube reliability. Successful studies were undertaken to improve the reliability of these devices. Around the same time, the military began to study the overall reliability situation in earnest. Its aim was to provide recommendations that would enhance the reliability of equipment while reducing maintenance. With the advent of the missile age characterized by "one-shot" no-maintenance requirements, interest in reliability became more intense. More scientific approaches, such as life testing, were applied to improve reliability. Both military and commercial products were assessed on their ability to operate successfully in the manner intended over a given time period when used in a specified environment. Furthermore, products failed less frequently, and their life was prolonged. *Reliability* had come of age with a tremendous boost from the military.

However, reliability was not a panacea to product integrity. Creating a 100-percent reliable product is virtually an unattainable goal. When a complex product did fail, it was often difficult and costly to repair. Those in the military became increasingly aware of the maintainability problem around 1954, particularly when they found out that maintenance costs for their complex systems were approximately one-third of the total operating costs, and that one-third of their personnel were involved in maintenance and support functions. Consumers had similar problems. With many products, they found that it cost more to fix them than to throw them away and buy new ones—if they could get them repaired at all. Equipment that was down was costly in terms of both dollars and aggravation. The consumer could not cut the grass if the lawnmower couldn't be repaired; the pilot at war could not fly the plane if spare parts were unavailable; and so on. Thus sprang forth another product assurance discipline—*maintainability*—to meet the challenge.

With the start of World War II, technological advances increased, resulting in a variety of new and complex products for both military and consumer use. However, it didn't take long to discover that many of these products were not properly designed for use by typical human beings. For example, operators made too many errors in the operation of radar equipment. Accidents were attributed to human mistakes caused by design deficiencies. The human aspect was also an important factor in maintainability and maintenance. For instance, if something failed in a piece of equipment and it was not within reach or was outside the capabilities of a human being, it would be difficult to fix. Therefore, consideration was given to the user and repairer through still another new discipline of product assurance—*human factors.*

Still, this wasn't enough to achieve total product quality. Who wants to use a product that is unsafe? You think you have a shock-free electric drill until you stand on a damp surface and begin to drill—and zap! Once again there was concern on the part of the military. The military began to demand equipment that was safe for the operator and the repairer and that would not damage other parts of the equipment. Similarly, the general buying public, thanks to activists like Ralph Nader, began to get the message in the consumer product area. Consumer liability suits are now commonplace in the case of damage, injury, or death due to faulty products. With these concerns came yet another discipline called product *safety.*

The computer age spawned a new generation of product quality problems and challenges. Until that time, product quality concerns focused on hardware. However, the horizon expanded with the use of computers. The dimension of software and the interaction of the software with hardware was added. Although the importance of computers was understood early in their history, particularly during World War II, it was not until the 1960s that their use became more common. As computer use became more extensive, so did the recognition of computer-related problems. System outages due to software bugs struck a serious note, which was amplified by software maintenance inadequacies. Finally, in the late 1970s, the military began a drive for software quality standards and a methodology to assure software quality. When related to software, the word *quality* took on a more encompassing meaning that included important software factors such as reliability, maintainability, portability, and robustness. In addition, the pursuit of software quality, when applied to interactive computers, required placing a heavy emphasis on the human aspects through design of user-friendly computer features. Thus, *software quality* came to embrace many of the product assurance disciplines under a single banner.

Back to Square One

During the development of the assurance sciences, it became abundantly clear that the human element is extremely important in assuring product quality. In the early days, the master craftsman's pride was key to achieving this objective. The Japanese have successfully resurfaced this ideal and have accomplished significant gains in all areas of product assurance, including quality and reliability. In the United States, we are rekindling the pride factor and restrengthening our commitment to product integrity. Quality improvement teams are springing up to provide a group focus on the solution of product integrity problems. An even more innovative approach is the use of a sociotechnical systems (also called high-performance work systems) concept in which an organization is arranged into self-managed work groups. Within these teams, employees work toward a common purpose and are given control over day-to-day decisions. The belief is that with more control over the decisions that influence their working lives, employees will achieve greater productivity and higher quality. Whatever the approach, the thought is the same—to get all workers to have pride in their work and to commit themselves to product quality as in the days of the master craftsman.

From Arts to Sciences

It is plain what has happened in the historical growth of product assurance. New disciplines grew to fill the voids not filled by other disciplines. Quality control took care of the quality characteristics of the product. But how about the product's durability? Reliability came along to fill that void. Still, when a product failed, repairability had to be considered. Maintainability and human factors filled that void. But was it safe to use? Maybe not—hence product safety. And so it went. Today we have even more related disciplines that are concerned with assuring product integrity, such as software quality assurance. The tree of product assurance (see Figure 1.1) has grown to the point where it is strong and viable, its many branches nurtured by strong roots.

Figure 1.1   The Assurance Sciences

Another factor in the growth of the assurance sciences that is obvious but certainly worth repeating is the role of the military and of military products. In the early days, the need for weaponry prompted the beginnings of the assurance sciences.

Later, the assurance sciences were continually pushed ahead through the concern of the military. Specifications, standards, and engineering/statistical techniques were developed by the military to address various facets of product quality. Commercial products contributed to this growth but primarily "rode the coattails" of the military. The military's need was more critical. In many cases it was truly a battle—a battle for survival!

Over time, we have seen an orderly transition of product assurance techniques from arts to sciences. In the beginning, we had craftsmen who employed highly developed skills to make their products. These craftsmen possessed the necessary aptitude, dexterity, and ingenuity to make the products of their day. But as products became more complex and intricate and were produced in greater volume, these characteristics were insufficient to meet the challenge of assuring product quality. Furthermore, existing product assurance approaches were inadequate for the increasingly difficult task at hand.

Today we have progressed to a point of assuring that product integrity is indeed a science. Science has been defined as a branch of knowledge dealing with a body of facts systematically arranged and showing the operation of general laws. And certainly, the disciplines of product assurance (such as quality control, reliability, maintainability, and product safety) employ scientific management and technical methods, techniques, principles, concepts, and approaches.

Chapter 2
Elements

What Is Product Integrity?

From a consumer's perspective, it is important to realize that functions exist that are necessary to assure a good product (that is, product integrity). Obviously the depth and scope of activities implemented within these functions will vary, depending on the product. For example, the effort that ensures that an automobile is easy and economical to repair has no relevance when the product is an aspirin; an effort aimed at assuring the quality of software is of no consequence if the product has no software. Nevertheless, the consumer should expect that these activities be performed by the manufacturer to the degree necessary, whenever applicable, to assure customer satisfaction. In order to understand these functions, we must know what product integrity is. Product integrity (see Figure 2.1) consists of a predetermined, optimum balance of performance; aesthetic appeal; reliability; ease, economy, and safety of operation; ease, economy, and safety of maintenance; software interaction (where software is employed); and consistency—all at a given cost, of course.

From the user's point of view, these product attributes can be defined as follows:

- *Functional performance*—the ability of the product to do what the user wants it to do

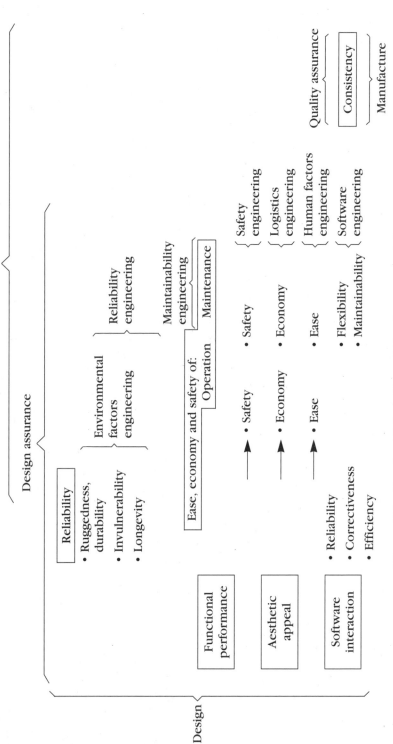

Figure 2.1   Product Integrity and the Assurance Sciences

- *Aesthetic appeal*—the ability of the product to please the human senses
- *Reliability*—durability, longevity, and freedom from failure
- *Ease, economy, and safety of operation*—(self-explanatory)
- *Ease, economy, and safety of maintenance*—(self-explanatory)
- *Software interaction*—characterized by reliability, correctness, and efficiency, while being flexible and maintainable
- *Consistency*—the ability to make any one copy of the product (and its constituent parts) the same as any other copy

Design Assurance

With the exception of *consistency* (which is primarily a function of manufacturing), the elements of product integrity are functions of product design. Integrity is achieved by *design assurance.* This function assures that design creation proceeds in a systematic, orderly fashion, achieving optimum design solutions for the other six product attributes previously defined.

Quality Assurance

It is the mission of the manufacturing function to fabricate the product as designed—in other words, to achieve consistency. This is accomplished by *quality assurance*—seeing to it that the as-designed integrity of the product is not degraded by the manufacturing process.

Assurance Sciences

So, given that the primary functions of design creation and product fabrication are performed, the integrity of the resulting product is assured by the *assurance sciences*—design assurance and quality assurance—which are detailed in the next sections. These are activities that any good manufacturer should implement to assure overall product integrity.

Assuring the Integrity of the Design

Design assurance is the process (or management mechanism) of creating a satisfactory and complete design. Design assurance is synonymous with design review in its larger sense and includes design review in its narrower sense (that is, formal examinations of the design). It seeks to make sure that nothing is forgotten or ignored. Further, it assures that the total design includes not only the engineering drawings and specifications necessary to describe the intended product physically and functionally but *all* documentation required to support the manufacture, test, delivery, use, and maintenance of the product. Design assurance embraces all of the design-related assurance science activities described briefly in the paragraphs that follow.

System reliability engineering influences the design toward a durable, long-lived product that rarely malfunctions. It seeks to minimize the frequency of component failures and to mitigate the effects of component failure on product function *by design.*

Components reliability engineering performs the same function, but in microcosm—that is, the "system" in this case (product) becomes a component part. The focus is on conservative component parts application to minimize overstress and eventual component failure.

Environmental factors engineering assures that the product, as designed, will withstand the rigors of any anticipated environmental stresses, within any required safety margins. An important aspect of this function is evaluation testing under the environments of sun, rain, wind, altitude, temperature extremes, shock, and vibration, separately or in any combination, depending on the products and environments of use.

Human factors engineering aims to design the product to fit the requirements and abilities of the user. Its major thrust is product design analysis from a people viewpoint—for instance, reach required, weight to be lifted, knobs to be turned, and so on.

The importance of *safety engineering,* at least in protecting the user from the product, is obvious. Not so obvious, perhaps, is the safety engineering concern with protecting the product from the user and from itself. The aim is to design the product so that it offers minimal risk to the physical well-being of the user, the surroundings, and itself.

Although a perfectly reliable product would never fail or wear out, such is not the case in the real world; products do fail and wear out. For most products, failure does not necessarily mean the end of that product's life—repair is possible. *Maintainability engineering* is concerned with the ease and economy with which a product can be restored to (corrective maintenance) and/or kept in (preventive maintenance) an operable condition.

Logistics engineering addresses an awakening realization that the even most reliable, safe, and maintainable product, built by the most quality-conscious company, is of little use without the proper support documentation, consumables, service, and spares. Logistics engineering creates product support documents such as user and maintenance manuals.

The past two decades have produced an amazing array of electronic products. The plethora of commonly used electronic systems and devices increasingly depends on two new "parts"— software and firmware. Software programs, either "burned" into an integrated circuit (firmware) or accessed as code by a system (software), are becoming as much a part of delivered products as the "hard" goods (hardware) themselves. Every design assurance and quality assurance issue in the design and manufacture of hardware also exists in the development of software. And just as in the case of hardware products, a variety of engineering approaches (such as design reviews) exists under the banner of *software quality assurance* for assuring the quality of software and its integration into the complete system (or end product, such as a personal computer).

Assuring that Designed-In Integrity Is Not Compromised

The foregoing assurance sciences, when performed in concert with each other and the other elements of the design process, give assurance that a *total design* exists—a design that embraces all parameters of goodness of the product within the full product life cycle environment. It remains, then, to convert this design to the physical/functional product it describes. Making sure that this conversion takes place properly and consistently is the responsibility of a function (management mechanism) we shall call *quality assurance.* Quality assurance comprises quality control engineering and quality control inspection activities.

Quality control engineering devises practical working procedures for achieving specific goals established by the quality

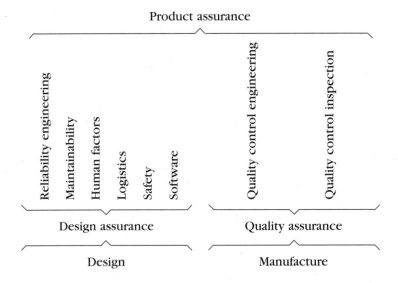

Figure 2.2   Relationship of the Assurance Sciences to Product Design and Manufacture

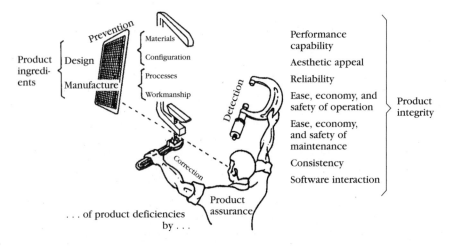

Figure 2.3   Product Integrity as a Function of Freedom from Product Deficiencies

assurance function. It establishes manufacturing operator and inspector skill and training requirements, the nature and points of inspections, sampling and accept/reject criteria, and so on. It also provides the direction for correcting deficiencies in the manufacturing process.

Quality control inspection, as we speak of it here, should not be thought of as merely visual. It includes all operations necessary to detect and measure conformance of the product to predetermined standards. The inspection and data reporting procedures established by quality control engineering are executed by the quality control inspection function.

Integrating Design Assurance with Quality Assurance

The assurance sciences are necessary, but not sufficient, to form a practical product assurance function. Assurance of overall product integrity requires the engineering techniques represented by the assurance sciences. However, effective product assurance also necessitates some coherent direction or management of their application to the product's design and manufacture. It should be clear from the previous discussion that the technical elements can be logically related, in some way, to the process of creating a product. Figure 2.2 illustrates the idea that these elements are neatly separable into those related to product design and those related to product manufacture. Figure 2.3 goes one step further and recognizes the commonality of purpose and approach of the assurance sciences across both design and manufacture; that is, prevention, detection, and correction of product deficiencies to achieve product integrity.

Further Reading

Carrubba, E. R., and R. D. Gordon. *Product Assurance Principles.* New York: ASQC Quality Press and McGraw-Hill Book Company, 1988: Chapter 2.

Chapter 3
World-Class Quality Viewpoint

World-Class Quality and Total Customer Satisfaction

Buying a product from a world-class quality manufacturer would assure that a consumer has a reasonably high chance of getting a high quality product. The trick is to determine which manufacturer, if any, within the product category of interest is world-class. Surely, there are certain attributes that distinguish a world-class quality manufacturer from one that is not.

In some respects, world-class quality is in the eyes of the beholder, in this case the consumer. If the consumer is not satisfied with the product that he or she has purchased, it really doesn't make any difference if the manufacturer is viewed as world-class by others. It comes down to the degree of total customer satisfaction. To a large extent, American consumers view Japanese products, particularly automobiles and entertainment products, as having world-class quality. Rightly or wrongly, the consumer's degree of satisfaction in his or her purchase is translated into the perception of total quality. The higher the degree of satisfaction, the higher the likelihood that a consumer will view that manufacturer as being at the world-class level. And Japanese products in general *do* provide a high degree of customer satisfaction.

Quality Recognition

For many years in Japan, the prestigious Deming Application Prize has been awarded to companies excelling in quality. This award is named in honor of one of the leading quality gurus in the United States, Dr. W. Edwards Deming. After World War II, the Japanese went through a painful reconstruction period to rebuild and revive their economy. Initially, their products were viewed as junk. Deming arrived on the scene and set in motion a quality revolution, largely based on the use of statistical quality control techniques, which Japanese manufacturers embraced. Through Deming's guidance and the unwavering commitment of the Japanese to religiously follow his lead, these products became the benchmark of high quality. In gratitude for Deming's contributions, this much-sought-after award is given annually in his honor.

Japanese manufacturers have been taking more market share away from American manufacturers in many product areas, such as automobiles and entertainment products. Quality has become a strong weapon of competition. In answer to this, many manufacturers in the United States have been working hard to improve their product quality and their quality image. As a result, quality levels of many of their products have risen dramatically in the last 10 years or so.

The U.S. government, eager to foster and continue this rejuvenated quality impetus, established its version of the Deming Prize, the Malcolm Baldrige National Quality Award (MBNQA). This award, signed into law in 1987, was named after the late Malcolm Baldrige, former secretary of commerce. The award recognizes companies in the United States that excel in quality from the viewpoint of both achievement and management. The award promotes the following:

1. Quality awareness as an increasingly important element in competitiveness

2. An understanding of the requirements for quality excellence

3. The sharing of information on successful quality strategies and on the benefits derived from implementation of these strategies

Up to two awards may be given annually in each of three categories: (1) manufacturing companies or subsidiaries, (2) service companies or subsidiaries, and (3) small businesses.

The award is managed by the U.S. Department of Commerce National Institute of Standards and Technology. It is administered by the American Society for Quality Control.

The MBNQA's *Award Criteria* spells out the application process in considerable detail. Companies vying for the award submit a formal application. This is followed by an evaluation (which can include a site visit) performed by trained examiners against established quality excellence criteria. The information provided by the applicants on their quality processes and quality improvements must demonstrate that the approaches used could be replicated or adapted by other businesses. Award winners receive worldwide recognition.

Award Examination Categories and Criteria

Over its history, the focus of quality has evolved. Initially, the focus was narrowly directed toward inspection activities—quality control. Then the focus was extended by coupling prevention and appraisal (inspection) activities—quality assurance. Now the focus is even more significantly expanded to cover all conceivable quality-related facets which influence customer satisfaction— *total quality management (TQM)*. The examination categories in the *Award Criteria* (1993 edition) encompass the major components of a TQM system. These criteria, itemized below, are dynamic and subject to continuing evolution. However, it is expected that the general content and basic structure will remain relatively unchanged.

1. *Leadership:* senior executive personal leadership; the company's quality values; how quality is managed; and extension of leadership to the outside community

2. *Information and analysis,* in terms of scope, management, and analysis of quality data

3. *Strategic quality planning,* covering the planning process; use of quality leadership indicators; and how priorities are set

4. *Human resource development and management:* how human resources are managed; employee involvement; education and training; employee recognition, performance measurement, well-being, and morale

5. *Management of process quality:* design and introduction of products and services; process and quality control; continuous improvement, assessment, and extension of these efforts into support services and business processes and to suppliers

6. *Quality and operational results* associated with products and support services; comparison with others; and providing a basis for improvement

7. *Customer focus and satisfaction,* to include a knowledge of customer requirements and expectations; managing relationships; established service standards; commitment; resolution of complaints; how customer satisfaction is determined; what the results are; and how these results are compared to others

The following sections provide further insight into these criteria as applied by the MBNQA examiners to judge applicants and select winners. As a consumer, you should expect no less. You should expect your chosen manufacturer to strive to meet these world-class quality standards of excellence. And why not? If you expect less, chances are you will get less!

Leadership

It has been said that management-related issues are responsible for over 85 percent of quality problems. Leadership by the senior executives, the people at the top of a company, goes a long way toward achieving world-class quality status. Therefore, the company's senior executives should endorse and commit to a strong quality value system and a supportive management system to drive toward quality excellence.

Senior executives should lead by example, being committed and personally involved and visible in the quest for quality excellence and total customer satisfaction. They should have a standard of quality values demonstrated through internal policies, mission, and guidelines. This leadership concept should also be extended downward to other management levels. Finally, quality leadership should be extended beyond the workplace and into the community.

Information and Analysis

Quality improvement depends greatly on data and its analysis. Improvement to be made should be based on fact, not hearsay and emotion. Since quality covers a lot of territory, the data should be far-reaching to cover both product and nonproduct (that is, administrative and service) quality areas such as the safety of employees. And the information should not only be collected but also acted upon (evaluated and appropriate action taken). It does no one any good to collect reams of data which then sit in a computer file or hard-copy file cabinet.

The data should be used to aid the management of total quality. The various kinds of data should be made available reliably and in a timely manner, and evaluated so that the results help meet the objectives of the company (which, by the way, should include total customer satisfaction).

Strategic Quality Planning

"Fail to plan, plan to fail!" This is an old yet oh-so-true statement. A good strategic quality planning process should be put in place and implemented. This process should result in plans that factor in quality-related data about competitors. In addition, since "to be the best is to know the best," quality planning should include benchmarks of the best-in-class companies. The resulting plans should address both short-term and long-term priorities of the company.

Strategic planning should be closely meshed with planning for the overall business. The planning process should not remain stagnant but rather be dynamic and continuously reviewed and improved.

Human Resource Development and Management

This criterion aims to ensure that the company's efforts are effectively focused on developing and realizing the full potential of the total work force. Tied closely to this aim is the importance of maintaining a conducive environment to achieve this end. A human resources plan should be be created, implemented, and managed. All employees should be involved in achieving the company's quality objectives. Quality education and training should be focused on, and related to, meeting the quality objectives of the company.

Human resources plans should be integrated with quality requirements into the company's business plan. Employee involvement in the pursuit of quality should be approached through team involvement encompassing suppliers and customers. Since a major way to encourage employees' quality contributions is to recognize their efforts, employee recognition should be an important element in the company's thinking. Still another important ingredient to achieving quality excellence is maintaining high morale among the work force.

Management of Process Quality

A world-class quality company should employ systematic approaches for total quality control of its products and, for that matter, its services as well. These approaches should begin with design and introduction of products to satisfy customer needs, expectations, and requirements. They should continue into the manufacturing process used to build these products and include the quality controls that are implemented. The products need to meet design specifications and be built using controlled processes. In addition, since the quality of components and materials used in the product are extremely important, an effective process should be in place to assure that suppliers (external providers of goods and services) meet the necessary requirements.

An important element throughout should be the continuous improvement (or *kaizen,* as the Japanese call it) of processes, products, and services. Regular assessments via product and systems audits of product quality, quality systems, and quality practices should provide a useful way of staying straight and honest.

Systems should document the various assessments and improvements as they provide a "lessons learned" filing of useful information. In addition to the quality assurance, assessment, and improvement of product, processes, and services, these activities should be extended to supporting services, such as sales and marketing, as well as to suppliers.

Quality and Operational Results

The measurement and knowledge of quality achievement are essential to quality improvement. Comparing these results against what are viewed to be the customer's requirements and expectations provides a good point of departure for getting better. These measures should be based on the customer's view of quality. Another important consideration should be the comparison of the company's current quality levels with those of the competition.

Trends in key product and service quality measures should be reviewed and acted upon routinely. When trends go awry, the reasons should be analyzed and understood, and appropriate actions should be implemented to bring them back in control and prevent their recurrence. Knowing what others (such as the competition, the industry as a whole, and the best-in-class), are doing and achieving can provide useful comparisons. These measures should not stop with product quality. They should include company operational results and extension to business processes, support services, supplier performance, and all elements (such as people or equipment) related to production of those products.

Customer Focus and Satisfaction

Last, but certainly not least, is how all this contributes to customer satisfaction. This MBNQA evaluation criterion on customer satisfaction carries the greatest weight in the scoring. And well it should. One should think of this element as the grand payoff. In this regard, the company should know its customers, be responsive, and meet their requirements and expectations. An aid to doing this effectively is the overall quality of the total customer service systems.

At the outset, there should be a strong knowledge of customer requirements and expectations (both current and future), something the Japanese do ever so well. The management of the company's customer relationships should also be considered essential. In line with the latter, it is important that standards for customer service be set high. It is also important that the company keep its commitments, such as those made in guarantees and warranties, if it is to maintain its credibility.

Timely and effective resolution of customer complaints is obviously an important aspect of total customer satisfaction. The company may believe that its customers are reasonably satisfied with its products. But to know for sure, it should conduct surveys that take the pulse of the customer. These customer satisfaction results should be tracked religiously, and any adverse trends addressed promptly and effectively. Finally, the results of the company's customer satisfaction studies should be compared with those of industry and world leaders as well as competitors. When it comes to total customer satisfaction, there is only one goal: to be at the top, to be the best, world-class.

Some World-Class Quality Companies

As of 1992, 17 companies out of 399 applicants have received the MBNQA since its establishment in 1988. Table 3.1 lists the winners and the category in which the award was made.

Together with Florida Power & Light Company, which won the prestigious Deming Application Prize, a first for a non-Japanese company, these 17 companies clearly are of world-class quality stature in the United States. Certainly there are other companies in the world, such as Toyota, which are also world-class. One thing is common to these companies—they are all implementing strong and effective quality initiatives. Motorola has its Six Sigma® quality program, aimed at achieving virtually zero defects in everything it does; Xerox has its "leadership through quality" program, focused on continuous quality improvement; and IBM has its "market-driven" quality program, which, like Motorola's, is directed toward cutting defects to near zero across the board. But the one point that sets the world-class quality companies apart from all the rest is that they consistently do all the right things from a total quality management perspective to achieve total customer satisfaction.

**Table 3.1   Malcolm Baldrige National Quality Award
Recipients**

Year	Category	Winner
1988	Manufacturing	Motorola, Inc.
	Manufacturing	Westinghouse Electric Corporation, Commercial Nuclear Fuel Division
	Small Business	Globe Metallurgical, Inc.
1989	Manufacturing	Milliken & Company
	Manufacturing	Xerox Business Products and Systems
1990	Manufacturing	General Motors, Cadillac Motor Car Company
	Manufacturing	International Business Machines, Minicomputer Division
	Service	Federal Express Corporation
	Small Business	Wallace Company, Inc.
1991	Manufacturing	Solectron Corporation
	Manufacturing	Zytec Corporation
	Small Business	Marlow Industries
1992	Manufacturing	AT&T Network Systems Group Transmissions Systems Business Unit
	Manufacturing	Texas Instruments, Inc., Defense Systems & Electronics Group
	Service	AT&T Universal Card Services
	Service	The Ritz-Carlton Hotel Company
	Small Business	Granite Rock Company

Further Reading

Award Criteria. Washington, D.C.: Malcolm Baldrige National Quality Award Office, 1993.

Steeples, M. M. *The Corporate Guide to the Malcolm Baldrige National Quality Award.* Rev. ed. Homewood, Ill.: ASQC Quality Press and Business One Irwin, 1993.

Part 2

The Manufacturer's Perspective of Quality

Part 2 provides important insights into what manufacturers should be doing to ensure quality. It serves as a point of reference to help a consumer weed out the potentially good manufacturers from the potentially bad. The chapters are presented in the order of a product's major life cycle phases. Chapter 4 reviews the design activities which occur up front in the product life cycle. Chapter 5 covers traditional quality control-related activities that take place as the product design is produced in many copies. Chapter 6 describes the various kinds of tests that are performed to verify and influence product quality. Finally, following these discussions of design, manufacture, and test activities, the role of customer service when the product is "fielded" is examined in chapter 7.

Chapter 4
Design

Emphasis on Prevention

Some of the more enticing and productive opportunities for truly useful work in product assurance are those influencing the design of a product. We have previously defined this segment of product assurance as design assurance. Design assurance is the companion to product design, as quality assurance is to product manufacture. The primary focus of design assurance is preventing or correcting design errors that lead to poor product integrity. If design errors can be prevented, fine; otherwise, the earlier they can be detected and corrected, the better. The concern here is with their prevention, detection, and correction before release to manufacturing, and surely before the consumer gets the product!

The quality of the craftsperson's work is highly dependent on the ability to select the right tool for the job at hand. So it is with the design assurance engineer. Knowing *why* a certain tool or set of tools is proper for a given situation is helpful. Above all, the techniques selected must be pertinent to the design problem at hand and to the current stage of solution of that design problem.

The design assurance treatment in this chapter is largely applicable to functional products such as automobiles, electronic products (like radios, TVs, and VCRs), and appliances (such as washing machines, dryers, refrigerators, and stoves) rather than to nonfunctional products (like a piece of furniture). Nevertheless, key concepts such as emphasis on prevention, customer needs and expectations, design guidance, and design review are fundamental to all products and need only be tailored to the product of interest.

Reflecting the Needs and Expectations of the Customer

Every new product, from the simplest device to the most complex system, begins as an idea. Likewise, every significant advance in designed-in product integrity begins with an idea. One of the more important ideas of design assurance is that it is not so much the absolute value of individual integrity parameters (such as reliability) that govern the "goodness" of a product as it is the proper *combination* of integrity parameters, together with the parameters of performance, capability, cost, and sometimes aesthetic appeal. Partial realization of this idea is attained by using such techniques as cost-of-ownership analysis (see chapter 12), to determine what it will cost the purchaser/user to buy, use, and maintain the product over its life. Full realization of this concept is achieved only by developing the optimum set of goals for product characteristics.

Knowingly or unknowingly, the customer is an important player in the process of establishing appropriate technical requirements. Ultimately, it is the customer who will have to live with the product as designed, built, and serviced. Consequently, the customer's perspective is an essential input that the manufacturer must fervently pursue. Fortunately, there are techniques such as the Japanese-developed quality function deployment (QFD) method which provide a means for examining and incorporating the customer view. An example of a simplified version of QFD on a screwdriver is given in Figure 4.1. In this example, the voice of the customer identifies the two most important product characteristics (those with the highest importance ratings) that the manufacturer needs to address: durability and price.

Once some understandable bounds have been determined for product performance, cost, and aesthetic characteristics and for product integrity characteristics, the assurance specialist must assist in determining optimum bounds on individual product integrity characteristics. The question must be: "What kind of

| Voice of the customer input | Product characteristics | | | | | | Importance rating (sum of weightings) | Priority ranking |
	Sales price	Interchangeable bits	Steel shank	Rubber grip	Ratcheting capability	Lexan handle		
Easy to use				1	3		4	3
Nonrusting			3			1	4	3
Durable			3			3	6	1
Comfortable				1			1	5
Versatile		3					3	4
Inexpensive	5						5	2

Importance weightings:

High importance = 5

Medium importance = 3

Low importance = 1

Figure 4.1   Simplified QFD Example: The Screwdriver

integrity is desirable for this product to achieve total customer satisfaction?" To find the answer, information such as the following must be determined.

- Is the product durable or consumable?

- Is product operation attended or unattended?

- Can the product be repaired when it fails? With or without interrupting product operation?

- What will it cost the user (customer) for each failure incident or each minute or hour or day that the product doesn't work? What are the consequences of product failure or inoperability?

Once answers to an exhaustive set of such questions pertinent to the product development at hand are secured, they can be properly quantified. The manufacturer can use these results with appropriately tailored models (such as a cost-of-ownership model) to develop product integrity requirements.

A usable set of product integrity requirements must be clear and unambiguous, preferably quantitative, and somehow measurable. The job of design assurance can now be pursued. In its simplest form, this job consists mostly of avoiding past mistakes.

Perennial Problems

Human nature being what it is, 80 percent of all problems are caused by 20 percent of the population (an expression of Pareto's Law). This is just as true for product designs as it is for the body politic. Over the years, a few classes of design errors have been found to cause a surprising amount of grief. Some examples of these kinds of design errors are discussed in the next sections.

Component Misspecification

Any component of a product that is purchased, rather than built by the product designer, is suspect—if for no other reason than the communication problem. It is difficult to determine exactly what one's requirements are and even more difficult to express these requirements in an unambiguous manner. As a result, component specifications can turn out to be incomplete, unenforceable, or improper, with dire consequences.

Part Misapplications

If a perfect set of specifications for purchased materials, parts, and components exists, there is still the opportunity to err by ignoring specified characteristics. An obvious consequence here is unacceptable operation outside specified bounds.

Design Oversight

By having a good set of specifications, and by assuring that each component and part in the design is assigned a proper function, we have gone a long way toward ensuring a reliable product. Nevertheless, in the interconnection of these parts into an overall performing product, there is still ample room for error which can thwart the intended function of the product.

Some Practical Solutions

If these are the kinds of design problems typically encountered, what should a good manufacturer be doing to solve them? There are two major categories of practical design assurance techniques that can be brought to bear: design guidance and design review. Very simply stated, design guidance attempts to *prevent* design error, and design review attempts to *detect* and *correct* design error. These pursuits cannot be successful unless the guidance and review techniques are thoroughly grounded in a combination of experience and sound basic design assurance analysis.

Design Guidance

Design guidelines and ground rules are among the most important products of design assurance engineering. On any new design project, the manufacturer should develop and disseminate relevant design guidelines and ground rules for the designers to follow.

Design guidance begins with design-to requirements for the constituent components of some larger product for which an overall goal or requirement has been previously established. These allocations are necessary so that the designer can design a component in such a manner that it and its "brothers" (or "sisters") collectively meet the overall design goals, requirements, and constraints.

Having established the design-to requirements, design guidance sets rules related to the component parts themselves. "A chain is only as strong as its weakest link" and "The whole is equal to the sum of its parts"—these old saws, though often misapplied, illustrate the point that the proper selection and application of component parts by the manufacturer is essential to product integrity. Part selection and application are not independent actions. Parts that are suitable for intended application must be selected. And the selected parts must be applied so that they are not expected to do something of which they are incapable.

Finally, design guidance needs to be provided for the physical being of the product. Too often, the first indication that anybody cares about the physical "building block" structuring of the product occurs at a formal design review, or worse still, after a user complains. If a reasonably complex product (say a personal computer) is being examined, the manufacturer should subdivide it into physical product groups (keyboard, monitor), sets, assemblies, and subassemblies. This is necessary to make the product easier for mass production, service and repair, and logistics support.

Design Review

In the absence of preventing design errors, the next best method that the manufacturer can apply is detecting and correcting them as early as possible—preferably before the design is released for manufacture. The design review process, which includes the application of specific analytical techniques, is the most effective known method for early detection of design errors. Examples of techniques the manufacturer can bring to bear in reviewing the design include the parts application review and the failure modes, effects, and criticality analysis.

Essentially, parts application review consists of determining to what extent the parts selection and application guidelines are being followed. An independent (of the designer) calculation of electrical, mechanical, and environmental part stresses verifies adherence to parts application guidelines and assures that no parts are being stressed at, near, or beyond their limits of endurance.

The failure modes, effects, and criticality analysis (FMECA) is another design analysis tool at the manufacturer's disposal. In an FMECA, the consequences of all potential failures are evaluated for their effect on product performance. The process is continued until all significant failure modes of constituent parts are accounted for, and their theoretical effects and criticality on higher levels of functional assembly are assessed. Table 4.1 provides a simple example of an FMECA as applied to a coffee percolator. In this example, the percolator has the job of brewing our coffee; if it doesn't work, we won't have our morning cup of coffee, with potentially dire consequences (particularly if we depend on that cup of coffee to keep us alert as we drive down the turnpike).

Table 4.1 FMECA Example: The Coffee Percolator

Item	Gross failure modes	Relative failure frequency	Failure effects	Failure criticality
Coffee percolator	1. Defective line cord	Low	Percolator remains cold →	Critical—no coffee to drink
	2. Defective brewing element	Low		
	3. Clogged valve	Medium	Water heats up but does not percolate →	
	4. Bent or broken valve	Low		
	5. Defective thermostat	High	Coffee boils	Major—coffee spills over; less than a full cup to drink
	6. Defective warming element	Medium	Coffee brews but is not kept warm	Minor—coffee cools quickly; can't savor coffee

Striving for Effective Design Assurance

In spite of every precaution, deficiencies will creep into product designs. Most of these deficiencies are of the sort that crop up time after time and that the standard design assurance techniques are supposed to prevent or correct. The standard techniques can, in fact, be effective in minimizing these deficiencies if properly applied. Effective design assurance comes about from the manufacturer selecting and applying the appropriate set of these techniques to a specific product.

Perhaps the single most important element of effectiveness for all of the design assurance techniques is *timeliness.* Even the simplest, riskiest, and most obvious conclusions and recommendations are better than no information at points where design decisions must be made. Conversely, even the most profound and confident conclusions are of little use once the manufacturer begins building the product.

Just as important as timeliness, but probably ignored less often, is *pertinence.* The technique and the manner of its application must be appropriate to the design problem as well as to the current stage of solution of that design problem.

Finally, there is the need for the "design-active" end of design assurance technique applications (published guidelines, corrective action recommendations, and so on) to be *provocative*—to get the attention of those who are in a position to make it happen, the designers.

Further Reading

Carrubba, E. R. and R. D. Gordon. *Product Assurance Principles.* New York: ASQC Quality Press and McGraw-Hill Book Company, 1988: Chapter 8.

Chapter 5
Manufacturing

What? You Have to Build It Too?!

Production, manufacturing, and *fabrication* are all names for a general process of assembling parts, materials, and components into some form of functioning item. The manufacturing process itself can vary from an extremely simple stamping operation resulting in a finished coin to a highly complex system of processes requiring many control techniques and resulting in, for example, a television set. Whatever the product and the process used, assurance activities will enter into the manufacture of that product. As a matter of fact, the assurance disciplines started with manufacturing, and the heaviest assurance effort is still concentrated in this part of the overall process of design, manufacture, and test.

Let's examine the quality of a manufactured product and how the manufacturer should assure that the requisite quality exists. Quality in manufacturing is the consistent conformance of the product to the design intent. Design intent invariably aims to eliminate all workmanship and process problems (caused by the manufacturing process) from the product. No designer of a portable radio intends any of his or her designs to fail, yet some will. No automobile company intends an axle to fracture in use because of a process defect, and yet some will. The function of manufacturing quality assurance, then, is to assure that the design intent is not degraded by workmanship or process-induced defects.

Quality is generally assured by employing a system that controls received parts/materials and the processes used to assemble the received items into the product. The control is almost always accomplished by measuring or testing something—the thread size of a screw, the tension of a spring, the radio frequency output of a transmitter, and so on. These measurements and tests detect unsatisfactory copies of the product at its various stages of fabrication.

The key word is *consistency.* It is preferable to have a consistent process, even if it is a somewhat poor process. For example, a process that consistently yields 95 percent good results is better than one that varies between 90 percent and 100 percent (even though it may average better than 90 percent). This is because the consistent process can be monitored on a small-sample basis with a higher confidence in the results.

Typical manufacturing functions all have some assurance activities associated with their operation. As shown in Figure 5.1, the activities come from both the design assurance and the quality assurance discipline areas. The controlled buying of parts/materials needed for the finished product should start with proper specifications, generally developed with heavy design assurance participation. These specifications form part of the design package that defines what is to be manufactured, from the parts through the completed product. The remainder of the drawing package are specifications also—manufacturing specifications that define the final form the assembled parts/materials are to take. The first direct assurance contact with the manufacturing process generally is the inspection of received parts and materials. Following production assembly operations, the manufacturer should be performing in-process inspection, equipment calibration, process control, and related assurance activities. Often there is some form of inspection and/or test applied to the finished product prior to its being considered ready for delivery to the customer. This can include the visual examination of a drawing requirement or a functional operation of some operational specification. This step is usually either witnessed or accomplished by a quality assurance function. In a well-controlled manufacturing cycle, a final assurance check should be made during packaging and shipping of the finished product. Again, this can be anything from a simple check of

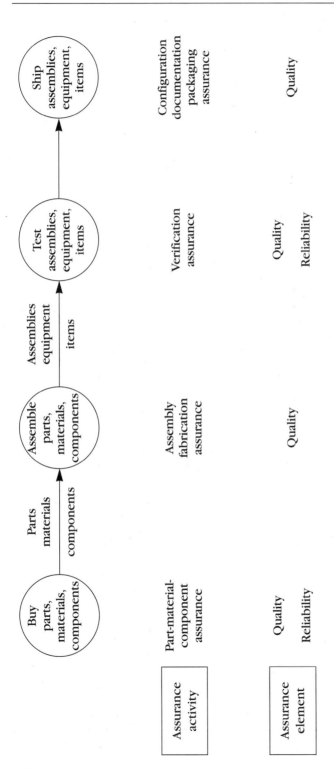

Figure 5.1   Assurance Elements for Manufacturing

shipping documentation all the way up to a complete inspection of the packaged product (with some product sampled by removal from the shipping package and complete reinspection).

It should be obvious that quality assurance activities are integral to the manufacturing process, being its watchdog, advisor, and conscience. All of these activities are aimed at measuring the consistent conformance of the product at all stages of manufacture to specifications developed during the design process. The inspection process includes visual examinations for obvious defects, mechanical measurements for dimensional variation from drawings, and functional testing to operational specifications. The types of testing are explained in chapter 6.

From all of this inspection and test comes considerable data on the operation of the finished product as well as outright defects and failures. Assurance functions should collect this data for additional analysis to determine root cause. One approach to determining root cause is through the use of the cause-and-effect diagram (or Ishikawa diagram, named after Dr. Kaoru Ishikawa). An example of a cause-and-effect diagram is given in Figure 5.2 for a wooden box manufacturer which is finding too many defective boxes at the end of the production line. The major causes related to the four Ms, Method, Manpower, Materials, and Machinery, are further subdivided into the specific causes that can contribute to the undesirable effect (result)—defective boxes.

This type of activity should be directed toward a corrective action to reduce or eliminate the possibility of a future occurrence of the same problem. Results should be used by manufacturing, engineering, and management personnel in accomplishing and monitoring progress of corrective actions as well as achieving satisfactory process and manufacturing control.

The later a problem is found, the more expensive it is to correct. Assurance activities, therefore, should be concentrated as early in the manufacturing process as practical. Figure 5.3 shows that the cost of finding and fixing these failures increases dramatically as the product proceeds along the manufacturing-use cycle. Costs accrue from the troubleshooting, repair, and retest involved, along with the operating and administrative expenses associated with maintaining repair parts, using special repair techniques, and

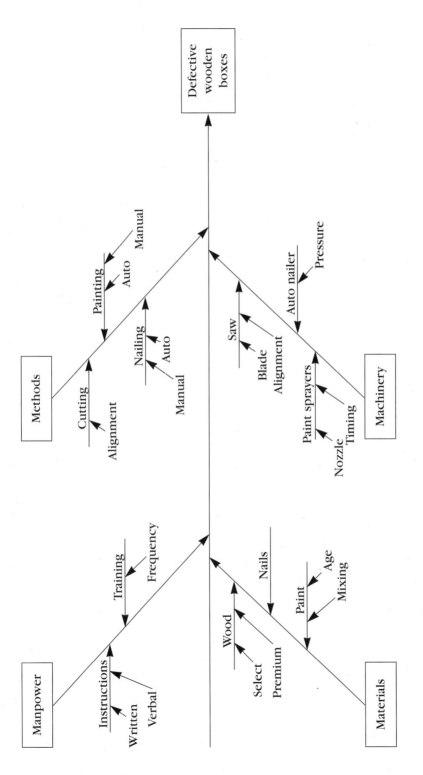

Figure 5.2   Cause-and-Effect Diagram Example: Defective Wooden Boxes

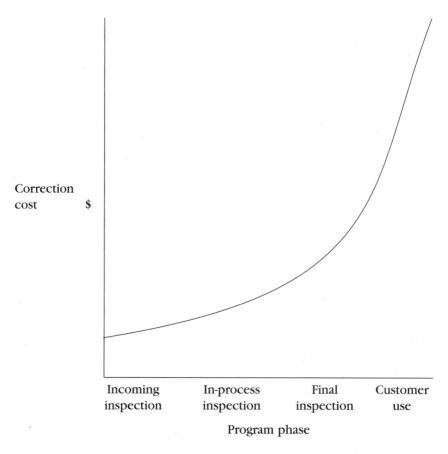

Figure 5.3   Correction Cost Versus Program Phase

maintaining customer liaison. Accurate knowledge of these costs makes it possible for a manufacturer to focus on appropriate areas.

Assurance Assessment

Incoming Inspection

Beginning with incoming inspection, the manufacturer should aim to identify parts/materials which might cause problems later in the manufacturing cycle. Significant parameters for each part should be selected for conformance to specifications and material content verified. The establishment of what to measure at incoming inspection is a somewhat ticklish problem. Assurance can be as minimal as making sure the part is the one ordered or as extensive as measuring every specified parameter on every part received.

In some instances where incoming inspection is impractical (such as destructive testing in which samples must actually be destroyed to verify that they meet specifications), on-site monitoring of a supplier's own assurance measurements is a practical method of inspection. In cases where a strong partnership has been forged between manufacturer and supplier, incoming inspection may be bypassed for a ship-to-stock program in which incoming parts/materials are sent directly to inventory without a verification.

In-Process Inspection

In-process inspection is established to assess the conformance of subassemblies (such as power supplies for personal computers) to design drawings. Here again, evaluation can take the form of visual examination, mechanical measurements, and functional testing. The same economic considerations exist for the assurance of subassemblies as for the parts and materials of which they are composed. One-hundred-percent inspection is rarely applied across all products; dependence is still on statistical sampling approaches. The statistical sampling techniques used at incoming inspection are entirely appropriate for in-process inspection. Although serving as an assurance check, in-process testing or visual examination is generally considered to be an integral part of the manufacturing process—under manufacturing direction and control. In fact, the growing trend is toward making the production line worker responsible for his or her step of the operation, as well as for its inspection.

Final Inspection

Final inspection is possibly the most important manufacturing assurance point of all. It is the last chance the manufacturer has to assure that the product conforms to all of the design-established requirements before the customer receives it. For this reason, at least on more complex products, some form of final inspection is frequently accomplished on each finished item. Again, as done in the subassembly activity, assurance checks can be accomplished in parallel with production measurements.

With some products (for instance, color television sets), samples are placed on extended life testing to assure consistent quality and reliability of delivered sets. There is an excellent reason for this type of assurance—warranties. For example, no television set manufacturer wants to be faced with a large and unpredictable number of television sets being returned within the warranty period. Similarly, manufacturers of automobiles, washing machines, stereo equipment, musical instruments, and hair dryers, to name a few, must also assure themselves of the quality of their delivered products. Inspection of the total delivered product, by definition, should include assurance that all necessary documentation (such as the owner's manual) is included in the delivery container and that the documentation matches the product being delivered.

Assurance Data and Analysis

One useful technique for presenting assurance data related to manufacturing is the control chart originated by Dr. Walter A. Shewhart. It is a statistical tool generally used to study and control repetitive processes. It allows for the establishment of a process standard and exists as a form for recording whether the standard has been attained. The control chart concept is based on the establishment of a desired standard value and of upper and lower control limits. These values describe a state of specified statistical process control over a time or ordered manufacturing base. In control chart theory, when actual values are between the upper and lower control limits, the process or events being measured are said to be stable and *in control.*

An example of a control chart for attributes appears in Figure 5.4. In this example, the established standard is 2.0 defects found per automobile inspected before shipment to the dealer; based on historical data, upper and lower control limits of 6.2 defects and 0 defects, respectively, are set up. The process used to build these cars stayed stable (that is, within the upper and lower control limits) until car 8 came off the assembly line, at which time the process went out of control. The number of defects (seven) observed in this automobile is significantly greater than the process has produced in the past. Corrective action is necessary to bring the process back in control.

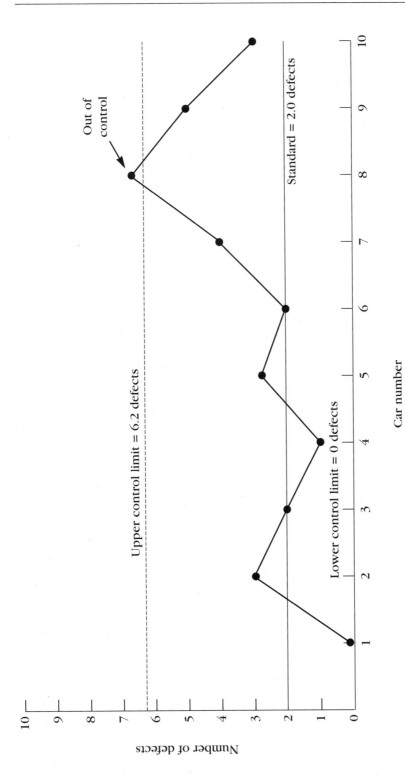

Figure 5.4 Sample Control Chart

All of these inspections, evaluations, and assessments provide data—either attributes data (go/no-go, yes/no, good/bad) or variable data (5.1 ampere, 0.3 volts, 51.7 pounds, 14.2 inches). These data are needed immediately (to decide whether to continue manufacturing) and should be analyzed to establish longer-term control and trend evaluation. In the case of some of today's highly automated processing and robotic equipment, it is not unusual to display data for critical variables in real time as they are being accumulated.

Nonconforming Parts and Materials Control

Another extremely critical assurance function throughout the manufacturing process is that of monitoring and controlling nonconforming parts and materials. At every stage of manufacturing, items will be found that do not conform to their individual requirements or the requirements of the end product. Before these items can be used, the manufacturer should decide whether they should be used at all. During this decision-making process, the manufacturer must control these items so that they do not inadvertently find their way into the end product.

Making It Happen!

Some of the more common homilies associated with manufacturing quality or product conformance assurance are as follows:

- "You can't inspect quality into your product."
- "Quality is everybody's business."
- "Control the process and you control the product."
- "Quality is an attitude."

Some of the more common misconceptions relating to manufacturing quality are as follows:

- "Increasing yield comes from lowering quality."
- "Quality is controlled by the quality organization."
- "Quality costs money."

The diametrically opposed views represented by these two groups of ideas show the problems associated with interpreting the meaning of quality. To some extent, the term's meaning is in the mind of the beholder. Therein lies the problem. Preconceived conceptions of manufacturing quality taint and, to an extent, direct the activities of all people associated with manufacturing. The success of any assurance program, therefore, lies in management's commitment to the concept of building quality into the product. The extent to which this attitude is positively reinforced is a large determinant of the attitude of all manufacturing personnel, from the very highest manager down to the lowest skilled assembler. Negative attitudes of manufacturing and management personnel can make producing quality products impossible. Over the past 25 years or so, a major public relations effort has been directed toward educating and convincing all levels of management and manufacturing personnel that their actions determine manufacturing quality. This effort is bearing fruit.

As a result of international economic competition and better quality of international imports, some innovative production approaches have been attempted. The most significant is the production team that combines most of the elements of manufacturing supervision and quality control. These teams are allowed to make decisions about working hours, production quotas, quality levels, and so on. They invariably are responsible for a much larger than normal portion of a complete production process—sometimes all of it. These teams compete with one another against a number of criteria (cost, defects, and others), and, of course, personal involvement is significant. This concept also is being used by companies in a number of other countries. For example, Japanese manufacturers have a quality circle approach. In all of these, there is the attempt to increase the motivation and empowerment of the hands-on workers to produce items with pride. This is the most solid indication of the recognition that manufacturing product integrity is the responsibility of the manufacturing organization, not the quality department.

Further Reading

Carrubba, E. R., and R. D. Gordon. *Product Assurance Principles.* New York: ASQC Quality Press and McGraw-Hill Book Company, 1988: Chapter 10.

Juran, J. M., ed. *Quality Control Handbook.* 4th ed. New York: McGraw-Hill Book Company, 1988.

Chapter 6
Testing

Is the Proof Really in the Pudding?

The most nearly unimpeachable source of product integrity information is testing. Personally, we tend to regard "proven-by-test" claims with the same suspicion generally accorded "proven-by-analysis" claims. Among the masses, however, "seeing is believing." Witness some television commercials in which the watch still runs after being fastened to the propeller that drives a racing motorboat to victory; the pen still writes after being used as a can opener; the leak-sealing antifreeze (with help from the laws of fluid mechanics) preserves the integrity of its punctured container; the upset-stomach remedy provides a protective (or at least opaque) coating on the inside of a beaker; the battery starts a fleet of automobiles simultaneously; the spray deodorant can make cotton balls stick to the inner elbow while another one can't . . . and so on, ad nauseam.

Advertising agencies have perceived that the consumer would like to "try before buy," even if only vicariously, via television. This natural and reasonable desire is the motivation for most testing. We applaud both the desire and the honest response to it, even by advertising agencies. (We have come to praise testing, not to bury it!) As far as we know, the watch, pen, and battery demonstrations cited were valid and to the point, if not comprehensive. Even the deodorant stickiness test is pertinent, if one considers stickiness and body odor to be equally odious. The upset-stomach remedy demonstration was not a test but merely a visual aid. It was graphic illustration of the nature of a claim—not substantiation. The attempt to imply substantiation was through the "demonstration" of the leak-sealing property of the antifreeze. In this case, the real hero was the partial vacuum formed in the top of the can.

Such demonstrations are not confined to the consumer market nor practiced exclusively by advertising people. Everything was open, documented, and approved by the proper authorities. It was all quite legal; it just wasn't *right.*

What is testing? According to our dictionary, *test* is a verb which means "(1) to try by subjecting to some experiment or trial, or by examination and comparison; (2) to subject to conditions that reveal the true character of, in relation to some particular quality." So, basically, testing consists of providing stimuli to the test subject and noting reactions.

Kinds of Tests

As you might expect, the manufacturer has a variety of tests to pick from. Proper selection will depend on the test objective(s). There are three primary reasons for testing: to seek knowledge, to verify a hypothesis, and to classify. In addition, there are test-like processes designed to eliminate inherent weaknesses, purify, and make better products. Motivation for testing comes in various combinations of these factors.

A test may be designed to destroy the test subject, either because of the nature of the subject (like a firecracker) or the objective of the test (such as determining how much weight a TV cabinet can bear before it breaks). It should be obvious that destructive tests relate to "class questions" about the test subject. If conclusions drawn from such a test cannot be applied to the test subject's brothers (or sisters) as well as to the test subject itself, then there is no point to the test. Nondestructive tests, on the other hand, might be directed to specific test subjects, with no extrapolation of results to others of their kind. Thus, there are really just two kinds of tests.

1. *Class tests.* Class-question testing seeks information or makes determinations related to item types, families, or classes (such as the Brand X 21-inch television set or the

Brand Y self-propelled lawn mower). As a consequence, it is important that the actual test subjects chosen be truly representative of the population about which information is sought or for which some determination is to be made. Class testing may be either destructive or nondestructive and applied to hardware or software.

2. *Item-directed tests.* Item testing makes determinations related to the specific item under test only and must therefore be nondestructive. Screening tests (for example, stress-type tests used to remove latent manufacturing defects in a product) are included in this category. These kinds of tests quite obviously have no effect on eliminating weaknesses from items not included in the processing (except as a by-product). These tests are solely hardware oriented.

For a worm's-eye view of the world of testing, see the "test apple" of Figure 6.1. It is shown here to demonstrate that there are a wide variety of tests for different purposes. It groups like characteristics in segments, with the most basic test characteristics at the core and characteristics growing more specific toward the outside. Design-related testing occupies the left hemisphere and manufacturing testing the right hemisphere. Those tests most closely related to the assurance of product integrity overlap both and occupy the lower hemisphere.

Ideally, from the point of view of accuracy and confidence of results, all testing would be conducted on each and every item of interest and, of course, be nondestructive. On the other hand, from an economic and practical point of view, it would be ideal if the results of testing a single representative item could be confidently applied to the entire parent population of that item. Both of these situations, and the many compromise positions in between, actually exist in the scientific/industrial environment.

Class Testing

Within the category of class testing, there are two major subclassifications. One is experimental testing; the other is verification testing.

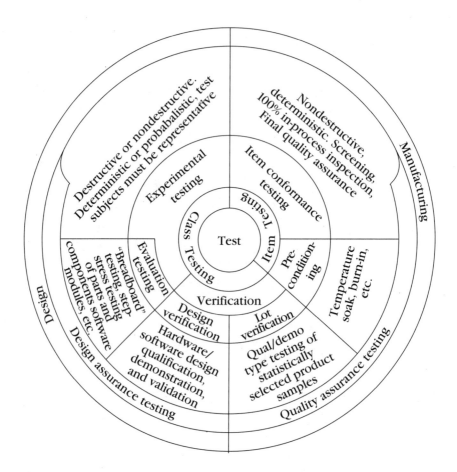

Figure 6.1 The Test Apple

Experimental testing fits the definition "to subject to conditions that reveal the true character of, in relation to some particular quality." It embraces design assurance evaluation testing, which is generally directed at determining the suitability of various parts/components (and software, where applicable) for inclusion in the product design. Evaluation testing can also be applied to the product itself; for instance, testing to determine how long a product will last.

Verification testing differs from experimental testing in that the objective is not to determine the true nature of the subject in relation to a particular quality. Verification testing is less ambitious, being content merely to determine whether the test subject meets certain preestablished criteria; for instance, that the operating software in a personal computer executes all the proper commands in the correct sequence.

An example of class testing is design verification testing performed on new products. This type of testing qualifies the product against a set of established requirements. As an example, TV advertisements show environmental testing of new automobiles. Manufacturers provide this type of advertisement as visual evidence that their automobiles can withstand the rigors of a wide set of environmental conditions. Examples include the torrent of water that pours on the Lexus, presumably without causing leaking inside, or the shopping cart that rolls down an incline and slams into the side of the Saturn without causing a dent. And then there are the countless other new car models which have their interior seats pounded on mercilessly; their exteriors exposed to the extremes of high and low temperature, humidity, icing, fierce winds, and sand blasting; their bodies bounced and tortured over surfaces resembling ski moguls; and even their windshield wipers cycled on and off relentlessly. All in the name of proof!

Item-Directed Testing

Item-directed testing, like class testing, embraces two major subclassifications. One is item conformance testing; the other is preconditioning or burn-in testing.

Conformance testing is applied to each item of the population of interest (such as all clothes dryers built by the manufacturer) and is go/no-go like verification testing (that is, the units under test are either good or bad). However, it is rather cursory in that ordinarily only major performance parameters are examined. Like verification testing, item conformance testing requires predetermination of accept/reject criteria.

On the other hand, in *preconditioning* or *burn-in testing,* all items of interest are subjected to controlled stress conditions so that weaknesses can be detected. Units found to be faulty are either discarded or repaired. The survivors are then known to be "tried and true."

Fail to Plan, Plan to Fail!

Now that we have completed this brief discussion of test varieties, let us raise some of the more important cares and cautions that a good manufacturer should consider in test planning. Few endeavors need more careful planning than a test and its associated documentation. If a test isn't documented, it isn't done, and that applies to the test plan, the test procedure, and the test results. Documentation doesn't necessarily have to be fancy, but it has to be done. It is easy to conceive of situations in which the absence of companion plans and procedures could render test results less credible or less useful.

There are a few basics to consider in planning any test. Is the test intended to find out something the manufacturer would like to know or needs to know (seek knowledge—experimental testing), to develop evidence that will substantiate some preconceived notion (verify a hypothesis—verification test), or to separate the apples from the oranges (remove manufacturing defects—screening test)? At this point, the manufacturer should be considering the alternatives. Does there exist any credible history which will supply these needs directly? Can previous or concurrent work of others be analytically extrapolated to satisfy these needs? What confidence (either qualitative or statistically quantitative) is required in the results?

Having established that a test is necessary, or at least desirable, the manufacturer should next survey the resources available and needed for performing the desired test. Consideration must be given to such factors as the following:

- Time—when and for how long the test will be run?

- Machinery—what test equipment will be needed to perform the test? What units and how many will be subjected to test?

- Personnel—how many people will be required to conduct the test? What skill levels will they need?

Even a well-planned test is not without problems. However, it should be recognized that there are many situations in which a properly planned, executed, and documented test is the best, and maybe only, available solution.

Consumers should not let paranoia about test flimflammery cloud the fact that there is no substitute for a properly conceived, planned, executed, and documented test. There are those who contend that the only real evidence of product "goodness" is a history of user satisfaction, particularly in regard to product integrity characteristics. While there is agreement that the best evidence of product integrity is continued user satisfaction, attempts to deny the efficiency of testing are largely without merit.

Further Reading

Carrubba, E. R., and R. D. Gordon. *Product Assurance Principles.* New York: ASQC Quality Press and McGraw-Hill Book Company, 1988: Chapter 11.

Gilmore, H. L., and H. C. Schwartz. *Integrated Product Testing and Evaluation.* Rev. ed. New York: Marcel Dekker, 1986.

Chapter 7
Customer Service

Quality and Service

The quality of a product is largely determined by how it is designed and manufactured, with the assurance activities providing a high confidence that the established requirements will indeed be satisfied. Yet, following the purchase and receipt of an item, and to some extent, prior to purchase, the customer's experience can be more influenced by service characteristics than the performance details of the product itself. Thus, the planning and delivery of service should be no less rigorous than the design, manufacture, and verification of product quality.

Service, as defined here, is the set of activities beyond the physical product that contribute to and facilitate successful intended use or enjoyment of a product. The quality of the service, when thought of in combination with the quality of the product, results in what can be called the *total customer experience.* The following areas, as appropriate for a given product, can be thought of as components of service.

1. *The sale*—includes accuracy of information to make an informed purchase decision, the ease of placing an order, and all the administrative processes which support the sale.

2. *The delivery*—includes the shipping method, the ability to fill an order on time and accurately, and the ease by which the customer can receive the delivered product.

3. *Installation and/or assembly*—includes the clarity of manuals and instructions, and the ease by which additional information can be obtained. When installation/assembly is not done by the customer, the competence of the installer is an important factor.

4. *Operation*—like installation, this includes the ability to obtain help when needed.

5. *Repair*—includes warranty policy and ease of obtaining warranty and gaining access to the repair resources. The competence of service resources and the ease of getting repair are important factors.

6. *Materials*—includes the ease of obtaining parts and supplies.

In the broadest sense, service can begin with how a product is marketed and sold and continue throughout the customer's total ownership experience. The product characteristics weigh heavily on a purchase decision, which is only a single moment. Yet service provided in the form of information prior to purchase, along with all additional service elements, constitutes the customer's ongoing experience with a product. Service that is adequate often goes unnoticed; superior service can make a product seem more desirable. A bad service experience can devalue a product, no matter how revered it may be in the marketplace.

Planning for Service

Service planning is a highly complex process that yields a cradle-to-grave support system for a product. It is influenced by the type and complexity of the product itself, the characteristics of the user, economic factors, and the service resources available. The planning process actually begins before the product is on the drawing board. The design of the product has to account for how it is to be serviced. Characteristics such as maintainability will determine whether repair is simple or difficult.

Above and beyond design, an entire support structure has to be considered to provide service that meets the customer's needs. Included in the planning for this support structure are the following:

- *Human resources*—The right people with the right skills in the right numbers form the service team that delivers the service. Service is most notably associated with people.

- *Training*—Salespeople, customer representatives, and repair technicians all need the proper training. Every product has its own unique characteristics, and quality service requires that all people who deliver service receive the appropriate training.

- *Spare parts*—Planning must ensure that parts are available on a timely basis to facilitate repair in accordance with customer expectations. Usually, the greater the need for speed, the more costly it is to provide needed parts. Companies generally balance parts availability against the costs of inventory and distribution.

- *Accessories and supplies*—Planning here is similar to that for spare parts. However, demand may be a bit more predictable, since consumption rates can be estimated more easily.

- *Facilities*—The locations and bases for service are a key element. Companies will decide how much of the service they will provide themselves and how much will be provided through others. Office space, factory space, and all equipment (computers, tools, test equipment, communications) associated with service are part of the planning.

- *Documentation*—The clarity, accuracy, and availability of written information play an important role in the service of a product. This includes sales literature, user instructions, warranty directions, and repair procedures.

- *Information*—Many types of information are needed to plan for a product. Customer data is one example. Product information in the form of technical assistance is another. The various forms of information are key elements of planning and delivering service.

The service planning effort is largely determined by the availability and type of service to be delivered. The service strategy is, in turn, influenced by a number of factors.

Product complexity and cost play an important role. Simple, inexpensive products that tend to have long, failure-free lives are not likely to have elaborate service networks. Conversely, complex items which require frequent maintenance or other service during their lives would require considerable planning. Competition is also an important factor. A leadership position in a particular market may require service to be the differentiator to a customer and therefore would necessitate a more elaborate service offering.

Maintenance Philosophy

Prior to exploring types of maintenance, we must examine the concept of maintenance philosophy. Maintenance philosophy is the set of norms by which maintenance will be performed on a product. The service planning effort will be largely determined by the maintenance philosophy.

One of the first considerations of the maintenance philosophy is determination of who is qualified or expected to do maintenance. This can be influenced by safety factors, skill requirements, or cost. If the philosophy is customer or user maintenance, then planning emphasis needs to be on instructions, technical support, and ease of obtaining parts. If the philosophy is maintenance by authorized representatives, then emphasis needs to be on training and human resource availability.

Another key area of the maintenance philosophy is the level of repair to be done on parts that can be repaired. For complex items, particularly electronics, faulty items can be identified by diagnosis and troubleshooting. Rather than removing a faulty module and repairing it, the alternative is to replace the module with a spare and repair the faulty item at another time and in another location (such as the factory). The service strategy to implement this philosophy would require various repair capabilities in support of each other focusing on maintenance for different levels of the product. This approach applies best to large, complex electronic products, because electronics are not subject to wearing out like mechanical items; therefore, the repaired parts can be considered "good as new."

The maintenance philosophy also influences product design. Careful consideration needs to be paid to testability (the ease of diagnosing problems), modularization (the ease of isolating a faulty item), and repairability (the ease of removing and replacing a faulty item).

Types of Maintenance

The area of service that presents the widest latitude of offerings is maintenance and repair. Each type of maintenance has unique elements that need to be considered, and the various types can be selected in combinations to round out a total strategy. The various types of maintenance are shown in Table 7.1.

The first type of maintenance is called *field service.* "Field" in this case refers to the actual environment of use, as in the "field of play" in a sporting event. It is characterized by the actual work or service performed at the location where the product is used. It may be a computer system in an office, an appliance in a person's home, or a tractor in a farm field. In field service, the service comes to the product rather than the product coming to the service. For many items, this may be the only practical approach, especially if the item is in a permanent location or cannot easily be

Table 7.1   Comparison of Maintenance Types

Maintenance type	Performed by	Where done	Advantages	Disadvantages
Field service	Field technician	Customer location	Competence Convenience	Waiting time Cost
Factory repair	Factory technician	Place of manufacture	Local skill resources	Turnaround Transit cost
Service center	Service center technician	Remote location	Accessibility	Less skills Parts stock
Self-maintenance	User or owner	Customer location	Cost	Skill requirements

brought to a source of service. The cost associated with field service is generally the highest, and the timeliness of obtaining service can vary with the degree of planning and the resources available. Field service certainly provides the most convenient source of service in cases where a choice of service can be made and cost is not a major factor. It can be performed by trained members of a manufacturer's service organization or by independent service providers who can meet the customer's needs. When field service is important, care should be given to the company's reputation and track record for time to reach the product location, ease of contacting the service provider, and how well repairs are accomplished.

Factory service differs from field service in that it is performed away from the location where the product is used. Although "factory" implies the manufacturing facility, it can mean any location controlled by the manufacturer which is dedicated to repair of a product. The key characteristic of factory service (or factory repair) is that the product, or a portion of the product, is brought to the repair location. For easily transportable items, factory repair can make a lot of sense, since savings can be realized when a service technician is not required to travel to and from the product site. This type of service can also be accomplished on large items; in most cases, troubleshooting or fault isolation can localize a problem to a smaller piece of the product, and that smaller item can then be shipped to the factory. The ability to determine a faulty assembly and remove it as a modular component is influenced by the maintainability requirements considered in product design.

Factory service is an effective method of repair, since it is likely to have available a concentration of resources and capabilities. For instance, if repair is done at the actual manufacturing factory, all of the test equipment, trained technicians, and procedures originally used to build the product are present to support the repair process as necessary. This is in contrast to a field service technician who is operating at some distance from factory resources.

Service center repair is performed neither at the normal location of the product nor at the factory. Generally, service centers are set up as an alternative to factory repair to make repair accessible in a greater number of locations. Service center repair is usually a more convenient way for consumers to obtain service at reasonable cost. Service centers usually provide a way for the user or owner to bring the product directly to the service provider. They are either run directly by the manufacturer or authorized by the manufacturer, and typically do warranty work as well as after-warranty repairs.

In terms of resources available, service centers are not thought of as being as well equipped as factory service. Furthermore, where spare parts are necessary to make repairs, service centers cannot realistically be expected to stock all parts for all products. Just as skills and diagnostic complexity can be established in tiers or echelons, so too can stocking of parts. With today's fast delivery services, it should never take very long to obtain needed parts. A possible delay is a small concession for the convenience of a service center.

The last type of maintenance to be considered is parts support or *self-maintenance*—service or repair is performed by the user or consumer. Assuming the right level of skill is available, this may be the most economical form of maintenance. Typically, the manufacturer will provide adequate instruction for service through documentation or formal training. (Documentation and training are often viable sources of income for the manufacturer.) It is also of prime importance to assure the availability of spare parts for the user. This form of maintenance is applicable to simple products that are relatively easy to repair or when an owner has many units and can justify the investment in training as an alternative to other forms of maintenance.

Customer Service and the Consumer

Service should play a significant role in the consumer's purchase consideration of a product. Customer satisfaction stands to be influenced just as much by the ease and quality of service as it is by the product itself. If a purchase decision is based exclusively on price and product features, then poor-quality or expensive, inconvenient service can cost the owner more in the long run. This factor, known as *cost of ownership,* takes into account the purchase price of a product plus the estimated cost of maintenance over the period of ownership. Cost of ownership is further defined and discussed in chapter 12. Other service considerations should also be taken into account, although they might not have a direct impact on cost. For instance, the types of maintenance available would not only determine the relative convenience but would also identify other areas of impact, like the possibility of being denied usage of the product while waiting for repair.

It is of obvious value to investigate and understand the service characteristics of a product before making a commitment. Sales literature often does not provide details of service, and salespeople may not be totally knowledgeable on the subject. Owner manuals and user manuals represent a source of data for terms and conditions of warranty as well as the availability of ongoing service. How frequently service may be required depends on the reliability of the product as well as the manufacturer's recommendation for scheduled maintenance. This information can be found through various consumer resources like publications and agencies, or through word of mouth. The additional time devoted to investigating customer service characteristics, and the use of the findings in an overall purchase decision, are important dimensions that you should be prepared to undertake.

Product-Focused Maintenance Thoughts

This section illustrates various types of maintenance as applied to several different product types. Each area has certain ramifications that can affect your overall experience with a particular product.

Small consumer products—This product category, which consists primarily of entertainment items and small appliances, is subject mostly to factory or service center repair. Although failures or problems are infrequent, maintenance can entail some inconvenience. You are generally required to package and ship a product at your own expense or to travel twice (drop-off and pickup usually are at different times, since maintenance is not immediate) to a service center, which could require a considerable trip.

In response to customer needs, more options are becoming available. Take the case of the cordless telephone. Early models required factory or service center replacement of the battery or antenna. In many designs, those parts are now user-replaceable and readily available from the manufacturer or retail stores.

Major appliance and large entertainment products— Products in this category generally do not lend themselves to easy transportation. Therefore, some form of field service will be the likely approach. For example, maintenance of your refrigerator would be done in your home by a technician representing the manufacturer or by a third-party repairer who is familiar with the product and has access to necessary parts.

*Personal computers—*This type of product can cover the whole range of maintenance types. While it is certainly easy to find sources of on-site service, most computers are either modular or small enough to facilitate factory or service center maintenance. And given the breadth of built-in diagnostics and detailed user manuals, self-maintenance is often possible. Many subassemblies are available for purchase, allowing significant savings over other forms of maintenance. And, if you attempt self-maintenance and are not successful, you can then seek the help of a service center.

Customer service remains an important component of the overall consumer experience. It is therefore important to carefully study all of the service considerations early in the evaluation of a product.

Further Reading

Zeithaml, Valarie, A. Parasuraman, and Leonard L. Berry. *Delivering Quality Service.* New York: Free Press, 1990.

Part 3

A Consumer's Guide to Quality

Part 3 offers a practical how-to treatment of quality from the consumer's perspective. It includes important guidelines and tips to help make the best decisions about the product being considered. It is the heart of this book. Chapter 8 discusses the meaning of and cautions related to warranties. Chapter 9 provides an understanding of the value, choice, and decisions surrounding service contracts. Chapter 10 examines the role of independent product testing and evaluation organizations as an important source of information in the product selection process. Chapter 11 provides a look at how the manufacturer measures and strives to achieve customer satisfaction. Chapter 12 gives a walk-through review of how to select quality products.

Chapter 8
Warranties and Guarantees

Why Have Warranties?

As we have seen, the consumer's view of quality is influenced by both product and service characteristics. When you make a purchase, you have established certain expectations; if they are not met, you expect the manufacturer to take some action. The warranty is the manufacturer's commitment to stand behind its products should they prove defective. It is common practice to provide buyers with written statements guaranteeing that the products will be of expected quality and describing the obligations of the manufacturer and the consumer.

In today's market, most products come with written warranties, although it is not absolutely required by law. The Magnuson-Moss Act ("federal warranty") requires only that warranties be available for you to read before you make a purchase. It is more for competitive reasons and consumer expectations that virtually all products come with a written warranty. The terms of protection do vary greatly, even within families of similar products. Therefore, as a consumer, you need to assess the importance of a warranty in any purchase decision and then investigate the specific choices and how they affect the overall product selection.

There are a number of reasons why manufacturers provide warranties on their products. Naturally, it would be difficult to instill consumer confidence in a product if the company wasn't demonstrating its own belief in the product in some fashion. It is more comforting for consumers to see a company standing behind its own products, and a written warranty is a way of accomplishing that. Secondly, there is a significant competitive value to a warranty. When product differentiation is small (for example, see the analysis of 19-inch color televisions cited in chapter 11), a warranty perceived as far superior to that of the competition could be a marketing advantage and thus would affect sales performance. Lastly, the warranty can explicitly define the limits of liabilities and responsibilities of the manufacturer. In the absence of definition of those limits, the manufacturer could conceivably be subject to obligations derived from the interpretation of varied legislation governing warranties.

Types of Warranty

The typical written warranty that accompanies most consumer purchases establishes a contractual obligation by which the manufacturer offers to remedy certain defects or failures in the product or to compensate the buyer for a predetermined time or usage factor following a sale. This is known as an *express warranty.* It is comprised of statements or promises made by the manufacturer or seller to the buyer that relate to the quality and other characteristics of the product. The commitments become part of the transaction, thus creating an express warranty that the product conforms to such promises or statements.

As stated earlier, written warranties are not required by law. However, every state has some law governing *implied warranties.* Two areas of implied warranties deal directly with every consumer purchase. They are

1. *Implied warranty of merchantability*—Simply stated, the manufacturer warrants that a product will do what it is designed to do; for instance, a washing machine will wash and a clock will tell the time.

2. *Implied warranty of fitness for a particular purpose*— This obliges sellers to know the purposes for which goods are purchased and to make their skills available in the

selection and furnishing of suitable goods; for example, a manufacturer warrants a specific space heater to warm a room of certain size.

The good news for consumers is that in the absence of a written warranty, implied warranties are in effect unless the manufacturer explicitly declares that no warranties are applicable. In the event that written warranties are not adequate, you should always pursue the protection afforded by your state's laws covering implied warranties. Often, implied warranties are in effect longer than written warranties provided by the manufacturer.

Warranty Features and Conditions

Given that the manufacturer can determine just about all the terms of an express warranty, we would expect a wide variation among warranties from product to product and manufacturer to manufacturer. As a consumer, you should view a warranty as a means of protecting your investment. Consequently, you should carefully investigate the terms of that protection. The following text describes various items to consider.

Extent of Coverage

It is important to understand what parts or types of problems are not covered by the warranty. While specific parts may be excluded from warranty coverage (for instance, the decorator light bulb in a newly purchased lamp), the more usual case is to provide different coverage for different components.

There are many examples of this in consumer products.

- Specialty muffler shops that offer a lifetime warranty on the muffler and 12-month coverage on everything else they replace
- The television set that provides a warranty of 90 days on all parts and 2 years on the picture tube
- The refrigerator that comes with a warranty of 12 months on the overall unit and 5 years on the compressor

Another situation in which there is different coverage in the same product occurs when more than one manufacturer covers different components of a product. For instance, a car manufacturer may advertise a particular warranty while the car's stereo system and tires are subject to the warranties of the stereo manufacturer and tire manufacturer.

It is important to check the extent of coverage thoroughly. You may assume that all parts are covered uniformly, but the risk exists that some of the most failure-prone or costly items may not be adequately addressed by the warranty.

Manufacturer's Obligations

In essence, a warranty states that a manufacturer agrees to remedy or compensate the buyer for certain defects or failures in the product for a specified time or amount of usage after the sale. How effectively the manufacturer chooses to define and administer the "remedies and compensations" will determine how useful the warranty is to the buyer. There are three basic choices available when it comes to warranty.

- *Repair*—fix the item using some combination of new parts and labor

- *Replace*—provide a whole new product in exchange for the old one

- *Refund*—return the buyer's money in exchange for the product

While the manufacturer generally decides on which course of action to take, you should be prepared to bring charges to bear if satisfaction cannot be achieved. For instance, if repeated repairs have not successfully solved a problem, you should seek replacement or refund instead of additional repair.

Another important consideration is whether a repair or replacement is totally free or prorated. Prorated replacements involve a cost to the consumer, depending on the measure of use at the time of failure. Automobile tires are generally prorated according to remaining tread thickness. If a defect occurs late in the prorated interval, the buyer may be virtually unprotected, even if the defect is unrelated to time or wear. This approach to warranty generally favors the manufacturer.

It is worth investigating the continuing warranty coverage of a product that has been repaired or replaced. An ordinary repair or replacement item has a warranty equal to the remaining length of the original warranty. This says that a new motor installed in a VCR during the 11th month of a 12-month warranty carries only a 1-month warranty. This is not desirable. On the other hand, an unlimited repair or replacement item carries a warranty identical to the original. The advantage should be obvious.

A common practice by manufacturers is to distinguish between parts and labor when specifying the extent of warranty coverage they will provide. The classic example of this distinction is the warranty that covers parts and labor for some initial period and then parts only for the balance of the warranty. This puts the manufacturer in a highly favorable position while permitting it to advertise a warranty that appears to be acceptably long even though coverage is "parts only" for the majority of the warranty period. Labor costs of a repair exceed parts costs so often that "parts only" coverage could be close to no coverage at all.

Consequential damage is another area that could have significant financial implications if not reviewed properly. In many circumstances, the failure of a product can damage other products or property. Some examples are a washing machine that rips clothing, a leaky battery that ruins an electronic device it was powering, and a smoke detector that fails and is responsible for the loss of a home. Consequential damage is often expressly limited by the manufacturer's statement that its responsibility is limited to the value of the original product. You should be aware of any risks that failure of a product might pose beyond the product itself and investigate what the manufacturer is willing to cover. And remember, in the case of consequential damage expressly limited by the manufacturer, your protection under implied warranties may be an avenue to pursue.

Consumer's Obligations

It is common for the terms of a warranty to place specific requirements on the consumer. In many instances, these requirements may be valid restrictions designed to minimize any problems with the product over its life, while in other cases they may be imposed simply to enhance profits.

One familiar example deals with the environment in which a product is used. The manufacturer can recommend a range or limit on elements of the environment, such as temperature, humidity, or sunlight and declare that exceeding these limits may void the warranty. This area should not be of major concern to you as a consumer, since the burden is on the manufacturer to declare when limits are exceeded. Although there are scientific methods that can tie certain failures to particular types of stress, the case would have to be fairly obvious for a manufacturer to void the warranty. Furthermore, the potential loss of goodwill might inhibit the manufacturer from taking action. In only the most obvious cases would the warranty be at risk.

Misuse or misapplication of a product and other consumer-induced problems are likely sources of invalidating a warranty. Although there may be some subjectivity involved in certain instances, there are cases where the manufacturer is clearly not responsible, such as when a washing machine is consistently loaded beyond capacity, or someone spills a glass of water on stereo equipment.

As was the case with the environmental restrictions, it may be difficult for the manufacturer to pinpoint or prove misuse, misapplication, and other consumer-induced problems.

An additional area of consumer responsibility is maintenance requirements and supplies. For instance, to maintain a warranty, you may be required to have the product serviced on a predetermined schedule by a specified service provider. This is common with automobiles; manufacturers recommend a schedule of oil changes and other maintenance actions. Although consumers typically are not required to show proof when obtaining warranty service, it is highly advisable to retain records and receipts of all maintenance in case a problem is attributed to insufficient maintenance. It is also advisable to follow the maintenance requirement specifically set forth by the manufacturer.

The choice and use of supplies can be just as important as following maintenance requirements. This can apply to the oil in a lawn mower, the various filters in a car, or the ribbon in a printer. The manufacturer can specify its own brand or another specific brand of supplies which must be used if the warranty is to be honored. This can be a legitimate requirement because of the concern that independent brands or generic supplies may be of lesser quality and thus create problems, or it may simply be a way for the manufacturer to sell more supplies. In any event, you should take care to understand such requirements and follow them carefully if there is a chance of needing work done under the warranty.

Premium Charge Cards

The highly competitive credit card market has added a potentially attractive warranty feature to many upscale cards available to consumers. The credit card company doubles the manufacturer's warranty for any product purchased with that card. While restrictions, requirements, and methods of honoring this benefit may vary, the extended coverage could prove highly worthwhile. This is particularly true for products that exhibit failure based on length of usage. It may prove desirable to investigate the cost and benefits of one of these cards.

Consumer Considerations

The warranty that accompanies a product is an important dimension of the whole consumer experience. It not only represents the manufacturer's commitment to you and to the product but also affords a level of financial protection should you need it. Therefore, the following considerations are important when investigating a warranty.

- *How is the warranty communicated?* It can be printed on packaging, contained on a separate card, or described in an owner's manual.

- *What is required of the consumer?* You may be requested to mail in a registration card to allow the manufacturer to have traceability (in case of a product recall, for example). Furthermore, you should be aware of all restrictions with regard to environment, maintenance requirements, or supplies. In addition, if this is the type of product you may resell, you should know whether the warranty is transferable.

- *How complete is the protection?* You should determine whether you incur any expense under warranty and be aware of the time periods for which you may be covered. Specific exclusions should be identified. Also, understand what the manufacturer will provide under warranty.

- *How is warranty service obtained?* There should be detailed instructions on how to file a claim and the specific locations where warranty service can be obtained. You should save all purchase and maintenance receipts.

- *What is the process for resolving warranty disputes?* You should identify what you would do if you were not satisfied with your warranty. This can take the form of calling a customer service support number provided by the manufacturer or appealing to government agencies.

Further Reading

Belli, M., Sr., and A. P. Wilkinson. *Everybody's Guide to the Law.* New York: Gramercy Publishing Company, 1989: Chapter 10.

Chapter 9
Service Contracts

Thinking About a Service Contract?

It has been shown that the manufacturer's warranty is your protection when a product fails to perform as expected. Yet with few exceptions, warranties are in effect for only a limited time and thereby only provide protection until the date they expire. It is important to understand the impact of quality when the manufacturer is no longer obligated to take some form of action in the event of problems. At that point you have to make some decisions that could have financial impact on your remaining years of ownership of the product. The options range from doing nothing (and incurring all out-of-pocket expenses) to entering into one of a variety of contract arrangements designed to make your expenses predictable. The key to deciding which is best for you depends largely on your ability to determine the quality and reliability of the product and using that information in conjunction with any maintenance cost estimates.

Service contracts are a common vehicle for obtaining maintenance once a manufacturer's warranty has run out. In effect, for a predetermined fee, you obtain a level of service beyond that of warranty coverage, subject to the terms and conditions of the agreement. Service contracts are often referred to as extended warranties because they are virtual extensions of the terms of the original warranty. Although this terminology is common, a service contract is technically not a warranty, because a warranty is included in the price of a product and is not sold separately. A service contract more closely resembles health insurance than a warranty.

Terms and Conditions

The terms and conditions of service contracts vary widely. Although we showed the complexity of basic warranty coverage, the variations of service contracts are even more complex. It is well worth the time to study the service contract as well as the performance of the product you are considering or already own. Only then can you make an informed decision about whether or not the contract is right for you.

There are two times when a service contract typically is available for purchase. The first opportunity is at the time of the original product sale. It is now common to have your salesperson try to persuade you to enter into a service contract just as you have made a new purchase. Often, retail stores display a separate tag on display models offering a service contract and advertising the annual cost or one-time fee in bold numbers. Now you must not only do your homework on the product itself; it's also to your advantage to also understand service contracts when you are making a purchase.

The other major opportunity to consider a service contract is when the manufacturer's warranty is about to expire. It is common to receive solicitations for service contracts as the expiration date of your warranty approaches. Whether it's a promotion through the mail or a telephone sales pitch, someone tries to sell you a service contract. As we shall point out later, there are large profits associated with service contracts. Therefore, aggressive sales tactics are not unusual. If you make a major purchase and a service contract is not offered at that time, you can expect to be contacted toward the end of the original warranty. The offer can come from the manufacturer or from an independent dealer of service contracts. Whichever is the case, careful consideration needs to go into the decision.

While dollars and cents play a large role in determining whether or not a service contract is right for you, it is important to understand just what you're getting for the money.

1. *Coverage*—Basic manufacturers' warranties cover parts and labor, sometimes for different time intervals (for example, parts and labor for 90 days and parts only thereafter). The same is true for service contracts. It is extremely important to know what is covered. Parts and labor may be covered for the first year, then parts only thereafter. Equally important is how many times or for how long a contract may be renewed. As a product gets older and is more likely to need service, there may be restrictions on renewability.

2. *Service source*—There is a range of possibilities for obtaining needed service, depending on who sold you the service contract. If it's the original manufacturer, the service source may be identical to the provider of service obtained under warranty (service center, factory, and so on). However, if someone other than the original manufacturer sold you the service contract, you may be required to take or send the product to an authorized dealer or some equivalent approved by your service contract.

    Issues to consider at this juncture are convenience and competence. If you are required to travel or to ship the product (or its elements) at your expense, this can be more costly than a minor repair. You should also know when on-site (as opposed to carry-in) service is available. Finally, as was the case with customer service, the skill level of those outside the control of the manufacturer can be unpredictable. If you must use the services of those directed by the contract, you may not have much recourse if you are not satisfied with the work provided.

3. *Compensation*—Service contracts are supposed to limit your out-of-pocket expenses in the event of problems with a product. In the simplest case, a problem arises, you obtain the necessary service, and no money exchanges hands. Unfortunately, this is not always the case. Some service contracts work on a reimbursement basis: you pay for the service and then get reimbursed under the terms of the contract. This is another case where it is important to be familiar with the specifics. There may be limitations on

amounts payable for service as well as a limited number of places that provide service. Furthermore, some contracts require approval before the actual work is performed. Also, many service contracts are subject to a deductible. This means that for any service, an initial, predetermined amount of money is the responsibility of the owner. The deductible applies regardless of how small the service is or how frequently it is required. Depending on the deductible amount, you may only receive compensation if your service cost is relatively high.

4. *Owner requirements*—Similar to basic warranties and depending on the type of product, there may be certain responsibilities placed upon the consumer to satisfy the terms of the service contract. Where the quality and reliability of a product could be influenced by scheduled maintenance, the service contract may require proof of recommended services to validate the contract. Examples of scheduled maintenance are oil changes in an automobile, head cleaning in a VCR, and filter cleaning in an air conditioner. One advantage to the consumer is that some contracts provide for, and actually include, scheduled maintenance as part of the overall service. This not only ensures meeting the terms of the contract, but also has the potential of maximizing the lifetime and enjoyment of the product. In addition, the user of the product should carefully consider the recommended environment. As was the case with warranty coverage, misuse of a product or operation beyond specified limits could invalidate the terms of a service contract.

5. *Portability*—It is important to consider the flexibility of a service contract in accommodating change. For instance, if you buy a product from a local retailer offering a service contract and you then move across the country, you should determine whether it would become more difficult to obtain service. If the contract specifies carry-in service to a local facility, you may be out of luck. Or what if you had purchased in-home scheduled maintenance and are now 2000 miles away? Another factor to evaluate is the

ability to transfer the service contract to another person if you sell the product. The possibilities of doing so range from automatic transfer to a flurry of paperwork and records. If transfer of a service contract is one of your selling points, you should have a clear understanding of whether or not it is permitted and the of complexity of the transfer to a new owner.

Making a Decision

Deciding whether or not to purchase a service contract should depend on product quality and the financial benefits received for the money paid. Since the cost of a service contract typically represents only a fraction of the original product cost, there may be a tendency to make a quick decision to buy the contract, since for a small additional expense you receive protection and peace of mind. Yet when you examine the financial benefits more closely, you may reach a different conclusion.

Consider the so-called "bathtub curve," which describes the reliability pattern of electronic products (see Figure 9.1). The tendency of the product to fail starts high in early life and decreases to a relatively constant and improved reliability (the bottom of the bathtub) until the product reaches a wear-out period and the tendency to fail increases. Since the manufacturer's warranty generally covers the early life failures, service contracts are really in effect during the most reliable period of product ownership and are probably not extended into the period during which wear-out failures increase. If you reflect on personal experience, it is likely that most products you have owned, whether or not they exhibited early problems, had a relatively failure-free existence for most of their time in service. In effect, a service contract may be protection against a rare, failure-prone product—a "lemon." Therefore, when considering whether a service contract's protection is really needed, we find it may be much rarer than believed.

It is no surprise that service contracts have become a major phenomenon in retailing. In fact, they are so lucrative that in some businesses, they can make the difference between profit and loss. In price-competitive commodity businesses, profit margins can be relatively low. A consumer who has spent considerable time doing

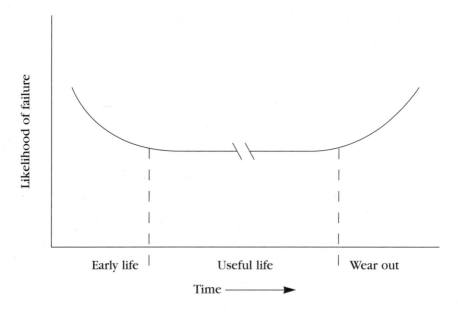

Figure 9.1   Bathtub Curve

comparison shopping for the best price will make a split-second decision to purchase a service contract. No wonder more and more dealers are offering their own contracts rather than merely representing a service company for a commission only.

The bottom line is not that service contracts are inherently bad. They represent a way to limit the cost incurred from failures after the warranty no longer protects you. However, you must carefully compare the out-of-pocket expenses of purchasing the service contract to the likelihood of service cost you will experience. Analysis shows that service contracts generally cost the average consumer more in the long run for the average product. While an occasional poorly performing product might cost more than planned, this should not justify an automatic decision in favor of all available service contracts. If the contracts were so beneficial to consumers, their high profitability for those who offer them could not be explained.

As a consumer, your best protection is knowledge of product quality and reliability. While price is an important factor, total cost of ownership takes into account the cost of service over the life of the product. Your efforts are best directed toward research into how products perform in the marketplace and how they are rated from a quality perspective. Arming yourself with this information should give you a greater sense of confidence in making an informed decision about the necessity of a service contract.

Service Contract Considerations for Typical Products

This section is designed to illustrate the thought process to follow for a variety of product types when considering a service contract. Remember, in practice, the decision should not be made solely on the advice of a salesperson or a solicitation. It is essential to ascertain sufficient information to make an informed decision. For any product under consideration, the factors to consider are generally (1) the product's reliability, (2) the cost of the product versus the cost of the contract, (3) the terms of the manufacturer's warranty, and (4) what repairs might cost in the event of failure.

Consumer electronic products (television, stereos, and so on)—Consumer electronic products especially those with few moving or mechanical parts, tend to be highly reliable. Under normal use, the tendency to fail following warranty expiration is rare. On that basis alone, service contracts are usually not a good investment.

Major appliances (washers, dryers, refrigerators)—The reliability of major appliances is good but cannot always be taken for granted. Moving parts are certainly more prone to failure than simple electronics. Yet most major appliances run for years with no problems. You may tend to favor a service contract if you've had any bad experiences. You may recall needing a new compressor for your refrigerator or a new motor for your washing machine. This is a case where some homework is in order. First, if you had that appliance problem, did the repair cost very much? How would the annual or total service contract cost compare with a typical repair cost? It's easy to be misled by the recollection of a problem product. Furthermore, you are likely to own several major appliances rather than just one. Would it make sense to have service contracts on all of them? The likelihood of all major appliances benefiting from a service contract is very small. The decision to risk a problem rather than buy a number of service contracts will usually be in your favor. You can certainly improve your odds by evaluating brand-name performance through consumer information or informal communication and selecting products that are least likely to fail in the first place.

Automobiles—The thought process and analysis for automobiles is similar to that of major appliances, but the stakes are higher—much higher! We are talking about service contracts that cost hundreds of dollars applied to products that cost thousands. This would suggest the need for more than casual thought.

Many folks can remember the expense of owning a "lemon" car and would have appreciated a service contract under the circumstances. Automobiles are complex machines, and repairs can often be complicated and expensive. Yet rising customer expectations have forced car manufacturers to dramatically improve quality and reliability, which has also influenced the increase of basic warranty duration on many vehicles.

The quality gap (whether real or perceived) between Japanese and other cars is rapidly disappearing. With regular maintenance, most automobiles are now pretty reliable.

It is important to do information gathering once again. Service and repair histories, like those published by *Consumer Reports,* can point to models that are more likely to need service than others. Yet even for the worst performers, there is no certainty that you will get the lemon. The temptation to buy the service contract is greatest here, but a careful analysis might just convince you to do otherwise.

The three examples provided here give you the range of thought processes that should go into a decision to buy a service contract. In addition to doing an analysis, it's equally important to bear in mind that industry estimates indicate that fewer than 20 percent of service contracts purchased are ever utilized. Buyer beware!

Chapter 10
Independent Assessments

Obtaining Objective Data

As we have seen, knowledge of a product's quality is most useful when making a purchase decision or in conjunction with numerous other aspects of product ownership such as warranty, maintenance, service contracts, and so on. Yet despite the importance of such information, its potential impact on customer satisfaction, and its relation to cost of ownership, there are not too many ways to obtain the comprehensive, objective data you may need.

The most common and familiar sources of product information may be word of mouth from other owners and manufacturers' claims of particular levels of quality or performance. While these may be better than nothing at all, they also can lead to less-than-the-best consumer decision. The data you need should be free from bias and subjectivity and should reflect a scientific methodology in their determination. Informal information obtained from other consumers can provide convincing arguments but must be carefully evaluated for objectivity and credibility. Problems could have been the fault of the user, or a salesperson may have misrepresented the product. Also, manufacturers' claims are designed to sell a product, not necessarily to provide useful data. It is wise to be wary of taking statements at face value. For instance, how do you interpret, "Eight out of ten auto mechanics prefer a Brand XYZ car"?

Among the best sources of objective data are organizations that provide independent assessment of products. These organizations typically operate separately from manufacturers and thus are viewed as objective, open, and fair. The assessments consist of laboratory tests and evaluations, simulated use in a typical environment, and analysis of user feedback, to name a few areas. The tests are generally performed against a standard or specification or, in some situations against customer expectations or requirements. The two major areas of evaluation are product safety and product performance. Each has value to consumer decisions and should be judged on that basis.

Is It Safe?

As a consumer, you expect products to be safe. If quality is defined in terms of meeting customer expectations, then safety should be a factor in how you judge the quality of a product. Yet how often do you consider safety among all the other factors when deciding to buy a particular product? Parents tend to be safety-conscious when evaluating children's products, but in the case of other products, safety may be assumed or just not considered, for whatever reason.

When you purchase an electrical product, you certainly expect to use it without concern about electrical shock or fire hazard. When you buy a gas stove or clothes dryer, you don't want to worry about gas leaks. The good news is that numerous organizations perform product safety assessments and therefore provide you, the consumer, with the means to differentiate products that have undergone a specific safety evaluation from those that haven't. Successful conformance to a set of standards or required features gives the product the right to display the seal of the testing organization. Labels commonly seen on consumer products are Underwriters Laboratories (UL), ETL Testing Laboratories, and the American Gas Association, to name a few. If safety is a consideration, then it's wise to be knowledgeable about the process of evaluating and labeling the product.

Interestingly enough, independent assessment and labeling for safety is voluntary, and the manufacturer pays the assessment organization to conduct the evaluation. It does, however, make good business sense for this assessment to be done. First, it provides a level of assurance that the product is safe and will not create a hazard to the user. Second, the appropriate label may represent a competitive advantage over another product that does not display a label.

Depending on the type of product, safety assessment can cover a multitude of areas, such as basic construction, heat source protection, wiring practices, and radiation exposure. Standards are usually established by government agencies or private organizations set up for that purpose. Two well-known examples of standards organizations are ANSI (American National Standards Institute) and ASTM (American Society for Testing and Materials). Their standards cover the entire spectrum of consumer products.

At this point, it should be noted that a safety assessment (and seal if appropriate) do not (and are not intended to) provide quality data about the product unless it is specifically related to safety. Once you have confidence in the product's safety, it is time to turn your attention to product performance.

Yes, But Does It Work?

Although safety is an important consideration, the myriad of independent assessments to validate compliance with safety standards is not intended to provide insight into, or make judgments about, the product's ability to perform its intended function. For the most part, organizations conducting safety evaluations do not concern themselves with performance. For instance, when a toaster or a washing machine is measured against appropriate safety standards, no consideration is given to how evenly toast browns or how clean the clothing comes out.

Once again, if we define quality in terms of customer expectations, then it is safe to assume that you expect any product to perform its intended function reliably over its useful life. To obtain the data you need to make that determination, you can turn to a number of organizations that do independent assessments of product performance. Performance assessment can be as complex and comprehensive as safely evaluation, and it also provides valuable information to guide you to the right purchase decision.

While safety assessment is generally performed against a set of standards for a product or product family, performance assessment requires a higher level of creativity to establish the basis by which a product is judged. Comparison to a safety standard is straightforward; you either meet it or you don't. When dealing with product performance, each product may have its own set of standards based on some combination of the manufacturer's goals and the market expectations. Evaluations of performance, whether based on facts or perceptions, can vary from a simple determination of "does or doesn't" to the more complex question of "how well?"

A product can be judged against a variety of criteria. It is important to recognize how these criteria are determined and to make judgments based upon the difficulty of the evaluation that has been done.

How Much Is Enough?

Independent assessment of product performance can be discussed in terms of three levels of criteria, each more encompassing and difficult than the one before it.

1. *Generic performance*—This simply verifies that a product performs its basic function. Independent assessment of basic functions would verify that a popcorn popper pops corn and that a clothes dryer dries clothing. This is not necessarily a sophisticated process, as one would well imagine. At its basic level, it is a protection against products that fraudulently claim to perform functions or grossly exaggerate or mislead consumers as to what they actually do. Naturally, subjectivity and judgment may enter into this type of assessment.

2. *Manufacturer's claims or product specifications*—This verifies that a product is capable of performing in accordance with specific requirements. These requirements can be derived from statements made by the producer about what the product can do or from the specification that was the basis of the product design. Assessment of performance claims and specifications can vary in accordance with the complexity of the product and the degree of difficulty of measuring the particular item. For instance, to

verify if a tire's tread is capable of lasting 40,000 miles, sophisticated testing in simulated road conditions might be necessary. In contrast, when testing the "snooze alarm" button on an alarm clock that is supposed to repeat every nine minutes for an hour, only a source of electric power and a stopwatch may be required. The information provided by this type of assessment will aid in purchase decisions, particularly if a certain product feature is a deciding factor in selecting that item.

3. *Customer expectations*—Perhaps the most difficult thing to assess, yet likely the most important, are your needs and wants associated with a product. These characteristics often are not covered by a manufacturer's claim or a product specification. For instance, you expect a clock radio to keep accurate time, a popcorn popper to pop corn thoroughly, and a washing machine to get clothing clean. Yet, in these examples, how do you define *accurate, thorough,* and *clean?* It is in this area that independent assessments can bridge that gap for you and remove much of the subjectivity in determining how well your expectations will be met.

In the case of the items mentioned, assessment would be based on a set of objective criteria that would measure the performance expectation and facilitate ease of measurement under controlled conditions. For the three examples, these criteria might be

- Clock radio: seconds gained or lost per day

- Corn popper: percentage of kernels popped

- Washing machine: brightness measurements of light reflected off clothes washed in machine

Thus, in determining whether or not customer expectations are met, subjectivity is kept to an absolute minimum. The most important role of the assessment organization, however, is first to determine those expectations important to the consumer. Without prior knowledge of key expectations on a product-by-product basis, the most creative ways of measuring and establishing criteria may never achieve their desired impact.

There is one customer expectation that may be considered universal: the reliability of the product. Consumers expect that a product will work the first time and continue to work when required, short of predictable items that wear out over time. Although assessment of reliability is frequently done by the manufacturer (see chapter 6), the test conditions and results may not be a good indicator of the reliability you will experience in actual use. Often, a manufacturer's evaluation will be performed in a laboratory under simulated conditions, whereas an independent assessment organization might go the extra distance to replicate the conditions under which the product will be used. Furthermore, the results can be correlated to statistical analysis of data from consumers' experience with the reliability of a product.

As with safety, unless a product turns out to be unreliable, you may have assumed it to have been reliable. It is important to verify reliability expectations as part of a purchase decision if cost of ownership is an important consideration. Independent assessment of product reliability is a valuable information source that is well worth investigating.

Which Is the Best?

The methods of independent assessment described thus far have focused on evaluating a product against a set of standard requirements or those derived from customer expectations. This approach helps determine whether the product measures up and certainly provides useful information which affects a purchase decision.

In reality, though, one does not compare a single product to a single set of requirements. We generally apply a set of needs and expectations to a family of products from which we eventually make a purchase decision. Independent assessment, therefore, can not only help when evaluating individual products but can also be of immense benefit in performing comparative analyses across families of competitive products. Not only can we see how products perform against requirements and standards, but we also get insight into how they perform against one another. If all products meet the same requirements, it's a safe bet that some exceed a portion of the requirements while others may not. For instance, two blenders may chop vegetables adequately, but one may be observably (or measurably) quieter. You may expect an automobile to get 25 miles to a gallon of gasoline; some may get 30, while others may get only 20.

The value of independent assessment over the spectrum of available products should be obvious. When you can base a purchase decision on a comparison of products using carefully selected areas of performance, choosing the one that will provide the highest satisfaction and quality is more likely.

Worth the Effort

Independent assessments provide some of the most crucial information to be taken into account when purchasing a product. In general, these data are a primary aid in making decisions that will minimize your cost of ownership over the life of the product and ensure that your expectations are achieved. It is worth the time and effort to acquaint yourself with the resources available and how to use them.

Organizations that perform independent assessment can have a general focus or a narrow industry-specific one. For example, Consumers Union and the Good Housekeeping Institute evaluate a wide range of products. While the Good Housekeeping Institute limits itself to testing performance of products advertised in *Good Housekeeping* magazine, Consumers Union looks at the whole range of consumer products. It does performance testing and comparative analysis as well as safety testing. Additionally, organizations tied to a specific product or industry do assessments in their area. The American Automobile Association (AAA) routinely examines new model cars, and *PC Magazine* awards the "editors' choice" designation to computer products that excel in comparative assessments. When making a product purchase decision, the wise use of independent assessments can go a long way.

Further Reading

Consumer Reports. Fairfield, Ohio.

Chapter 11
Customer Satisfaction

Quality and Customer Satisfaction

Customer satisfaction is the outcome of a quality product and quality service. It can be thought of as the result of meeting or exceeding customer expectations. In the 1990s, customer satisfaction is becoming the driving force behind many industries rather than an abstract concept casually considered and associated with a customer's experience with a product. Although customer satisfaction can be defined in relatively simple terms, the ability to measure, understand, manage, and improve it is a highly complex process. Historically, customer dissatisfaction has been considered the more obvious customer indicator, and customer satisfaction has simply been the absence of customer dissatisfaction. This chapter demonstrates that customer satisfaction has become a systematic, scientific process with a broad perspective that influences all aspects of product quality and service.

The notion of customer satisfaction is not new. Indeed, it was real and significant to craftsmen who passed their product directly to the customer. The closeness of relationships provided easy access to the opinions of the customer, and certainly the consumer could easily express wants and expectations, thus influencing the product directly. Given the size and complexity of today's business organizations, customer satisfaction inadvertently evolved into a concept which may have partially overlooked the customer.

Who's the Customer?

To further complicate the picture, the concept of a customer may vary from situation to situation. Naturally, the person who buys an item is a customer. However, the person who actually uses the item may be different from the buyer. When a parent purchases a stereo system for a teenage son or daughter, elements of satisfaction that are important to the parent could be different than those important to the teen. In this case, the parent is the buyer and the teen is the user. Both must be thought of as customers when considering customer satisfaction.

Another consideration may be the sequence or layers of customers involved in a single product. The person who buys a finished product is obviously a customer. Yet that person, the consumer, is the customer not only of the retailer but also of the distributor, the wholesaler, the manufacturer, and any party that has contributed to that product reaching the consumer. Furthermore, in many respects, the retailer is the customer of the wholesaler, the wholesaler or distributor is a customer of the manufacturer, and the manufacturer is a customer of its suppliers. In fact, the consumer is at the end of a chain of customers and providers in which the role flip-flops at each step in the chain. This illustrates the complexity of customer satisfaction, given all who actually contribute, as well as the difficulty in communicating customer expectations throughout this pipeline.

Defining Quality

To discuss the relationship of customer satisfaction and customer expectations to quality, it is important to discuss the concept of quality and the evolution of its definition. Historically, quality has been associated with value and expense. A luxury car or designer clothing, for instance, would be called high-quality. In this context, the term means "quality of grade"; that is, a quality item is of a higher grade than its counterparts. A bejeweled Swiss watch is considered to be of higher quality than an inexpensive electronic watch, although both keep accurate time.

When quality is viewed at the other end of the spectrum, the same associations do not necessarily hold true. For instance, an economy car in perfect working order is not typically considered to be of poor quality. Yet a top-of-the-line appliance that requires frequent repair would be called poor quality. When used this way, quality is associated with conformance to specifications, the basic requirements the product must satisfy. For example, the basic requirements of a washing machine may be to get clothes clean without breaking down. If the washing machine was not getting clothes clean, it would not be conforming to its basic requirements; thus, it would not be considered good quality regardless of its value or associated expense. This conformance view of quality has been the view traditionally taken by manufacturers.

From the manufacturer's point of view, quality has been associated with how well a product performed against the requirements established by the manufacturer. If the product worked right, the quality was good; if it didn't work right, the quality was inadequate. The quality department tested or inspected products so that only the good ones would get to customers. It was assumed that ensuring the shipment only of good products would assure customer satisfaction.

Industry is learning that the consumer's view of quality is different than that of the manufacturer. As people become more educated and sophisticated and competition drives up the stakes, consumers recognize that they can get more for their money and therefore come to expect it. Customer expectations need to be thought of as continuously rising. A manufacturer producing products that merely conform to a specification is overlooking the changing market, and hence, the changing customer expectations. Therefore, customer satisfaction, if defined by the manufacturer, may be shortsighted. Indicators of quality should be obtained directly from the customer if they are to be effective. Quality must be defined as *meeting customer expectations.*

Customer Satisfaction as a Distinguishing Factor

As previously stated, treating quality as conformance to specification addresses, at best, the basic needs of the consumer. Since the specification is generally composed of basic needs, meeting those requirements satisfies what the customer must have, not necessarily what the customer wants. An organization expends energy to meet the requirements of the specification when that energy could be better used to determine customer expectations. Expectations may be thought of as the wants and desires that are above and beyond requirements. When all manufacturers satisfy the same basic set of requirements, it begins to become difficult to distinguish one from the other. Color televisions are an excellent illustration of this point. The industry reached a point at which just about any 19-inch set had a clear picture, good color, and easy controls, and would run for many years with no problems. Prices were relatively close, and the product seemed like just another commodity. Manufacturers were designing and building their sets to a simple set of requirements. While all this was happening, customers' expectations and needs were changing to the point that the products available would no longer satisfy them. Today, the color televisions that sell well offer distinguishing features like electronic tuning, remote control, and cable-readiness in response to customer desires. Quality, defined in terms of meeting customer expectations, can be seen as the key to market share and a company's business success. Companies that put the consumer ahead of profit will be around for the long haul.

Dimensions of Customer Satisfaction

When customer satisfaction is viewed through the eyes of the consumer, it is difficult to put limits on how it is perceived. Every customer is satisfied for different reasons. More importantly, the interplay of product characteristics and service characteristics is an undeniable element of customer satisfaction. In the case of the 19-inch televisions that all looked alike, the manufacturer that offered the most generous warranty, or who delivered and set up the set in the consumer's home, would be seen as achieving a higher level of customer satisfaction. It's important, as a consumer, not to restrict customer satisfaction to the product alone. World-class quality performance takes all dimensions of customer satisfaction into account and includes customer expectations beyond the boundaries of product features and performance.

Measuring Customer Satisfaction

Consumers know when customer satisfaction has been achieved. They also know when it hasn't. Before the "age of consumerism," manufacturers rarely asked consumers if they were satisfied; the most dissatisfied consumers were expected to complain without being asked. In reality, satisfied consumers might tell others, but more likely, dissatisfied consumers would tell many. Hence, the manufacturer could be losing significant business without any access to the consumer-based reasons. Opportunities to make true improvements and achieve customer loyalty were lost. Fortunately for the consumer, this trend has changed. Defining quality in terms of meeting customer expectations and recognizing that world-class quality performance is the key to survival have necessitated a major effort by industry to continuously measure customer satisfaction and to use the results of those measures to determine how well customer expectations are being met.

Given that every customer may have different expectations, the challenge for the manufacturer is to find a meaningful way of measuring customer satisfaction. This is further complicated by the fact that customer satisfaction is a state of mind, often based upon intangible factors; quality is very much a perception. Yet the relationship between achieving customer satisfaction and measuring customer satisfaction is so important that a wide variety of techniques and approaches are employed.

Indirect Measures

Some measures of customer satisfaction are not necessarily obtained directly from the customer. These are often financial or other business measurements that are considered indicators of customer satisfaction. One key characteristic is that they are usually developed by the manufacturer and do not involve the customer's input at all. The main drawback of such indirect methods is that while they are useful in showing gross trends, it is virtually impossible to use them to pinpoint specific problem areas and take appropriate actions.

Some examples of indirect measures are

- *Service calls*—By employing some automated data system tied into a company's customer service network, it is relatively easy to track the number of times service is required. Using the number of products sold as the base, service call trends can be an indicator of customer satisfaction.

- *Product returns*—Products are returned to a manufacturer or point of sale for a wide variety of reasons. Naturally, not all returns are from dissatisfied customers. For instance, sometimes people receive duplicates of an item as gifts. However, if the proportion of returns due to dissatisfaction is always roughly the same, then comparing return trends to sales volumes can be an indicator of customer satisfaction. This is a fairly common measure employed by manufacturers.

- *Warranty expense*—Companies generally budget and carefully watch warranty costs. It is presumed that warranty cost is incurred for reasons connected with customer dissatisfaction. Therefore, some form of month-to-month or year-to-year measure based on warranty is used as an indicator of customer satisfaction.

- *Customer-oriented inspections*—Manufacturers inspect products prior to shipping against criteria based on the company's best understanding of customer expectations. The results of these inspections are considered an indication of customer satisfaction.

Again, it needs to be pointed out that these indirect measures of customer satisfaction, although widely used, do not by themselves enable a company to achieve world-class quality. Two ingredients that are absolutely essential are (1) measures of customer satisfaction derived from customers and (2) the means for the manufacturer to use those data to increase and sustain customer satisfaction.

Direct Measures

The premise of direct measures of customer satisfaction is simple: If you want to know whether your customers are satisfied, ask them. There is no substitute for having the customers measure customer satisfaction. Although it may be more costly and complicated to obtain information, the benefits of not having to second-guess and interpret, combined with the opportunity for usable detail and perspectives, certainly justify the investment of time and money. Two ways of obtaining direct measures are customer surveys and customer assistance numbers.

Customer surveys can take many forms and utilize a variety of media, but the common characteristic is that the customer provides direct responses to a series of questions. Surveys can be conducted directly by the manufacturer or by consulting firms that specialize in the field. These surveys can be written or verbal. One advantage of the survey process is that the survey can be structured to seek out specific information that the manufacturer knows is more indicative of customer satisfaction than other data. Furthermore, since specific customer sources are used, the manufacturer knows exactly where to go to obtain more detail or clarification. With creative and effective techniques of quantifying the information, surveys can provide a good measure of customer satisfaction.

In the case of customer assistance numbers and hot lines, companies generally keep careful records of customer calls. The calls are often categorized so that areas of customer dissatisfaction can be identified. When measured against quantities sold, not only can this be an indicator of customer satisfaction, but sources of more detailed information also become readily accessible. This measure is often known as complaint tracking.

One of the key opportunities for the manufacturer is to take what amounts to after-the-fact measures of customer satisfaction and probe further into the reasons for dissatisfaction. That information can then be used not only to fix existing problems but also to eliminate the sources of dissatisfaction in future products. In order to be world-class, companies must continuously look to the future and focus on meeting customer expectations. To affect future direction, indicators of customer satisfaction need to be direct customer measures if a leadership position is to be attained.

Corrective Action

Despite the effort a manufacturer puts into achieving customer satisfaction, things can and will go wrong. If for any reason the consumer believes the product is not right the first time, then the importance of getting the "second chance" right is paramount. Everyone can relate to an experience where something had to be fixed, returned, exchanged, or modified. If that effort turned out to be simple and painless, often the original problem would be forgotten and forgiven. Corrective action needs to account for customer satisfaction just as product performance does. The car owner who makes multiple visits to the dealer to repair the same problem each time is made more dissatisfied by the corrective action than by the original problem.

Naturally, if all things were perfect, there would be no need for corrective action. However, as close as products get to not needing corrective action, there will still be some level required somewhere, and it will affect overall customer satisfaction. The essence of the word *corrective* suggests that a customer expectation was not met, and hence, needs to be corrected. How this is accomplished is the manufacturer's opportunity to restore confidence in the product.

Corrective action, which is defined as things required to meet customer expectations if for any reason they have not been met previously, can take two forms. The first is *remedial* corrective action. This addresses the problem by dealing with its symptoms in a timely manner. Remedial corrective action means correcting something that is wrong without regard to what caused it. An illustration of remedial corrective action would be a light bulb that keeps burning out prematurely. Remedial corrective action would be to replace the bulb each time it goes out. Yet the reason it goes out may be frayed wiring that should have been replaced. Remedial corrective action is a quick way to restore customer satisfaction but may be shortsighted in cases where the real goal is world-class quality for the consumer. If the bulb was under the dashboard of the car and each replacement required a service appointment with a dealer, failure to solve the real problem (frayed wiring) would not lead to customer satisfaction, even though the bulb worked when replaced.

The other type of corrective action is *preventive*. The principal difference is that it goes beyond the symptoms and addresses the root cause of the problem. It is aimed at preventing any recurrence of the source of customer dissatisfaction. World-class quality performance strives toward preventive corrective action. Certainly, customer expectations would dictate that if a problem exists, it should be corrected once and for all. Preventive corrective action not only achieves a higher level of customer satisfaction, but in the long run, it is in the best interests of the manufacturer as well, in terms of cost and goodwill.

The Role of the Consumer

At an ever-increasing rate, businesses are awakening to the connection of customer satisfaction and quality to their own profitability and long-term survival. Therefore, the expectations, perceptions, and experiences of the consumer represent the basic information a company must work with to be successful. Communication between consumers and manufacturers is critical. Consumers should assume that companies now want to listen to them. Consumerism is no longer limited to a vocal few lobbying for change. Today, everyone can participate, and their contributions will be valued. Opportunities will exist to state expectations and provide feedback. This information is treasured as never before. True customer satisfaction can be achieved as the consumer becomes part of the process.

Further Reading

Harris, R. L. *The Customer Is King!* Milwaukee, Wis.: ASQC Quality Press, 1991.

Chapter 12
Product Selection Process

The Chance to Buy

Consumers consume! The average person makes hundreds of purchases in a lifetime. In this common activity, there is not only a set of complex thought processes at work, but also a series of choices, priorities, and decisions that take place. From the perspective of the consumer, quality, in its broadest sense of customer satisfaction, value, and long life, can best be achieved by viewing the purchase process as a systematic approach. Product selection can be broken into a set of steps, as depicted in Figure 12.1, which we refer to as the *product selection how-to's.*

To help you better understand the process, we have provided an example: the Jack-and-Jill story. Follow them through their automobile selection process.

Do You Really Need It?
Step 1: Need

> *"Jack, now that the kids are in school and I'm going back to work, I'm going to need a car to get there. I'm afraid to drive 60 miles round-trip in the old clunker. It makes me queasy just thinking about it, especially in the winter when the weather gets bad. I don't want to get stranded!"*

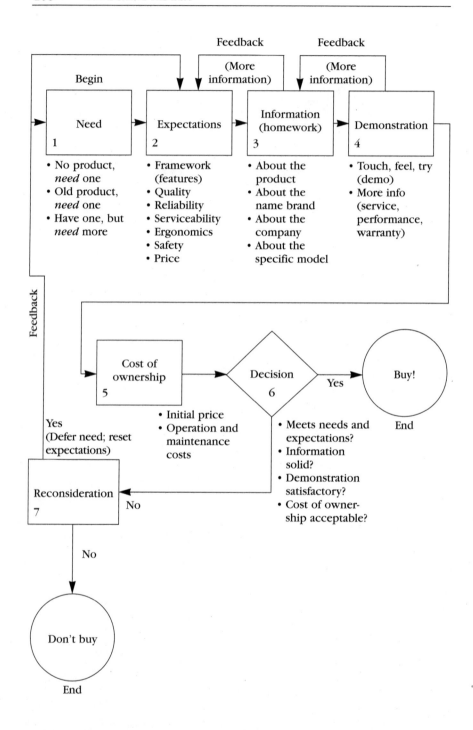

Figure 12.1   Overview of Product Selection and Purchase Steps

*"I think you're right, Jill. We're going to have
to get another car. Why don't you get a com-
pact wagon? That way, we'll have a way to
chauffeur the kids around as well as haul
large things that won't fit in my car."*

*"Do you think we should buy a new car, Jack,
or a used one?"*

*"Let's see how much a new one costs and go
from there."*

"OK!"

The first determination in the process is to establish a need.
When you look closely, this may be more complicated than you
might expect. A need may involve a specific product or a more
general desire. For instance, the need for music in a room of the
home could be satisfied by a radio or a stereo system; the need for
exercise equipment could be satisfied by a bicycle or a rowing
machine. Narrowing the more general desire to a product type is
the first step. It is largely the result of a wide range of personal
factors beyond the scope of this chapter. Once a product need
has been identified, confirmation of the actual need should be
established.

The first thing to consider is whether the product is filling a
void that cannot be satisfied in any other way. For instance, before
the need for a washing machine is established, the availability of
laundry services could be investigated. The determination of need
could then be based upon cost and convenience. Another basic
need can be based on replacement of an existing product. This
common situation could involve a car or appliance that is showing
signs of wear. The need decision here should be based on a comparison of the cost and convenience of maintaining the existing
product versus replacing it. The final area of need involves requiring more of a particular product or a greater capacity of an existing
product. This could be the case of needing a second car to satisfy
family transportation needs or greater capacity because of an
increase in family size. The determination here is similar to the
first. Careful consideration should be given to alternative ways to
achieve the need identified. Only then should you pursue a product.

Establishing Your Expectations

Step 2: Expectations

> *"What features do you think we ought to look for, Jill?"*
>
> *"I want it to be safe and reliable and to have a good radio. I also like blue!"*
>
> *"Well, that's fine, but we don't want to have to pay a mint to buy it. Plus, we don't want to have to spend a lot every time we have to get it serviced."*

Once you have established the need to pursue a particular product type, it is time to reflect specifically on exactly what you want to get from that product. World-class quality manufacturers understand that quality is defined in terms of customer expectations and strive to offer a product to meet or exceed the expectations of the marketplace. However, you need to establish your own unique set of requirements and expectations as an initial basis of evaluation for the product type under consideration. This ultimately enables you to make a decision based upon what you want and not necessarily simply on what's available.

The framework of forming expectations lies within the determination of product features. These are functional characteristics unique to the type of product. For a washing machine this may be load capacity, while for a television it could be cable-readiness. Once you identify the product features that relate to the operation of the particular function of the product, you can identify and establish the range of more generalized characteristics. As the total set is formed, it is then possible to establish priorities and weigh each feature against the others to decide which are particularly important.

Product quality and reliability are key considerations. Product quality, in this context, is related to how well the manufacturing process creates products without defects. In today's marketplace, many products are manufactured virtually defect-free. It is hard to imagine freedom from defects *not* being an expectation. Yet explicitly stating this expectation reminds you to consider it when comparing one product to another. Reliability relates to a product's ability to perform over time without failure. It can affect your ability to enjoy and/or use a product and can heavily influence the cost of owning a product over time. Both quality and reliability are legitimate expectations and, as such, are valuable criteria in product selection.

An expectation of serviceability deals with both product design and customer service. Maintainability determines how well a problem can be detected, diagnosed, and fixed. Customer service (as described in chapter 7) deals with resources provided to effectively accomplish repair. Serviceability can significantly influence your enjoyment as well as ease and cost of ownership, particularly if maintenance is a key issue.

Ergonomics take into account how well the product interacts with its expected environment and particularly with the human being using it. This includes comfort, ease of use, and other factors related to the senses. Ergonomic design can contribute heavily to the overall enjoyment of a product and should be considered as part of your expectations.

Safety is generally not something that one would explicitly state as an expectation. It's assumed. Yet some products meet safety standards while others exceed them. For instance, some cars have two air bags, some have one, and others have none. Therefore, if safety is an area of concern, it should be one of your expectations.

Once you have established product features and general characteristics, you should set an expectation regarding price range. After all, it often comes down to price. However, now you can make judgments in light of these expectations. Thus, you can make systematic decisions against differences in price; that is, you have a better idea of what you are willing to pay for.

Doing Your Homework
Step 3: Information

> "You know, Jill, I hear the Toyota Camry is a good car. Let's see what we can find out about it."

> "I agree. Toyota makes high-quality cars, and the Camry's a good one. Bill Jones and

*Jimmy Capshaw both have one, and they
love it."*

*"Let's go to the library tonight and see if we
can find an evaluation of the Toyota Camry
wagon in* Consumer Reports."

Later that night:

*"Sounds like a pretty good choice to me! It's
got a lot of cargo space, real good visibility,
good headroom and leg space, pretty good
pickup, and the gas mileage isn't bad."*

*"Right! I particularly liked the fact that it
holds its value well, and on top of that, its
repair record looks super. The only thing I'm
concerned about is that it might be too pricey
for us. Let's go take a look at one anyway
down at Johnson Toyota Motors tomorrow
after work. But before we go there, using the*
Consumer Reports *guidelines, we should figure out what the dealer's cost is and what
we should pay to get a good deal."*

You've established your expectations; that's wonderful! Not
only have you identified the characteristics you want, but you have
established priorities to help you systematically determine which
product best meets those expectations. The next phase of product
selection is the collection and review of information. Each expectation now needs to be objectively evaluated for the given product
based upon the range of information available.

General product information can be a valuable source to
begin the process. Consumer-oriented stories and articles on television and in magazines and newspapers can provide some broad
pointers that help you assess your expectations. For instance, this
information may alert you that a product is new, unproven, potentially unpopular, or difficult to service. Consumers who invested in
videodisk players instead of VCRs probably wish they had done
this information gathering. Not only does this information apply
to a product type, but it could also influence your opinion of a

particular brand. The early 1990s have seen the introduction of a number of new automobiles. Yet some of these new brands have been referred to as "stealth" cars because despite an array of advertising hardly a dealership can be found. This can be a significant factor when it comes to service.

As you begin to narrow your choices and become more knowledgeable about general product characteristics, the level of information can become more focused and specific. Sales brochures, product evaluations, and informed discussions can provide a level of detail for making an initial assessment against your expectations. Another valuable avenue to aid you in selecting a product is obtaining information about the manufacturer. If a company has a fine reputation for some of its products, then the good points probably apply across the board. Conversely, if there are some negative points, the same is probably true of its other products. In addition to the sources previously mentioned, various agencies (the Better Business Bureau, your state attorney general's office, and others) can point to consumer experience with numerous manufacturers.

Try Before You Buy
Step 4: Demonstration

> "Well, here we are. Jill, before we go in and a salesperson jumps on us, let's take a walk around the lot and look at a few of them."

> "Wow, I like it! It's really a great-looking car! Look at this blue one—my favorite color!"

> "Yeah, but look at the sticker price. They ain't cheap! By the time they add in all these options, and we include all the things we want in the car, it's mighty expensive."

> "Let's go inside and see what kind of a deal we can get before we get excited and walk away."

> "Hi. Welcome to Johnson Toyota Motors. My name's Darren Thomas. What kind of car are you folks interested in?"

"I'm Jack Stillson, and this is my wife, Jill. We're interested in a Toyota Camry wagon. We've done a lot of research on it and we think it would be the car for us."

"Well, let me tell you more about it, and then you folks ought to take one out and drive it— see how you like it. Believe me, this car is really built to last; it's got . . ."

Some 20 minutes later:

"Gee, the car handles and rides well. It's got nice pickup. All the controls are easy to find and use. The radio sounds great. I like it, don't you, Jill?"

"Yes, I do!"

"Let's go talk dollars and cents."

Some 30 minutes later:

"So it'll cost $12,000 and our car to get the Camry we want? Can't you do any better, Darren?"

"I wish I could, folks, but I've gone as low as I can considering what you have to trade in and the small margin we have on a Camry. And don't forget, Toyota offers a real good warranty."

"Well, tell us about your service department."

"Johnson Toyota Motors has a great service department. We've won the 'best service dealer of the year' award three years in a row. Bill Constance, our service manager, has been with us for 21 years. All our mechanics are Toyota-certified, with a lot of experience, too. Best of all, our service and parts departments are open from 7:30 A.M. to 5:30 P.M. Monday, Tuesday, Thursday, and Friday, and Wednesday nights till 8:30 P.M. We're even

open on Saturdays from 8 A.M. to noon. So if
you ever need service, you can count on us."

"Pretty impressive! Well, we're going to go
away and think about it. We'll call you,
Darren, as soon as we make a decision."

"OK, folks. I'll be waiting for your call!"

Seeing is believing! This statement rings true in the process of selecting a product. Let's face it, there is only so much information that can be compiled about a product without coming into contact with the product. While collection of information is an important step in the process, demonstration and trial of the product provide a valuable perspective for the consumer to uncover important facts that would not have been available otherwise.

Getting the touch and feel of a product through simulated or actual use is an excellent means of investigating whether some of your expectations are met. Characteristics like "comfortable" or "simple to use" can be evaluated through the judgments and opinions of others. Yet given how personal those considerations are, you can be the final arbiter of whether or not they are true. What is simple to you may not be simple to another person.

The more complex or expensive a product, the greater the tendency to want to see it first. It is extremely unlikely that you would purchase a car or a personal computer without some level of firsthand exposure. Even if you don't go as far as test driving a car, you will most likely sit in a representative model and "get a feel" for it. As you move down the line in product complexity, there is still good reason to have some contact with products. The whole concept of retail sales is based on this. Salespeople stand ready to demonstrate how a host of vacuum cleaners can suck up dirt, while stereo equipment stores have special acoustic rooms so you may listen to products without interference.

Another advantage of product demonstrations or customer trials is the opportunity to develop new ideas for consideration as a result of seeing or using the product. "Auto-reverse," the feature of a stereo tape deck that allows continuous play without having to flip over the cassette, is still not a given on the majority of cassette decks currently on the market. Therefore it may not have been one of those expectations considered early on. The chance to investigate products with this feature would have pointed to the significant benefit of auto reverse; without a demonstration, it may have been overlooked entirely.

Lastly, a product demonstration generally provides the opportunity to interact with a salesperson who has additional knowledge and information. While you are trying the product, questions may arise regarding certain features or considerations related to service or warranty. In one brief experience you not only get a hands-on feel but continue to build an information base that will ultimately lead to a best selection.

How Much Will It Really Cost Me?
Step 5: Cost of Ownership

> *"Jack, I love the Camry, but can we really afford it? It costs so much, and then we have to pay to run and service it."*
>
> *"Let's sit down and figure out the total cost of ownership and find out."*
>
> *"How do we do that?"*
>
> *"Well, first you have to understand that there is a difference between the initial price and the after-cost of the Camry. The initial price is what we have to pay the dealer to take the car off the lot. The after-cost is what we have to pay to own, operate, and maintain the car over its lifetime. Together, the initial price and the after-cost are our total cost of ownership."*
>
> *"Is it hard to figure out?"*
>
> *"Not too bad. Let's work it out together. We already know the initial price, $12,000. Now we have to include the after-cost factors: depreciation, insurance, financing, license and registration fees, fuel, repairs, and maintenance. We'll have to make some estimates, but we can work it out, and put it on a cost-per-mile basis over a five-year ownership period."*

About an hour later:

*"Wow, that's expensive, isn't it? I didn't think
it was going to be that much."*

"Neither did I."

At this point in the product selection process, you've established the need for the product, developed a set of expectations, and collected a range of information. If applicable, practical, and possible, you've also seen the product demonstrated or had an opportunity to use it yourself. Given all this, you probably have a reasonable idea of how well your expectations can be met. Although price may have been one of those expectations, or perhaps, a constraint on the process, it's important to examine the concept of the true cost. This factor in the selection process is referred to as the cost of ownership.

Cost of ownership considers all categories of expense associated with a product over its lifetime. It goes well beyond the price tag we normally consider when evaluating a product.

Most people have had the misfortune of owning a lemon, a product that is a continuous source of trouble and aggravation. Often, the repair bills exceed what the product may have originally cost or what it is worth. In that situation the initial price may not be as significant as the cost incurred by repairs and routine maintenance. The cost of ownership of that product would actually be the sum of price and repairs plus any other costs associated over the product lifetime. In general, we say

Cost of ownership = initial price plus after-cost (for the number of anticipated years of ownership)

where

Initial price consists of your actual cost of purchase

After-cost is the sum of the ongoing expense of operating and servicing a product

Initial price consists of the purchase price, the cost of any required or optional accessories, sales tax, and any other costs paid at the initial transaction. After-cost represents the regular and the unexpected expenses you experience after your initial purchase.

For many products, it's the after-cost that is more of a determining factor in product selection than purchase price. Let's examine a number of after-cost items.

Repairs and Maintenance

Product reliability and quality can heavily influence the cost of repairs and maintenance. In addition, recommended maintenance schedules can drive up the cost. It's important to understand which selections have the best chance of being trouble free. Also, take the time to review and compare recommended maintenance schedules. These areas tend to have a big swing with automobiles but certainly apply to any product. Learn about maintenance and service resources as well as differences in warranty. In the case of any product, the more failure-prone the product, the more important the warranty. Thus, the cost of ownership should consider the potential after-cost savings of a longer warranty. This is also a factor in service contracts (see chapter 9). While the service contract fee could be considered part of the initial price, its value needs to be weighed against the estimated after-cost savings.

Consumables

A consumable is anything that is regularly used and consumed to operate a product. In the case of a car, gasoline is a consumable that can greatly affect the after-cost because fuel efficiency varies so greatly among automobiles. If you have the opportunity to buy a so-called gas guzzler at a low initial price, the after-cost associated with higher fuel consumption may more than offset the initial price savings. The same is true of other products. Air conditioners display an EER (energy efficiency ratio) rating and a related estimate of electricity consumption. This is important information. A cheaper, but more inefficient air conditioner could present a greater cost of ownership because of high electric bills. There are other types of consumables to be considered when reviewing cost of ownership. If the cost of a particular brand of vacuum cleaner bags or typewriter ribbons were many times the norm, they too could adversely affect the cost of ownership.

Financial Considerations

There are areas greatly influencing cost of ownership that are not directly tied to product operation or performance. If a consumer loan is involved, the interest rate and term of the loan are factors that determine interest paid over the loan duration. The initial price range will affect the amount you might need to borrow; the more you invest in initial price, the less the after-cost due to interest. Another area is depreciation. If you are not likely to keep a product over its expected lifetime (for example, by upgrading your basic stereo system or trading in your car), then the amount you would lose due to depreciation should be factored into after-cost. You can influence this at the time of your initial purchase by selecting a product that is likely to retain more value over time. One way to accomplish this is to avoid technologies that are unproven and may have no market in the future (for example, the videodisk). It may also involve selecting a product with features that have a broad appeal or a product with the best reputation for durability.

Cost of ownership is a key determining factor in product selection. Yet in the absence of all those later expenses, initial price often is used as a sole decision criteria. To get the most value, it becomes important to take a broader view of product ownership and consider the real cost that will be incurred. This will ensure the best selection for your dollar.

Make a Decision

Step 6: Decision

> *"The Camry's just what we need, and it is everything that we could ever expect in a car."*
>
> *"Yeah, except the price and the total cost of ownership are too high."*
>
> *"Too bad. Toyota's a good company, the Camry's a great car, and it runs great."*
>
> *"I hate to say this, but I think we'd better go for something less expensive."*
>
> *"Heck, you're right."*

You've gone through the product-selection steps and are now a well-informed consumer ready to make a purchase decision. You may be convinced that your expectations are met and that you have enough information to satisfy yourself. If all is well thus far, determine whether the cost of ownership is acceptable. If so, it's time to buy; if not, don't.

Step 7: Reconsideration

> *"We're sold on Toyota as a company and Camry as a car, so let's think about a used Toyota Camry wagon. We'll also save on some of the after-cost items like insurance and financing."*
>
> *"Sounds good. Let's call Darren Thomas and go look at a two-year-old Camry wagon. It's got better-than-average reliability and a good repair record."*

If uncertainties still exist, it's worth your effort to go through a reconsideration process. This may begin with revisiting the initial need and then possibly reprioritizing your expectations. It may require the assimilation of more data. In any event, the decision to buy should be rendered only when you are satisfied you've gone through these steps. The product selection how-to process will help ensure your ultimate enjoyment and the satisfaction that you've received value for your dollar.

> *Finally, Jack and Jill went up the hill and bought a used two-year-old Camry wagon and lived happily ever after—for the ownership period of the car!*

Further Reading
Consumer Reports. Fairfield, Ohio.

Part 4

A Consumer's Recourse for Quality Problems

Part 4 gives some get-well approaches that can be pursued to remedy after-the-fact (post-purchase) quality problems; it acts as a safety net, given that the consumer is stuck with a less-than-acceptable situation. Chapter 13 discusses the help that can be obtained through consumer assistance groups and the employment of legal remedies. The book concludes with chapter 14 and a step-by-step plan of action that can be followed to increase the chances of customer satisfaction.

Chapter 13
Consumer Assistance

Doing the Right Thing

Products can have defects related to their design or manufacturing. Products can also be defective if inadequate instructions or warnings are provided for their use or maintenance. The severity of the effect of the product defect on the consumer can range from simply being a nuisance to causing personal injury or even death. In any event, preventing these defects should be the responsibility of the manufacturer.

Design defects can be attributed to errors of commission or omission. Errors of commission can be the result of inadequate or incomplete product specifications. An example of such an error would be a chair specification that calls for the use of a lightweight wood (such as balsa wood) that breaks under the weight of an adult. On the other hand, an error of omission can be the result of oversight or purposeful exclusion of a required feature. In the case of safety features intended to protect against injuries, omission can prove fatal. On the other hand, manufacturing defects can be attributed to products not being made to proper specifications and then shipped in a defective condition. The defective condition can be deadly to the consumer, say in the case of an improperly grounded electric drill.

Products that are defective because they lack adequate instructions or warnings for their use can be attributed primarily to oversight or just plain carelessness. The manufacturer must provide the consumer with complete instructions and warnings on correct product assembly, use, and maintenance (if it is a consumer maintainable product). The manufacturer needs to tell you, for example, that it is hazardous to stand in a bathtub full of water while using your hairdryer.

Furthermore, it's up to the manufacturer to do all the right kinds of things described in the earlier chapters on design, manufacture, and test. The types of activities described in these chapters can go a long way toward protecting both the consumer and the manufacturer. From your end, however, you need to do all the right things with regard to your purchase, or shame on you!

Post-Purchase Things to Do

As a consumer, you have an obligation to do certain things after you purchase the product. You have to use the product in the way it was intended to be used. For instance, if you buy an electric drill to drill holes in sheet metal, and the manufacturer has instructed that you use safety glasses to prevent metal fragments from flying into your eyes, then use safety glasses. You should also use the product for the purpose for which it was intended to be used; that is, don't use your microwave oven to dry clothes or the cat! Make sure you know and follow the specific conditions of warranty for the product you bought. If you are required to change the engine oil in your new car every 6000 miles or 6 months, whichever comes first, then do it, so you don't void the warranty. Finally, keep a file of the relevant documentation pertaining to your purchase—sales slips, warranty documents, maintenance invoices, and so on.

There's More Help Available Than You Think!

Sometimes, even after you've done all the right things with respect to your purchase, you still end up with an unsatisfactory product. You went through all the right steps, but alas, all is not well. Fortunately, there are a number of organizations that can help you. Surprisingly, some may exist within the company which manufactured or sold you the product in the first place!

Here is an overview of organizations, some of which are more specifically focused than others, that can help resolve product complaints.

- Company consumer affairs or customer relations departments
- Automobile manufacturer regional offices
- Better Business Bureaus
- Trade associations and other dispute-resolution organizations
- State, county, and city government consumer offices
- Federal agencies
- Media programs

Company Consumer Affairs or Customer Relations Departments

This is a good place to start. You might even have your complaint resolved at this point. These departments take on different titles in various companies, including customer service, customer satisfaction, customer assistance, customer response, consumer relations, consumer affairs, and even quality assurance. Whatever the name, the goal is the same (or at least should be)—to turn a dissatisfied customer into a satisfied one.

Appendix A lists the addresses and telephone numbers of more than 750 companies. In many cases, the name of a contact person is also given. For product names not listed in the appendix, check your product label or warranty for the name and address of the manufacturer. Another way to get the information you need is through your public library. Public libraries usually have several sources that you can utilize.

- *Standard & Poor's Register of Corporations, Directors and Executives*
- *Trade Names Directory*
- *Standard Directory of Advertisers*
- *Thomas Register of American Manufacturers*
- *Automobile Manufacturer Regional Offices*

Appendix B lists the names, addresses, and telephone numbers of the various automobile manufacturer regional offices. You should also check the warranty information which was provided to you when you purchased your car (or, with a trade-in, check the glove compartment.)

Due to significant consumer and consumer advocacy group pressure, most foreign and American car manufacturers have established regional offices to address complaints not resolved by your local dealer. If the regional office doesn't resolve your problem, you can seek help from a dispute-resolution organization such as the following:

- Automobile Consumer Action Program (AUTOCAP)
- BBB Auto Line (for certain car brands)
- Chrysler Motor Customer Relations
- Ford Consumer Appeals Board
- National Tire Dealers and Retreaders Association

Information on these organizations is provided in Appendix C (together with dispute-resolution programs for other product types). Another thing you can do is to work through your state's automobile dispute-resolution arbitration office. You can determine whether such a program exists in your state by checking the listing of state consumer affairs offices in Appendix D.

Better Business Bureaus

Better Business Bureaus, or BBBs, are known to many people. Although you may not yet have used the services of a BBB, you've certainly heard about them. There are over 200 BBBs in the United States. BBBs are nonprofit organizations sponsored by local businesses that offer a variety of services. Appendix E provides the addresses and telephone numbers of various BBBs.

Although they serve primarily as an information source for complaints made against a specific business, some BBBs also process complaints. If you have a problem, contact your local BBB and see whether it will accept your (written) complaint and contact the company on your behalf. In addition, many BBBs offer binding arbitration which serves as a form of dispute resolution to those who ask for it.

Trade Associations and Other Dispute-Resolution Programs

There are many of these programs—over 40,000 trade and professional associations in the United States. They represent a wide variety of interests, not only of products but also of services (such as banks and insurance companies). Some of them have programs to help consumers with problems at the point of purchase. As noted earlier, Appendix C gives the addresses and telephone numbers of these trade associations and other sources of dispute-resolution programs.

The dispute-resolution procedures offered by these programs fall into three types: arbitration, conciliation, and mediation. Check the particular program's rules before you file your complaint. Generally, an arbitrator's decision is binding and must be accepted by the consumer and the manufacturer. However, in the other two forms of dispute resolution, the decision may be binding only on the manufacturer, or it may not be binding on either party.

State, County, and City Government Consumer Protection Offices

As a taxpayer, you would expect to have consumer assistance offices available to you at the state, county, and city government levels—and typically you do. You should begin at the city or county level first. If you can't find a local consumer protection office in your area, contact a state consumer office. One point to remember: you should contact the consumer protection office in the state where you made your purchase, rather than in the state where you live. In any event, these offices will tell you how to file a complaint. Appendix D provides a listing of the various levels of consumer protection offices, state by state.

Federal Agencies

A last major source of consumer assistance is available through the federal government, which has agencies that deal with a variety of consumer problems. In addition, many of these federal agencies offer consumer information to help in making purchase decisions. A list of federal information centers is provided in Appendix F, while Appendix G gives a list of agencies that can be helpful to you in handling complaints.

The fact is that there are plenty of sources of help, but it's up to you to take the initiative and use them if you have a problem. If you don't, shame on you!

Pushing You Over the Edge

When all else fails, you may have no choice but to follow the legal process. You've tried to enlist the help of various organizations but to no avail. Your seemingly simple-to-resolve complaint is still unresolved. And, worse still, it doesn't look like it will be resolved. You are definitely dissatisfied!

Beyond the relatively simple complaint involving failure of a product to satisfy the purchaser is the larger and more serious issue of product liability. If the product causes injury or death, legal recourse will be the prime course to follow. The laws have been changed to make it easier to pursue and even recover damages related to injury or death resulting from a defective product. Under the doctrine of strict product liability, a manufacturer has the responsibility to market and sell defect-free products that do not cause injury or death.

Since defects that can cause injury or death can be due to poor design, faulty manufacture, or inadequate instructions or warnings (for use or assembly), astute manufacturers have taken heed. The type of quality activities described in Part 2 and implemented during design, manufacture, and testing go a long way toward protecting both the manufacturer and the consumer.

In any event, whether it be the simple unresolved complaint or product liability, you're convinced that the time has come to pursue legal action. Go for it!

Legal Options

Product liability claims are increasing tremendously, and awards are growing in number, amount, and variety. Of particular significance is the change in interpretation of the law. Personal injury claims having any reasonable basis almost invariably are winners. One case, Henningsen v. Bloomfield Motors (1960), established the landmark precedent of not requiring proof of negligence to win a personal injury product liability award. Ten days after Henningsen bought a new Plymouth, his wife was driving the car when it allegedly went out of control and struck a stone wall, injuring his wife. Henningsen sued both Chrysler and Bloomfield Motors. A negligence count was not sustained by the evidence, but the trial court instructed the jury on breach of implied warranty of merchantability, and the jury held both defendants liable. This case clearly shows judicial attempt to protect consumers. It established that the disclaimer in the automobile express warranty is not all-inclusive due to the unequal bargaining position of a consumer and the manufacturer or dealer.

Strict liability is now the rule, not the exception. Claims are now being won for faulty products which have caused no loss other than money. An example of this, Santor v. A. and M. Karagheusian, Inc. (1965), involved a Gulistan rug purchased from a dealer. The rug soon revealed flaws, and a claim was directed against the manufacturer. The New Jersey court found for the plaintiff's economic loss—the difference between the present value of the carpet and its worth had it been a good carpet. Thus, as far as the individual consumer is concerned, adequate legal protection exists now and is getting more inclusive all the time. Producing and selling a product having less-than-adequate integrity is a serious thing.

You have several legal options. You can use a small claims court if your claim is sufficiently small. Another avenue is to avail yourself of Legal Aid offices which serve those who cannot afford private lawyers. Still another possibility is the use of the Legal Services Corporation. Finally, you can employ a private lawyer. In some cases, though more expensive than the other tactics, this may be the best and only reasonable alternative to select (for example, if the claim is large and you can afford a private lawyer).

As you might expect, small claims courts are in existence to resolve disputes involving small amounts, with the maximum amounts that can be claimed or awarded varying from state to state. For example, in Massachusetts the maximum claim/award amount is $1500 (except in special cases where double and triple damages are allowed). Pursuing legal action through a small claims court is well worth the effort. Court procedures are simple, inexpensive, quick, and informal. Court fees are minimal, and typically you won't need a lawyer. You can find the listings for small claims courts in your phone directory under municipal, county, or state government headings.

If you feel compelled to use a lawyer but can't afford one, don't stop there. Try a Legal Aid office, of which there are over

1000 in the United States, all offering free legal services to those who qualify. These offices are staffed by highly dedicated lawyers, paralegals, and law students. One caution: not all offices handle all types of cases, but as a minimum, they will provide advice on other local, state, or national organizations that might be able to help you. Again, check the phone directory or call your local consumer protection office to find the address and phone number of the Legal Aid office nearest you.

The Legal Services Corporation (LSC), which was established by Congress in the mid-1970s, has offices in all 50 states as well as in Puerto Rico, the Virgin Islands, Guam, and Micronesia. Check the phone directory for an office near you, or call the LSC Public Affairs Office at (202) 863-4089.

Finding a private lawyer is easy; finding a good and reasonably priced one who will handle your case may be more difficult. Check around; ask friends; or try the lawyer referral service of your state, city, or county bar association. Know what the fee arrangement will be up front to avoid surprises later when the bill comes. These concerns notwithstanding, if you have a large claim, this might still be your best alternative. Just go into this arrangement with your eyes and ears open!

Further Reading

Bell, M., Sr., and A. P. Wilkinson. *Everybody's Guide to the Law.* New York: Gramercy Publishing Company, 1989: Chapter 10.

Consumer's Resource Handbook. Pueblo, Colo.: Consumer Information Center.

Chapter 14
Get-Well Plan

You Thought You Did Everything Right, But . . .

You've done all the right things (you think!) both before and after you made the purchase. However, you experience a problem with your product and you feel like you got stuck. The seller (store or dealer) won't do anything about the problem or won't/can't resolve it to your satisfaction. You are not a happy customer!

This chapter provides you with a step-by-step get-well plan in the event you find yourself in this situation. Admittedly, at times, in trying to make things right, you may feel it's a hopeless case. But hang in there; right will prevail.

Chapter 13 gave you some background material that forms an important part of the get-well plan. This chapter folds in these avenues of assistance, together with other venues, so that they become an integral part of a plan of attack. Remember, as a consumer, you have the right to expect quality products (and at fair prices). And if you don't get what you expected, you should not feel bashful about complaining. In fact, there's a saying: "If you don't open your mouth, you will open your pocketbook."

A Reminder

Remember, there are three phases of interest: (1) pre-purchase, (2) post-purchase, and (3) problem.

In actuality, the problem phase is really a subset of the post-purchase phase in which the customer experiences varying degrees of dissatisfaction. In earlier chapters, you were given guidelines that you should have followed in the pre-purchase and post-purchase phases. Although the focus of this chapter is on the problem phase, it is nevertheless worthwhile to remind you what you should have done in those two phases. If the pre-purchase and post-purchase phases are handled effectively, the degree of pain in the problem phase will be greatly diminished.

Pre-Purchase Phase

In chapter 12, some tips were given for making the right decisions in buying a quality product. Some of the highlights were

1. Decide what you want in and from the product.
2. Carefully compare product brands.
3. Diligently compare stores or dealers of the product.
4. Know the total product cost.
5. Understand the product warranty conditions.
6. Know the seller's return or exchange policy.

Post-Purchase Phase

Chapter 13 provided some details on what to do after you buy the product. These are summarized below.

1. Use the product the way it's intended.
2. Use the product for the purpose for which it's intended.
3. Know the warranty conditions.
4. Maintain files of all relevant documentation.
5. Carefully follow the get-well plan in this chapter if you have an unresolved problem.

Problem Phase

In this phase, you should pursue four major steps.

1. Contact the seller.
2. Contact the company's headquarters.

3. Contact consumer assistance organizations.

4. Pursue legal aid.

It should be noted that these steps need not be taken sequentially; in some cases, they can and should be executed in parallel. Within these major steps, though, there are some essential substeps that must be followed diligently. This is the only way you are going to resolve your problem to your satisfaction.

Figure 14.1 lays out the major steps and associated substeps that should be followed in the problem phase and that form an integral part of the get-well plan. These steps and substeps are discussed in more detail in the next section.

Get-Well Plan

In this section, the get-well plan is explained step by step to ensure clarity and complete understanding of what to do to gain problem resolution.

Step 1: Contact the Seller

Step 1A: Get Your Records Together

You need to assemble all the records pertaining to your complaint. This documentation should include copies of sales receipts, repair orders, warranties, canceled checks, credit purchase slips, and so on. You need to draw from the documentation file you started to maintain in the post-purchase phase. This information will support your complaint and help get it resolved, if not at this step, then later. In any event, this first substep is one of the important keys to resolution in any of the major steps.

Step 1B: Report the Problem to the Seller

You should start with the person who sold you the product, or talk to customer service, but in any event, keep going until you get to the top of the seller hierarchy. Explain the problem and what action you would like taken. Be calm and collected, and above all be accurate in your facts; this is where your records come in. If you started at a lower level in the chain of command (such as with a sales clerk), and that person is not helpful, go up the chain of command. Ask for the supervisor or owner (or even company president!) and restate your case emphatically. Don't take no for an

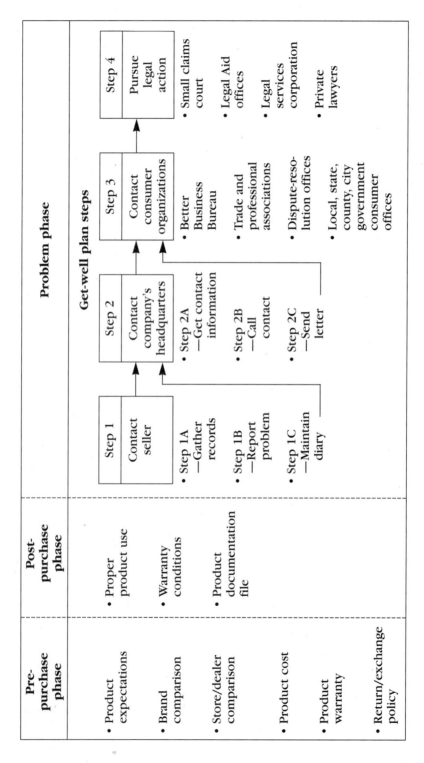

Figure 14.1   Get-Well Plan Overview

answer. Be patient but persistent. Allow each person you talk to a reasonable amount of time ("reasonable" will vary greatly depending on your prior efforts and tolerance level) before contacting someone else for help.

Step 1C: Maintain a Diary

Keep a running account of your efforts. This is almost like keeping a diary that will help you provide accurate facts all along the way not only in this major step but also in later steps if this step is futile. Include notes about who you spoke to and what was done about the problem. Refer to any letters you sent to the seller or company, as well as any letters they have sent to you. Keep track of everything. The best rule to follow is "When in doubt, write it down." It's better to have too much information than too little.

Step 2: Contact the Company's Headquarters

Step 2A: Get Contact Information

If you're not satisfied with the response you've received at the local level where you bought the product, you're going to have to raise the level of your complaint a notch to the manufacturer's/company's headquarters. This contact will most often take the form of telephone calls or letters. You'll have to know where and with whom this contact should be made. The person to contact will be the one responsible for customer complaints—and remember, ultimately this may turn out to be the company president. Check the information (such as the product label and warranty) that came with the product for company contact names, addresses, and telephone numbers. Public libraries also have sources such as *Standard & Poor's Register of Corporations, Directors and Executives* and the *Standard Directory of Advertisers* which provide this kind of information. Sometimes the company will have toll-free 800 numbers; check your local library for a directory of toll-free telephone numbers, or call directory assistance at 800-555-1212 to determine if the company has a toll-free number. Appendix A gives a comprehensive list of corporate consumer contacts, and Appendix B provides similar contact information for car manufacturers. It should be noted that contact names, job functions, and telephone numbers may change over time.

Step 2B: Call the Identified Contact

Using the information you've compiled in the previous substep, call the person who helps resolve customer complaints. Be sure that you make the following quite clear to this person.

- What you've already done to resolve the problem (refer to your diary)
- What you think will be a fair solution
- Whether you want your money back
- Whether you want the product repaired (if that's possible)
- Whether you want the product exchanged

Step 2C: Send a Letter to the Identified Contact

Again employing the information you pulled together in step 1C, send a letter to the person or function who helps resolve customer complaints. If you've already called this person or function, at this point you may want to write directly to the company president. Make sure you refer to your diary for pertinent information you'll need to compose your letter. An example of the letter you write is given as Figure 14.2. The letter should reflect certain information and features.

- Provide basic personal information, including your name, address, home and work telephone numbers, and account number (if appropriate).
- Keep the letter brief and to the point, listing important facts about your purchase such as date and place of purchase, and model and serial number of the product.
- Give a summary of what you've already tried to do to resolve the problem, and who you've contacted.
- State specifically what you want done to resolve your problem, and how long you're willing to wait to get resolution (remembering to be reasonable).
- Attach *copies* (not originals!) of all documents pertaining to your problem.
- Write in a calm tone (not angry, sarcastic, or threatening), so that the person to whom you're writing (who is probably

• Describe your purchase

• Name of product, serial numbers

• Include date and location of purchase

• Ask for specific action

• Enclose copies of documents

(Your address)
(Your city, state, ZIP code)
(Date)

(Name of contact person)
(Title)
(Company name)
(Street address)
(City, state, ZIP code)

Dear (contact person):

On (date), I purchased (or had repaired) a (name of product with serial or model number or service performed). I made this purchase at (location, date, and other important details of the transaction).

Unfortunately, your product (or service) has not performed well (or the service was inadequate) because (state the problem).

Therefore, to resolve the problem, I would appreciate your (state the specific action you want). Enclosed are copies (*not* originals) of my records (receipts, guarantees, warranties, cancelled checks, contracts, model and serial numbers, and any other documents).

I look forward to your reply and a resolution to my problem, and will wait (set time limit) before seeking third-party assistance. Please contact me at the above address or by phone at (home and office numbers with area codes).

Sincerely,

(Your name)
(Your account number)

• State the problem

• Give the history

• Allow time for action or response

• Include how you can be reached

Keep copies of your letter and all related documents.

Reproduced from *Consumer's Resource Handbook.* Pueblo, Colo.: Consumer Information Center.

Figure 14.2 Sample Complaint Letter

not the person directly responsible for your problem) will feel more motivated to help resolve it.

- Type your letter if at all possible. If you must write by hand, make sure the letter is neat and easy to read.

- Make and keep a copy of this and any subsequent letters.

Be sure you incorporate copies of all letters sent and received as attachments to your diary. In addition, send a copy of your correspondence to the company president (if he or she wasn't the recipient of the letter) and another copy to the appropriate consumers assistance organization(s).

Step 3: Contact Consumer Assistance Organizations

As noted in chapter 13, a number of organizations can provide aid in the event of unresolved product problems. These include non-profit organizations sponsored by private local businesses; trade and professional associations; state, county, and city government consumer organizations; and selected federal agencies. These consumer assistance organizations may sometimes be contacted in parallel to the activities pursued in steps 1 and 2. However, it is wise to expend some effort to resolve your problem before contacting these organizations.

You need not follow a step-by-step procedure (that is, contacting one before another) to deal with them. Call or write to them, but above all contact them. Draw from your diary for information about your problem, and give them the facts.

Step 4: Pursue Legal Action

You may have no choice but to pursue legal action. You may be able to go the small claims court route; or, if you meet the qualifications, use a lawyer provided by your local Legal Aid office; or bite the bullet and hire a private attorney. Except for the product liability situation, in which you will probably want to take the legal route directly, make sure you've first followed steps 1 through 3. In the case of the private lawyer option, by doing some things up front yourself (as spelled out in the earlier steps), you may save yourself a great deal of money and perhaps even negate the need for an attorney. In any event, you will need to get all your ducks in a row (that is, have the facts). Your diary will provide the facts you will need to present your case.

Epilogue

This book has attempted to give you, the consumer, a better appreciation of product quality from your perspective. We started by providing you with some important background material about quality. We then gave you some insight into what manufacturers should do to assure quality. We followed this with some practical how-to guidelines and tips to help you make the right decisions about the product you might want to buy. Finally, we wrapped it up with some post-purchase product remedies for you to use if a problem ensued.

Maybe this book hasn't transformed you into an expert in buying a quality product. Hopefully, though, it has made you more aware. If it has made you a more intelligent consumer from a quality perspective, then we have succeeded in our mission. An educated consumer is a better consumer. We hope you'll agree!

Further Reading

Belli, M., Sr. and A. P. Wilkinson. *Everybody's Guide to the Law.* New York: Gramercy Publishing Company, 1989: Chapter 15.

Consumer's Resource Handbook. Pueblo, Colo.: Consumer Information Center.

Appendixes

Consumer Assistance Directory

Appendix A:
Corporate Consumer Contacts

This section will help you resolve a complaint about a product or service. First, be sure to go back to the place where you bought the product or service.Try to resolve the complaint with the seller. If that does not work, the next step is to write or call the company's headquarters.

This section lists the names and addresses of more than 750 corporate headquarters, and in many cases, the name of the person to contact. Most listings also include toll-free 800 numbers.

Unless otherwise noted, all 800 numbers can be used from anywhere in the continental United States. Many companies have Telecommunications Devices for the Deaf (TDDs). All TDD and 800 numbers are in bold type.

In some cases, you will see a company name or brand name listed with the instructions to see another company listed elsewhere in this section. For example: Admiral, see Maycor. This means questions about Admiral products should be directed to the consumer contact at Maycor because Maycor handles the complaints for the Admiral brand.

If you do not find the product name in this section, check the product label or warranty for the name and address of the manufacturer. Public libraries also have information that might be helpful. The *Standard & Poor's Register of Corporations, Directors and Executives, Trade Names Dictionary, Standard Directory of Advertisers,* and *Dun & Bradstreet Directory* are four sources that list information about most firms. If you cannot find the name of the manufacturer, the *Thomas Register of American Manufacturers* lists the manufacturers of thousands of products.

Remember, to save time, first take your complaint back to where you bought the product. If you contact the company's headquarters first, the consumer contact probably will direct you back to the local store where you made the purchase.

A _____

Ms. Anna Wright
Agency Complaint Coordinator
AAMCO Transmissions, Inc.
One Presidential Boulevard
Bala Cynwyd, PA 19004-9990
(215) 668-2900
1 (800) 523-0401 (toll free)

Audience Information
ABC Inc./Capitol Cities
New York, NY 10023
(212) 456-7777

Mrs. Susan Shaw
Consumer Affairs Assistant
AETNA Life and Casualty
151 Farmington Avenue
Hartford, CT 06156
(203) 273-2645
1 (800) 243-0185
(toll free outside CT)

AJAY Leisure Products
1501 East Wisconsin Street
Delavan, WI 53115
(414) 728-5521
1 (800) 558-3276 (toll free)

Ms. Susan Mach
Director of Consumer Affairs
AT&T
295 North Maple Avenue
Room 2334F2
Basking Ridge, NJ 07920
(201) 221-4003

Customer Service
Ace Hardware
2200 Kensington Court
Oak Brook, IL 60521
(708) 990-6600

Admiral
see Maycor

Airwick Industries, Inc.
see Reckitt & Colman
Household Products

Ms. Patricia E. Arnold
Director, Consumer Affairs
Alaska Airlines
P.O. Box 68900
Seattle, WA 98168
(206) 431-7286 (consumer affairs)
(206) 431-7197 (customer relations/
baggage, air cargo, and freight claims)
(206) 431-3753 (existing refunds
and lost ticket applications file
information)

Ms. Michelle Evans
Manager, Consumer Relations
Department
Alberto Culver Company
2525 Armitage Avenue
Melrose Park, IL 60160
(708) 450-3000

Mrs. Leah Reed
Supervisor, Customer Service
Department
Allied Van Lines
P.O. Box 4403
Chicago, IL 60680
(708) 717-3590

Mr. Michael Foort
Customer Relations Manager
Allstate Insurance Company
Allstate Plaza—F4
Northbrook, IL 60062
(708) 402-6005

Ms. Lydia Morikawa
Manager, Customer Relations
Aloha Airlines
P.O. Box 30028
Honolulu, HI 96820
(808) 836-4293

Mr. Tom Onushco and
Ms. Gail Donnelly
Consumer Representatives
Consumer Services
Alpo Pet Foods
P.O. Box 2187
Allentown, PA 18001
(215) 395-3301
1 (800) 366-6033 (toll free)

Mrs. Kathy Ford
Manager, Customer Relations
Amana Refrigeration, Inc.
Amana, IA 52204
1 (800) 843-0304
(toll free—product questions)

Ms. Susan M. Sampsell
Manager, Consumer Affairs
America West Airlines
4000 East Skyharbor Boulevard
Phoenix, AZ 85034
(602) 894-0800

Ms. J.L. Ferguson
Manager, Consumer Relations
American Airlines, Inc.
P.O. Box 619612 MD 2400
DFW International Airport, TX
75261-9612
(817) 967-2000

Approved Auto Repair
**American Automobile
Association**
Mailspace 15
1000 AAA Drive
Heathrow, FL 32746-5063
(written complaints only)

**American Cyanamid Company
see Lederle Consumer Health
Products Division**

Mr. Martin J. Hummel, Vice President
Corporate Customer Relations
American Express Company
American Express Tower
World Financial Center
New York, NY 10285
(212) 640-5619
1 (800) 528-4800
(toll free—green card inquiries)
1 (800) 327-2177
(toll free—gold card inquiries)
1 (800) 525-3355
(toll free—platinum card inquiries)

Customer Service
American Family Publishers
P.O. Box 62000
Tampa, FL 33662
1 (800) AFP-2400 (toll free)

Ms. Sue Holiday
Consumer Correspondent
American Greetings Corporation
10500 American Road
Cleveland, OH 44144
(216) 252-7300
1 (800) 321-3040
(toll free outside OH)

Ms. Linda Mulrenan
Director, Consumer Affairs
**American Home Food
Products, Inc.**
685 Third Avenue
New York, NY 10017
(212) 878-6323

**American Learning Corporation
see Encyclopaedia Britannica**

Mr. Ronald J. Fojtlin, Manager
Customer and Product Services
American Standard, Inc.
P.O. Box 6820
Piscataway, NJ 08855-6820
1 (800) 223-0651
(toll free in NJ)
1 (800) 223-0068
(toll free outside NJ)
(608) 787-2000 (Trane/CAC, Inc.)

Mr. Troy D'Ambrosio
Vice President, Corporate
Communications
American Stores Company
P.O. Box 27447
Salt Lake City, UT 84127
(801) 539-0112
1 (800) 541-2863 (toll free)

Mr. Anthony L. Fera
Manager, Consumer Relations
American Tourister, Inc.
91 Main Street
Warren, RI 02885
(401) 247-2100
1 (800) 635-5505
(toll free outside RI)

Mr. Peter Lincoln
Director of Corporate Communications
Ameritech
1050 Connecticut Avenue, NW
Suite 730
Washington, DC 20036
(202) 955-3058

Amerongen, Inc.
see Budget Rent-A-Car Corporation

Mrs. Joanne Stevens, Manager
Customer Relations and
Consumer Affairs
Amoco Oil Company
200 East Randolph Drive
Chicago, IL 60601
(312) 856-4074

Mr. Alex T. Langston, Jr.
Director, Customer Relations
Amtrak
Washington Union Station
60 Massachusetts Avenue, NE
Washington, DC 20002
(202) 906-2121
1 (800) USA-RAIL
(toll free reservations and information)
1 (800) 356-5393
(toll free—credit card inquiries only)

Mr. John Brown, Manager and
Senior Corporate Counsel
Corporate Government Affairs
Amway Corporation
7575 East Fulton Road
Ada, MI 49355
(616) 676-6733
1 (800) 548-3878 (toll free TDD)

Mr. Jeff Solsbig, Supervisor
Product Service and Repair
Andersen Corporation
100 4th Avenue, North
Bayport, MN 55003
(612) 439-5150

Mr. Craig Hetterscheidt
Manager, Consumer Relations
Anheuser-Busch, Inc.
One Busch Place
St. Louis, MO 63118-1852
(314) 577-3093

Corporate Relations
Aon Corporation
123 North Wacker Drive
Chicago, IL 60606
(312) 701-3000
1 (800) 621-2108 (toll free)

Customer Relations Department
Apple Computer, Inc.
20525 Mariani Avenue
Cupertino, CA 95014
1 (800) 776-2333
(toll free—complaints and questions)
1 (800) 538-9696
(toll free—dealer information)

Aramis, Inc.
see Estee Lauder, Inc.

Customer Service
Arizona Mail Order
3740 East 34th Street
Tucson, AZ 85713
(602) 748-8600

Arm & Hammer
see Church & Dwight Co., Inc.

Mr. Harry Robinson
Consumer Relations Administrator
Armorall Products Corporation
6 Liberty
Aliso Vijo, CA 92656
(714) 362-0600
1 (800) 747-4104
(toll free outside CA)

Consumer Services
Armour Food Company
9 Conagra Drive
Omaha, NE 68102-1679
(402) 595-7000

Mr. Fred Fuest
Manager, Consumer Affairs
Armstrong Tire Division
Pirelli/Armstrong Tire Corporation
500 Sargent Drive
New Haven, CT 06536
1 (800) 243-0167 (toll free)

Ms. Jane W. Deibler
Manager, Consumer Affairs
Armstrong World Industries
P.O. Box 3001
Lancaster, PA 17604
(717) 396-4401
1 (800) 233-3823 (toll free)

Mr. Lawrence Seigel
Atari Video Game Systems
330 North Eisenhower Lane
Lombard, IL 60148
(708) 629-6500

Ms. Alice Benzing
Consumer Compliance Officer
Atlantic Financial
2401 Walnut Street
Philadelphia, PA 19103
(215) 972-4530
1 (800) 233-1198 (toll free)

Mr. Thomas C. Butler
Manager, Customer Relations
Atlantic Richfield Company
ARCO Products Company
1055 W. 7th Street
Los Angeles, CA 90051-0570
1 (800) 322-ARCO (toll free)

Mr. J.R. Patterson, Vice President
Customer Service and Insurance
Atlas Van Lines
1212 St. George Road
P.O. Box 509
Evansville, IN 47703-0509
1 (800) 457-3705 (toll free)

Ms. Lynne Lappin
Supervisor, Customer Service
Avis Rent-A-Car System
900 Old Country Road
Garden City, NY 11530
(516) 222-4200

Customer Service
Avon Fashions, Inc.
5000 City Line Road
Hampton, VA 23661
(804) 827-9000

Ms. Lynn Baron, Manager
Consumer Information Center
Avon Products, Inc.
9 West 57th Street
New York, NY 10019
(212) 546-7777

B _____

Mr. Frederick J. Wilson
Assistant General Counsel
Bacardi Imports Inc.
2100 Biscayne Boulevard
Miami, FL 33137
(305) 573-8511

Bali
Sara Lee Corporation
3330 Healy Drive
P.O. Box 5100
Winston-Salem, NC 27103
(919) 768-8611
1 (800) 654-6122 (toll free)

Corporate Communications
Bally Manufacturing Corporation
8700 West Bryn Mawr
Chicago, IL 60631
(312) 399-1300

Quality of Services
Bank of America, NT & SA
Bank of America Center
555 California Street, 19th Floor
Department 3538
San Francisco, CA 94104
(415) 622-3590

Mr. Michael Pascale, Vice President
Public and Investor Relations
The Bank of New York Company
48 Wall Street, 16th Floor
New York, NY 10286
(212) 495-2066

Barnett Banks, Inc.
P.O. Box 40789
Jacksonville, FL 32231
(904) 791-7720

Mr. John Clapp
Quality Assurance Manager
R.G. Barry Corporation
13405 Yarmouth Road, NW
Pickerington, OH 43147
(614) 864-6400
1 (800) 848-7560
(toll free outside OH)

Bass Pro Shop
1935 South Campbell
Springfield, MO 65898
1 (800) BASS-PRO (toll free)

Customer Service
Eddie Bauer
1330 5th Avenue & Union Street
Seattle, WA 98101
(206) 622-2766

Ms. Karen Haase
Manager, Consumer Affairs
**Contact Lens & General
Eye Care Products
Bausch and Lomb**
Personal Products Division
1400 North Goodman Street
Rochester, NY 14692
1 (800) 553-5340 (toll free)

Ms. Janice Glerum
Director, Customer Service
**Contact Lenses
Bausch and Lomb**
Professional Products Division
1400 North Goodman Street
Rochester, NY 14609
1 (800) 552-7388 (toll free)

Ms. Ethel Killenbeck
Manager, Consumer Affairs
**Sunglasses Division
Bausch and Lomb**
P.O. Box 478
Rochester, NY 14692-0478
1 (800) 343-5594 (toll free)

Customer Service
L.L. Bean, Inc.
Casco Street
Freeport, ME 04033-0001
(207) 865-9407 (TDD)
1 (800) 341-4341 (toll free)

Customer Service Department
Bear Creek Corporation
2518 South Pacific Highway
P.O. Box 299
Medford, OR 97501
(503) 776-2400

Beatrice Cheese, Inc.
Cheese Division
770 North Springdale Road
Waukesha, WI 53186
(414) 782-2750

Mr. Charles F. Baer, President
Consumer Products Division
Becton Dickinson and Company
One Becton Drive
Franklin Lakes, NJ 07417
(201) 848-6800
1 (800) 627-1579 (toll free)

Beiersdorf, Inc.
P.O. Box 5529
Norwalk, CT 06856-5529
(203) 853-8008
1 (800) 233-2340
(toll free outside CT)

Mr. Fred Cooke
Assistant to the President
Bell Atlantic Corporation
1133 20th Street, NW
Washington, DC 20036
(202) 392-1358

BellSouth Telephone Operations
(Southern Bell and South Central Bell)
Consumer Affairs Manager
600 North 19th Street, 12th Floor
Birmingham, AL 35203
(205) 321-2892
1 (800) 251-5325 (toll free TDD)
1 (800) 544-5000 (toll free voice line
for disabled customers)

Mr. Keith Kard, Director
Marketing and Public Relations
Benihana of Tokyo
8685 Northwest 53rd Terrace
Miami, FL 33166
(305) 593-0770
1 (800) 327-3369 (toll free)

Ms. Sue B. Huffman
Director, Consumer Affairs
Best Foods
CPC International, Inc.
P.O. Box 8000 International Plaza
Englewood Cliffs, NJ 07632
(201) 894-2324

Mr. John Morgan
Manager, Customer Service
Best Western International
P.O. Box 10203
Phoenix, AZ 85064-0203
(602) 780-6181

Consumer Relations Department
BIC Corporation
500 Bic Drive
Milford, CT 06460
(203) 783-2000

Bird's Eye
see General Foods

Mr. Floyd Coonce
Manager, Consumer Assistance
Black and Decker Home Appliances
6 Armstrong Road
Shelton, CT 06484
(203) 926-3218

Consumer Services
Black and Decker Power Tools
626 Hanover Pike
Hampstead, MD 21074
(301) 527-7100
1 (800) 762-6672 (toll free)

Mr. Jerry Weber
Senior Vice President of Operations
Blockbuster Entertainment
Corporation
901 East Las Olas Boulevard
Ft. Lauderdale, FL 33301
(305) 524-8200

Ms. Lori Hunt
Customer Services Representative
Block Drug Company, Inc.
257 Cornelison Avenue
Jersey City, NJ 07302
(201) 434-3000, ext. 308
1 (800) 365-6500
(toll free outside NJ)

Customer Service Department
Bloomingdale's by Mail, Ltd.
475 Knotter Drive
P.O. Box 593
Cheshire, CT 06410-9933
(203) 271-1313
(mail order inquiries only)

Ms. Allison Rader
Consumer Relations
Blue Bell, Inc.
P.O. Box 21488
Greensboro, NC 27420
(919) 373-3564, 4036

Consumer Affairs
Blue Cross and Blue Shield
Association
655 15th Street, NW, Suite 350
Washington, DC 20005
(202) 626-4780

Ms. Karen Braswell
Marketing Manager
Bojangles
P.O. Box 240239
Charlotte, NC 28224
(704) 527-2675, ext. 226

Consumer Response Department
Borden, Inc.
180 East Broad Street
Columbus, OH 43215
(614) 225-4511

Boyle-Midway Household
Products, Inc.
see Reckitt & Colman
Household Products

Ms. Stephanie Smith
Manager, Consumer Affairs
Bradlees Discount Department
Stores
One Bradlees Circle
P.O. Box 9015
Braintree, MA 02184-9015
(617) 380-5468

Breck Hair Care Products
see Lederle Consumer Health
Products Division

Customer Service
Brights Creek
5000 City Lane Road
Hampton, VA 23661
(804) 827-1850

Mr. Raymond Heimbuch
Manager, Consumer Affairs
Bristol-Myers Products
685 Routes 202/206 North
Somerville, NJ 08876-1279
1 (800) 468-7746 (toll free)

Mr. John L. Skule, III
Vice President, Industry
and Public Affairs
Bristol-Myers Squibb
Pharmaceutical Group
P.O. Box 4000
Princeton, NJ 08543-4000
(609) 921-4000
1 (800) 332-2056 (toll free)

Brita, USA
see Clorox Company

Customer Relations
British Airways
75-20 Astoria Boulevard
Jackson Heights, NY 11370
(718) 397-4000

Ms. Deborah A. Volz
Consumer Relations Manager
Brown-Forman Beverage
Company
P.O. Box 1080
Louisville, KY 40201
1 (800) 753-1177 (toll free)

Consumer Care Information
Brown Group, Inc.
P.O. Box 354
St. Louis, MO 63166
1 (800) 766-6465 (toll free)

Customer Relations
Budget Rent-A-Car Corporation
P.O. Box 111580
Carrollton, TX 75011-1580
1 (800) 621-2844 (toll free)

Investor Service Center
Bull & Bear Group, Inc.
11 Hanover Square
New York, NY 10005
(212) 363-1100
1 (800) 847-4200 (toll free)

Manager, Customer Relations
Bulova Watch Company
26-15 Brooklyn Queens
Expressway East
Woodside, NY 11377
(718) 204-3300 (consumer relations)
(718) 204-3222 (repairs)

Mr. Monroe Milstein, President
Burlington Coat Factory
Warehouse Corporation
1830 Route 130 North
Burlington, NJ 08016
(609) 387-7800

Public Relations
Burlington Industries
3330 West Friendly Avenue
Greensboro, NC 27420
(919) 379-3376

Mrs. Dorie Monroe
Professional Services Manager
Burroughs Wellcome Company
3030 Cornwallis Road
Research Triangle Park, NC 27709
(919) 248-3000

C

Mr. Ray Faiola, Director
CBS Broadcast Group
Audience Services
Program Information Office
524 West 57th Street
New York, NY 10019
(212) 975-3166

CIBA-GEIGY Corporation
Agricultural Division
410 Swing Road
Greensboro, NC 27409
(919) 632-6000
1 (800) 334-9481 (toll free)

CIBA-GEIGY Corporation
Pharmaceuticals Division
556 Morris Avenue
Summit, NJ 07901-1398
(908) 277-5000

CIBA Vision Corporation
2910 Amwiler Court
Atlanta, GA 30360
1 (800) 241-5999 (toll free)
1 (800) 227-1524, ext. 4828
(toll free—consumer relations)

Customer Service
CIE America
2515 McCave Way
P.O. Box 19663
Irvine, CA 92713-9663
1 (800) 877-1421 (toll free)

CIE Terminals
see CIE America

Mr. Mark A. Whiter
Director, Customer Relations
CIGNA Property and Casualty
Companies
1600 Arch Street
Philadelphia, PA 19103
(215) 523-2729

Consumer Affairs Department
CPC International Inc.
International Plaza
Box 8000
Englewood Cliffs, NJ 07632
(201) 894-4000

Mr. Paul Reisbord
President and Chairman of the Board
C&R Clothiers
8660 Hayden Place
Culver City, CA 90232
(213) 559-8200

CVN
see QVC Network

Customer Relations Department
CVS
One CVS Drive
Woonsocket, RI 02895-0988
(401) 765-1500
1 (800) 444-1140 (toll free)

Cabela's, Inc.
812 13th Avenue
Sidney, NE 69160-8888
1 (800) 237-8888 (toll free)

Ms. Darlene Stovall
Consumer Affairs Analyst
Cadbury Schweppes
Beverages Division
High Ridge Park
P.O. Box 3800
Stamford, CT 06905
(203) 968-7673
(203) 968-5895 (consumer affairs)
1 (800) 426-4891 (toll free)

Cadbury Schweppes Confections
see Hershey

Ms. Kathleen Ellwood
Manager, Consumer Relations
Caloric Modern Maid Corporation
403 North Main Street
Topton, PA 19562-1499
(215) 682-4211

Mr. Drew Fox
Director, Consumer Relations
Campbell Soup Company
Campbell Place
Camden, NJ 08103-1799
(609) 342-3714

Mr. Lloyd Rockwell
Vice President, Winery Operations
Canandaigua Wine Company
116 Buffalo Street
Canandaigua, NY 14424
(716) 394-3630

Corporate Consumer Affairs
Canon U.S.A., Inc.
One Canon Plaza
Lake Success, NY 11042-9960
(516) 488-6700

Ms. Pat Biederman
Passenger Service Manager
Carnival Cruise Lines
3655 Northwest 87th Avenue
Miami, FL 33178-2428
1 (800) 327-7373 (toll free)

Mr. James Witz
Consumer Relations Manager
**Carrier Air Conditioning
Company**
P.O. Box 4808
Syracuse, NY 13221
1 (800) 227-7437 (toll free)
Bryant Heating and Air Conditioning
1 (800) 428-4326 (toll free)
Day & Night Heating and
Air Conditioning
1 (800) 428-4326 (toll free)
Payne Heating and Air Conditioning
1 (800) 428-4326 (toll free)

**Carte Blanche
see Diners Club**

Ms. Mary Mumolo
Senior Manager, Consumer Relations
Carter Hawley Hale Stores
388 North Mission Road
Los Angeles, CA 90031
(213) 227-2423

Consumer Affairs Department
Carter-Wallace Inc.
1345 Avenue of the Americas
New York, NY 10105
(212) 339-5000

Retail Operations
Carvel Corporation
201 Saw Mill River Road
Yonkers, NY 10701
(written inquiries only)

Customer Service Department
Casio, Inc.
570 Mount Pleasant Avenue
Dover, NJ 07801
(201) 361-5400

Mr. Bruce Wagner
Customer Service Supervisor
Champion Spark Plug Company
P.O. Box 910
Toledo, OH 43661
(419) 535-2458
1 (800) 537-8984
(toll free outside OH)
1 (800) 537-9996
(toll free in OH)

Ms. Stacey French
Customer Relations Coordinator
Chanel, Inc.
9 West 57th Street, 44th Floor
New York, NY 10019
(212) 688-5055

Ms. Lila A. Lesley, Consumer Affairs
Consumer Products Division
Chattem, Inc.
1715 West 38th Street
Chattanooga, TN 37409
(615) 821-4571, ext. 211
1 (800) 366-6833
(toll free outside TN)

Mr. Walter Dabek
Director, Consumer Information
Cheesebrough-Pond's, USA.
33 Benedict Place
Greenwich, CT 06830-6000
1 (800) 852-8558
(toll free in CT)
1 (800) 243-5804
(toll free outside CT)

Ms. Kathy Yeu
Director, Consumer Affairs
Chemical Bank
277 Park Avenue
New York, NY 10172
(212) 310-5800

ChemLawn Services Corporation
8275 North High Street
Columbus, OH 43235
(614) 888-3572
1 (800) 888-3572 (toll free)

Mr. W. P. Howell, Supervisor
Dealer and Consumer Affairs
Chevron U.S.A. Inc.
P.O. Box H
Concord, CA 94524
(415) 827-6412
1 (800) CHEVRON (toll free)

Complaint Department
Chi-Chi's, Inc.
10200 Linn Station Road
Louisville, KY 40223
(502) 426-3900

Chuck E. Cheese
see Integra

Mrs. Cathy R. Marino, Manager
Consumer Relations
Church & Dwight Company, Inc.
469 North Harrison Street
Princeton, NJ 08540-7648
(609) 683-5900
1 (800) 624-2889 (toll free in NJ)
1 (800) 524-1328
(toll free outside NJ)

Church's Fried Chicken, Inc.
see Popeye's

Cincinnati Microwave
One Microwave Plaza
Cincinnati, OH 45249-9502
(513) 489-5400
1 (800) 543-1608 (toll free)

Circuit City Stores, Inc.
2040 Thalbro Street
Richmond, VA 23230
(804) 257-4292
1 (800) 251-2665 (toll free)

Ms. Dinah Nemeroff, Vice President
Corporate Director of
Customer Affairs
Citicorp/Citibank
399 Park Avenue
New York, NY 10043
(212) 559-0043

Ms. Ellen Peressini, Executive Secretary
Citizen Watch Company of
America, Inc.
8506 Osage Avenue
Los Angeles, CA 90045
(213) 215-9660
1 (800) 321-1023 (toll free)

Ms. Carol Leet, Director
Consumer Affairs Dept.
Clairol, Inc.
345 Park Avenue
New York, NY 10154
1 (800) 223-5800
(toll free voice/TDD)
1 (800) HISPANA
(toll free Spanish voice/TDD)

Clinique Laboratories, Inc.
see Estee Lauder, Inc.

Ms. C. Kay Whitehurst
Consumer Services Manager
Clorox Company
1221 Broadway
Oakland, CA 94612-1888
(415) 271-7283
1 (800) 292-2200
(toll free—laundry brands)
1 (800) 537-2823
(toll free—charcoal and food brands)
1 (800) 227-1860
(toll free—household surface cleaners)
1 (800) 426-6228
(toll free—insecticides)
1 (800) 242-7482
(toll free—water purification systems)

Consumer Affairs Department
Club Med Sales, Inc.
40 West 57th Street
New York, NY 10019
(212) 977-2100

Mr. Roger Nunley, Director
Industry and Consumer Affairs
Coca-Cola Company
P.O. Drawer 1734
Atlanta, GA 30301
1 (800) 438-2653 (toll free)

Coldwell Banker
see Sears, Roebuck and Co.

Ms. Grace Richardson
Vice President, Consumer Affairs
Colgate-Palmolive Company
300 Park Avenue
New York, NY 10022-7499
1 (800) 221-4607
(toll free—oral care products)
1 (800) 338-8388
(toll free—household products)

Mr. Tom Kelly
Senior Vice President, Operations
Colonial Penn Group, Inc.
11 Penn Center Plaza
1818 Market Street, 26th Floor
Philadelphia, PA 19181
(215) 988-8531
1 (800) 523-1700
(toll free—auto and homeowner
customer service)
1 (800) 523-4000
(toll free—health customer service)
1 (800) 523-9100
(toll free—life customer service)

Columbia House
A Division of SONY Music
Entertainment, Inc.
P.O. Box 4450
New York, NY 10101-4450
1 (800) 457-0500
(toll free—records and tapes)
1 (800) 457-0866
(toll free—videos)

Ms. Teresa C. Infantino
Executive Vice President
Combe Incorporated
1101 Westchester Avenue
White Plains, NY 10604-3597
(914) 694-5454
1 (800) 431-2610 (toll free)

**Combined Insurance
Company of America
see Aon Corporation**

**Commerce Drug Division
see Del Laboratories, Inc.**

Ms. M. Teresa Abreu
Manager, Customer Relations
**Commodore Business
Machines, Inc.**
1200 Wilson Drive
West Chester, PA 19380
(215) 431-9100

Customer Relations Department
Compaq Computer Corporation
P.O. Box 692000
Houston, TX 77269-2000
1 (800) 345-1518 (toll free)

Comprehensive Care Corporation
1795 Clarkson Road
Chesterfield, MO 63017
(314) 537-1288
1 (800) 678-2273 (toll free)

Ms. Janet M. Venditti
Manager, Consumer Affairs
Congoleum Corporation
Technical Operations Center
861 Sloan Avenue
Trenton, NJ 08619
(609) 584-3000
1 (800) 274-3266 (toll free)

**Consumers Products Group
see Commodore Business
Machines, Inc.**

Supervisors Department
Contempo Casuals
5433 West Jefferson Boulevard
Los Angeles, CA 90016
(213) 936-2131
1 (800) 368-5923 (toll free)

Ms. Ann R. Yanulavich
Director, Customer Relations
Continental Airlines, Inc.
3663 North Belt East, Suite 500
Houston, TX 77032
(713) 987-6500

Ms. Barbi Rose 2CR
Manager, Consumer Affairs
Continental Baking Company
Checkerboard Square
St Louis, MO 63164
(314) 982-4953

Control Data Contact Center
Control Data Corporation
8100 34th Avenue South
P.O. Box 0
Minneapolis, MN 55440-4700
(612) 853-3400
1 (800) 232-1985 (toll free)

Customer Service
Converse, Inc.
One Fordham Road
North Reading, MA 01864-2680
1 (800) 545-4323 (toll free)
1 (800) 533-8656 (toll free)

Conwood Company, L.P.
813 Ridge Lake Boulevard
Memphis, TN 38120
(901) 761-2050

Ms. Margie Hausburg
Quality Assurance Analyst
Coors Brewing Company
Consumer Hotline
Golden, CO 80401
1 (800) 642-6116 (toll free)

Coppertone
see Schering-Plough
HealthCare Products, Inc.

Ms. Suzanne Scannelli, Supervisor
Corning/Revere Consumer
Information Center
Corning Incorporated
1300 Hopeman Parkway
Waynesboro, VA 22980
(703) 949-9143

Ms. Connie J. Shelby
Director, Consumer Affairs
Cosmair, Inc.
P.O. Box 98
Westfield, NJ 07091-9987
1 (800) 631-7358 (toll free)

Ms. Aggie Merkel, Supervisor
Member and Consumer Relations
Cotter & Company
2740 North Clybourn Avenue
Chicago, IL 60614-1088
(312) 975-2700

Service Department
Craftmatic/Contour
Organization, Inc.
2500 Interplex Drive
Trevose, PA 19053-6998
(215) 639-1310
1 (800) 677-8200 (toll free)

Consumer Affairs Division
Jenny Craig International
445 Marineview Avenue
Del Mar, CA 92014
(619) 259-7000

Mr. George Turner
Assistant Vice President, Operations
Crown Books
3300 75th Avenue
Landover, MD 20785
(301) 731-1200
1 (800) 835-7300 (toll free)

Mr. Peter Cammarata
Director, Sales and Marketing
Operations
Cuisinarts Corporation
P.O. Box 120067
Stamford, CT 06913-0741
(203) 975-4600
1 (800) 726-0190
(toll free outside NJ)
(609) 426-1300 (in NJ)

Ms. Kathleen Bayer
Special Assistant to the President
for Consumer Affairs
Culligan International Company
One Culligan Parkway
Northbrook, IL 60062
(708) 205-5757

Mr. Marvin E Eisenstadt, President
Cumberland Packing Corporation
Two Cumberland Street
Brooklyn, NY 11205
(718) 858-4200
1 (800) 336-0363 (toll free in NY)
1 (800) 231-1123 (toll free outside NY)

Mr. Tony Saulino
Department Head, Customer Service
Current, Inc.
P.O. Box 2559
Colorado Springs, CO 80901
1 (800) 525-7170 (toll free)

Customer Care Department
Curtis Mathes Corporation
1450 Flatcreek Road
Athens, TX 75751
(214) 675-6886
1 (800) 326-1920 (warranty processing)
1 (800) 736-1920 (technical services)
1 (800) 473-1920 (customer care)
1 (800) 326-1920 (parts administration)

D _____

d-Con
see L&F Products

Ms. Joan Calkins
Manager, Customer Service
DHL Corporation
1820 Gateway Drive, Suite 300
San Mateo, CA 94404
1 (800) CALL-DHL (toll free)

Dairy Queen
see International Dairy Queen

Ms. Becky Ryan
Director, Consumer Relations
Dannon Company, Inc.
P.O. Box 44235
Jacksonville, FL 32256
1 (800) 321-2174 (toll free)

Ms. Stephanie McDermott, Manager
Customer Service Department
Danskin
P.O. Box 15016
York, PA 17405-7016
1 (800) 87-DANSKIN (toll free)

Ms. Avis Carlson, Manager
Central Consumer Relations
The Department Stores of the
Dayton Hudson Corporation
Box 875
700 Nicollet Mall
Minneapolis, MN 55402
(612) 375-3382

Dean Witter Financial
Services Group
see Sears, Roebuck and Co.

Dearfoam
see R.G. Barry Corporation

Deere & Company
John Deere Road
Moline, IL 61265-8098
(309) 765-8000

Ms. Margaret Sanders
Consumer Relations Department
Del Laboratories, Inc.
565 Broad Hollow Road
Farmingdale, NY 11735
(516) 293-7070

Ms. Janet M. Acklam
Manager, Consumer Affairs
Del Monte Corporation
P.O. Box 193575
San Francisco, CA 94119
1 (800) 543-3090 (toll free)

Public Relations
Delco Remy Division
General Motors Corporation
2401 Columbus Avenue
Mail Code 1-310
Anderson, IN 46018-9986
(317) 646-2000

Mr. Fred Elsberry
Director, Consumer Affairs
Delta Air Lines
Hartsfield Atlanta International Airport
Atlanta, GA 30320
(404) 715-1402

Ms. Barbara Smith
Product Service Manager
Delta Faucets
P.O. Box 40980
Indianapolis, IN 46280
(317) 848-1812

Operations
Denny's, Inc.
P.O. Box 3800
Spartanburg, SC 29304-3800
(803) 596-8000

Mr. George Andrassy, Vice President
Research and Development
Dep Corporation
2101 East Via Arado
Rancho Dominguez, CA 90220-6189
(213) 604-0777
1 (800) 367-2855 (toll free)

Ms. Julie Jason
Manager, Customer Service
DeVry, Inc.
2201 West Howard Street
Evanston, IL 60202
(708) 328-8100
1 (800) 225-8000 (toll free)

Ms. Lisa L Ridle, Director
Consumer Information Center
The Dial Corporation
Dial Tower
Phoenix, AZ 85077-1606
(602) 207-5518
1 (800) 528-0849 (toll free—
foods division)
1 (800) 45-PUREX (toll free—
household and laundry division)
1 (800) 258-DIAL (toll free—
personal care division)

Customer Relations
Diet Center, Inc.
921 Penn Avenue
Pittsburgh, PA 15222-3814
(412) 338-8700
1 (800) 333-2581 (toll free)

Customer Assistance Department
Digital Equipment Corporation
40 Old Bolton Road
Stow, MA 01777-1215
(508) 493-7161
1 (800) 332-4636 (toll free)

Customer Relations
Dillard Department Stores, Inc.
1600 Cantrell Road
Little Rock, AR 72201
(501) 376-5200

Ms. Betsy Seeley
Vice President, Customer Service
Diners Club International
183 Inverness Drive West
Englewood, CO 80112
(303) 799-9000
1 (800) 525-9135 (toll free)
(303) 649-2824 (TDD)

**Discover Credit Card
see Sears, Roebuck and Co.**

Ms. Helen Robinson
Manager, Consumer Response
Dole Packaged Foods
Attn: Consumer Response
Department
50 California Street, 19th Floor
San Francisco, CA 94111
1 (800) 232-8888 (toll free)

Mr. David Black, President
Operations
Domino's Pizza, Inc.
P.O. Box 997
Ann Arbor, MI 48106-0997
(313) 930-3030

Mr. Robert J. Posch, Jr.
Vice President, Legal Affairs
**Doubleday Book & Music
Clubs, Inc.**
501 Franklin Avenue
Garden City, NY 11530-5806
(516) 873-4628

Ms. Sharon Clark
Manager, Consumer Affairs
DowBrands
P.O. Box 68511
Indianapolis, IN 46268-0511
1 (800) 428-4795 (toll free)

Mr. Jim Ball, Vice President
Corporate Communications
Ms. Wynema Hamilton, Coordinator
Consumer Affairs
**Dr. Pepper Co./The Seven-Up Co./
Premier Beverages**
P.O. Box 655086
Dallas, TX 75265-5086
(214) 360-7000

Customer Service Department
Walter Drake & Sons
Drake Building
Colorado Springs, CO 80940-0001
(719) 596-3140

Ms. Jane Lagusch
Corporate Secretary to the President
Drug Emporium, Inc.
155 Hidden Ravines Drive
Powell, OH 43065
(614) 548-7080

Dulcolax
Boehringer Ingelheim
90 East Ridge
P.O. Box 368
Ridgefield, CT 06877-0368
(203) 798-9988

Mr. Robert M. Rosenberg
Chairman of the Board
Dunkin Donuts of America
P.O. Box 317
Randolph, MA 02368
(617) 961-4000
1 (800) 6-DUNKIN (toll free)

Mr. Thomas M. Johnson
Manager, Consumer Affairs
Dunlop Tire Corporation
P.O. Box 1109
Buffalo, NY 14240-1109
(716) 879-8258
1 (800) 548-4714 (toll free)

Product Information Center
E.I. duPont de Nemours & Co.
1007 Market Street
Wilmington, DE 19880-0010
1 (800) 441-7515 (toll free)

Consumer Affairs Department
Duracell USA
Division of Duracell, Inc.
Berkshire Industrial Park
Bethel, CT 06801
(203) 796-4000
1 (800) 551-2355
(toll free—8:30 A.M.–5 P.M. EST)

Consumer Affairs Department
Durkee-French Foods
A Division of Rickett & Colman Inc.
1655 Valley Road
P.O. Box 939
Wayne, NJ 07474-0939
(201) 633-6800

E —————————————————

Mr. John Vaeth
Eastman Kodak Company
343 State Street
Rochester, NY 14650-0811
1 (800) 242-2424 (toll free)

Ms. Nancy J. Avino
Customer Service Representative
Eckerd Drug Company
8333 Bryan Dairy Road
P.O. Box 4689
Clearwater, FL 34618
(813) 397-7461

Customer Service
Edmund Scientific Company
101 East Gloucester Pike
Barrington, NJ 08007-1380
(609) 573-6260

Electrolux Corporation
2300 Windy Ridge Parkway
Suite 900
Marietta, GA 30067
(404) 933-1000
1 (800) 243-9078 (toll free)

Customer Relations
Emery Worldwide
A CF Company
3350 West Bayshore Road
Palo Alto, CA 94303-0986
(415) 855-9100
1 (800) 443-6379 (toll free)

Ms. Martha S. Yocum
Director of Consumer Affairs
**Encore Marketing
International, Inc.**
4501 Forbes Boulevard
Lanham, MD 20706
(301) 459-8020
1 (800) 638-0930 (toll free)

Mr. Norman Braun
Vice President, Public Affairs
Encyclopaedia Britannica, Inc.
310 South Michigan Avenue
Chicago, IL 60604-4293
(312) 347-7230

Mr. Labat R. Yancey
Assistant Vice President
Office of Consumer Affairs
Equifax
P.O. Box 4081
Atlanta, GA 30302
(404) 888-3500

Ms. Carolann V. Mathews
Vice President, Customer Relations
Equitable Life Assurance Society
135 West 50th Street
New York, NY 10020
(212) 641-7700 (collect calls accepted)

Retail Customer Service Department
Esprit de Corp.
900 Minnesota Street
San Francisco, CA 94107-3000
(415) 648-6900
1 (800) 777-8765 (toll free)

Ms. Theresa Sullivan
Vice President, Consumer Relations
Estee Lauder Companies
767 Fifth Avenue
New York, NY 10153-0003
(212) 572-4455

Ms. Carol Archer
Supervisor, Consumer Affairs
Ethan Allen, Inc.
Ethan Allen Drive
Danbury, CT 06811
(203) 743-8553

Mr. Rick Gremer
Consumer Relations Manager
The Eureka Company
1201 East Bell Street
Bloomington, IL 61701-6902
(309) 823-5735
1 (800) 282-2886
(toll free—warranty center)

Mr. Dan Evans, Chairman of the Board
Bob Evans Farms, Inc.
3776 South High Street
P.O. Box 07863
Columbus, OH 43207
(614) 491-2225
1 (800) 272-PORK
(toll free outside OH)

Mr. W.D. Dermott, Manager
Consumer and Regulatory Affairs
Exxon Company U.S.A.
P.O Box 2180
Houston, TX 77252-2180
(713) 656-3151

F

Ms. Erin Sparks
Consumer Affairs Coordinator
FMG/Tsumara
Jonathan Industrial Park
Chaska, MN 55318
(612) 448-4181

Ms. June Golden
Family Circle Magazine
110 Fifth Avenue
New York, NY 10011
(212) 463-1063

Consumer Affairs Department
**Faultless Starch/Bon Ami
Company**
1025 West Eighth Street
Kansas City, MO 64101-1200
(816) 842-1230

**Fayva Shoe Stores
see Morse Shoe Company**

Mr. John R. West, Manager
Corporate Quality Improvement
Federal Express Corporation
P.O. Box 727, Department 2605
Memphis, TN 38194-2605
(901) 922-5454
1 (800) 238-5355 (toll free)

Ms. Patricia Ikeda, Director
Community Relations and Operations
Federated Department Stores
7 West Seventh Street
Cincinnati, OH 45202
(513) 579-7000

Ms. Cathy Sharkey
Manager, Consumer Relations
Fieldcrest Cannon, Inc.
60 West 40th Street
New York, NY 10018
(212) 536-1284
1 (800) 841-3336
(toll free—Fieldcrest Stores)
1 (800) 237-3209
(toll free—Cannon Stores)

Ms. Mary Luethmers
Customer Relations Manager
Fingerhut Corporation
11 McLeland Road
St. Cloud, MN 56395
(612) 259-2500

Consumer Affairs
Firestone Tire & Rubber Co.
205 North Michigan Avenue
Chicago, IL 60601-5965
1 (800) 274-1344 (toll free)

Mr. Lee Mann
Director, Consumer Affairs
First Brands Corporation
88 Long Hill Street
East Hartford, CT 06108
(203) 728-6000

Mr. Patrick J. Swanick
Senior Vice President,
Customer Services
Customer Service Center
First Fidelity Bancorporation
100 Constitution Drive
Upper Darby, PA 19082-4603
(215) 734-5090
1 (800) 345-9042 (toll free)
(215) 734-5599 (TDD)

Consumer Affairs Department
First Interstate Bank of California
707 Wilshire Boulevard, W35-13
Los Angeles, CA 90017
(213) 614-3103
1 (800) 626-3400 (toll free)

Ms. Susan Alcorn, Director
Consumer, Government and
Media Center
First National Supermarkets, Inc.
17000 Rockside Road
Cleveland, OH 44137-4390
(216) 587-7100

Mr. Michael Cisneros
Consumer Affairs Officer
First Nationwide Bank
135 Main Street, 4th Floor
San Francisco, CA 94105-1817
1 (800) 237-0756 (toll free)

Customer Service
**First Union National Bank
of Florida**
P.O. Box 2870
Jacksonville, FL 32231-0010
(904) 361-6996
1 (800) 735-1012 (toll free)

**Fisher
see SFS Corporation**

Ms. Carol Steck
Manager, Consumer Affairs
Fisher Price
636 Girard Avenue
East Aurora, NY 14052-1880
1 (800) 432-5437 (toll free)

Ms. Kathryn McDonald
Consumer Affairs Manager
Florida Power and Light Co.
P.O. Box 029100
Miami, FL 33102-9100
(305) 227-4646
1 (800) 432-6554 (toll free TDD)

Ms. Monica Schmelter, Manager
Customer Relations
**Florists' Transworld Delivery
Association (FTD)**
29200 Northwestern Highway
P.O. Box 2227
Southfield, MI 48037-4077
(313) 355-9300
1 (800) 521-4366 (toll free)

Florsheim Shoe Company
130 South Canal Street
Chicago, IL 60606-3999
(312) 559-2500

Mr. Heeth Varnedoe, President
Flowers Industries, Inc.
P.O. Box 1338
Thomasville, GA 31799-1338
(912) 226-9110

Mr. Leonard H. Yablon
Executive Vice President
Forbes Inc.
60 Fifth Avenue
New York, NY 10011
(212) 620-2248

Customer Service
Foster & Gallagher, Inc.
6523 North Galena Road
Peoria, IL 61632
(309) 691-4610
(Monday–Friday, 8:30 A.M.–5 P.M.)
(309) 691-3633
(Monday–Friday, after 5:15 P.M.)

Marketing and Customer Service
Fotomat Corporation
201 Prestige Park Road
East Hartford, CT 06108
(203) 291-0100
1 (800) 842-0001
(toll free in CT)
1 (800) 243-0003
(toll free outside CT)

Mr. David Listman, Vice President
Customer Service/Operations
The Franklin Mint
U.S. Route One
Franklin Center, PA 19091
(215) 459-6000

Frank's Nursery and Crafts, Inc.
A Division of General Host Corporation
6501 East Nevada
Detroit, MI 48234
(313) 366-8400

Customer Service Department
Freeman and French Shriner Shoes
1 Freeman Lane
Beloit, WI 53511-3989
1 (800) 456-9745 (toll free)

Customer Relations
Fretter Appliance Company
14985 Telegraph Road
Redford, MI 48239
(313) 537-3701
1 (800) 736-3430 (toll free)

**Frigidaire Appliances
see White Consolidated Industries**

**Frontier Airlines
see Continental Airlines**

Ms. Janet Rosati
Director, Consumer Services
Fruit of the Loom, Inc.
One Fruit of the Loom Drive
Bowling Green, KY 42102-9015
(502) 781-6400

Ms. Marianne Salembene
Associate Manager, Customer
Service Department
Fuji Photo Film U.S.A., Inc.
800 Central Boulevard
Carlstadt, NJ 07072-3009
1 (800) 526-9030 (toll free)

Customer Resource Center
Fuller Brush Company
P.O. Box 729
Great Bend, KS 67530-0729
1 (800) 523-3794 (toll free)

G

GTE Corporation
One Stamford Forum
Stamford, CT 06904
(203) 965-2000

Ms. Millie Roberson
Director, Consumer Relations
Ernest & Julio Gallo Winery
P.O. Box 1130
Modesto, CA 95353
(209) 579-3111

Ms. Jeannine Collins, Supervisor
Consumer Service Department
Lewis Galoob Toys, Inc.
500 Forbes Boulevard
San Francisco, CA 94080
(415) 952-1678
1 (800) 4-GALOOB
(toll free outside CA)

Ms. Sheila Gibbons
Director, Public Affairs
Gannett Company, Inc.
1100 Wilson Boulevard
Arlington, VA 22234
(703) 284-6048

General Electric Company
For information on GE consumer
products and services, call:
GE ANSWER CENTER® service
1 (800) 626-2000 (toll free)

Mr. Donald L. Mayer
Director of Consumer Response
and Information Center
General Foods Corporation
250 North Street
White Plains, NY 10625
1 (800) 431-1001
(toll free—desserts)
1 (800) 431-1002
(toll free—beverages)
1 (800) 431-1003
(toll free—meals and Post cereals)
1 (800) 431-1004
(toll free—Maxwell House
and Bird's Eye)
1 (800) 424-BAKE
(toll free—Entenmann's)
1 (800) 431-POST
(toll free—Post cereals)
1 (800) FOR-WACKY
(toll free—Kool-Aid)

General Host Corporation
P.O. Box 10045
Stamford, CT 06904
(203) 357-9900

Ms. Sandy Weisenburger
Assistant Manager, Consumer Services
General Mills, Inc.
P.O. Box 1113
Minneapolis, MN 55440-1113
(612) 540-4295
1 (800) 328-6787
(toll free—bakery products)
1 (800) 231-0308
(toll free—cereals)
1 (800) 222-6846
(toll free—Gorton's)
1 (800) 231-0308
(toll free—snacks)

Customer Relations Department
**General Motors Acceptance
Corporation (GMAC)**
3044 West Grand Boulevard,
Room AX348
Detroit, MI 48202
(313) 556-0510
1 (800) 441-9234 (toll free)
1 (800) TDD-GMAC (toll free TDD)

Customer Service
General Tire Inc.
One General Street
Akron, OH 44329-0006
1 (800) 847-3349 (toll free)

Ms. Lori Thies, Vice President
Customer Service
Generra
278 Broad Street
Seattle, WA 98121
(206) 728-6888

Sales Department
Genesee Brewing Company, Inc.
445 St. Paul Street
Rochester, NY 14605
(716) 546-1030

Ms. Denise Irish (paper products)
Ms. Janet Folk (building products)
Georgia-Pacific Corp.
P.O. Box 105605
Atlanta, GA 30348-5605
(404) 521-4708 (building products)
(404) 527-0038 (paper products)

Mr. L. James Lovejoy, Director
Corporate Communications
Gerber Products Company
445 State Street
Fremont, MI 49413-1056
(616) 928-2000
1 (800) 4-GERBER
(toll free—24 hours)
1 (800) 421-4221
(toll free, 24-hour breastfeeding advice)
1 (800) 828-9119
(toll free—baby formula)

Ms. Odonna Mathews
Vice President for Consumer Affairs
Giant Food Inc.
P.O. Box 1804, Department 597
Washington, DC 20013
(301) 341-4365
(301) 341-4327 (TDD)

Gibbons Greenvan
see Budget Rent-A-Car
Corporation

Gibson Appliances
see White Consolidated Industries

Ms. Beverly Smart
Manager, Consumer Affairs
Gillette Company
P.O. Box 61
Boston, MA 02199
(617) 463-3337

Glenbrook Laboratories
see Sterling Drug Inc.

Mr. James Sainsbury
Manager, Product Regulation
The Glidden Company
925 Euclid Avenue
Cleveland, OH 44115
(216) 344-8818

Mr. M.F. Smithson, Director
Consumer Relations
Goodyear Tire & Rubber Co.
1144 East Market Street
Akron, OH 44316
(216) 796-4940
(216) 796-6055 (TDD)
1 (800) 321-2136 (toll free)

Mr. Michael Legrand
Vice President, Operations
Gordon's Jewelers
A Subsidiary of Zale Corporation
901 West Walnut Hill Lane
Irving, TX 75038-1003
(214) 580-4924

Consumer Affairs
Greensweep
800 North Lindbergh
St. Louis, MO 63167
1 (800) 225-2883 (toll free)

Ms. Janna Willardson
Manager, Customer Relations
Greyhound Lines, Inc.
901 Main Street, Suite 2500
Dallas, TX 75202
(214) 744-6500

Guess? Inc.
1444 South Alameda Street
Los Angeles, CA 90021
(213) 231-2385

Guinness Import Company
Six Landmark Square
Stamford, CT 06901-2704
(203) 323-3311
1 (800) 521-1591 (toll free)

H _____

Ms. Marti Johnson
Director of Client Relations
H&R Block, Inc.
4410 Main Street
Kansas City, MO 64111-9986
(816) 753-6900
1 (800) 829-7733 (toll free)

HVR Company
see Clorox Company

Mr. Don Freberg
Manager of Consumer Affairs
Hallmark Cards, Inc.
P.O. Box 419034
Kansas City, MO 64141-6034
(816) 274-5697

Halston
see Revlon

Hanes
see L'eggs

Mr. Fred Gould
Director, Consumer Service
Hanover-Direct Inc.
340 Poplar Street
Hanover, PA 17333-9989
(717) 637-6000

Hardwick
see Maycor

Mr. Jim Round
Vice President, Advertising
Hartmarx Specialty Stores, Inc.
101 North Wacker Drive, 20th Floor
Chicago, IL 60606-7389
(312) 372-6300

Ms. Nancy Moland
Hartz Mountain Corporation
700 Frank E. Rodgers Blvd. South
Harrison, NJ 07029-9987
(201) 481-4800

Ms. Bonnie Fisher
Supervisor, Consumer Service
Hasbro, Inc.
P.O. Box 200
Pawtucket, RI 02861-0200
(401) 431-8697
1 (800) 237-0063 (toll free)

Hathaway Shirts
see Warnaco Men's Apparel

Mr. Jim Lytle, Vice President
Direct Marketing
Heath Company
Benton Harbor, MI 49022
(616) 982-3672

Mr. Thomas J. Rattigan
Chairman and CEO
G. Heileman Brewing Company
100 Harborview Plaza
La Crosse, WI 54602-0459
(608) 785-1000

Ms. Donna Elliott
Manager, Consumer Relations
Heinz U.S.A.
P.O. Box 57
Pittsburgh, PA 15230-0057
(412) 237-5740

Consumer Affairs Department
Consumer Products Division
Helene Curtis, Inc.
325 North Wells Street
Chicago, IL 60610-4713
(312) 661-0222

Ms. Lael M. Moynihan
Manager, Consumer Relations
Hershey Foods Corporation
P.O. Box 815
Hershey, PA 17033-0815
1 (800) 468-1714 (toll free)

Ms. Leslie Rotonda, Manager
Executive Customer Relations
Hertz Corporation
225 Brae Boulevard
Park Ridge, NJ 07656-0713
(201) 307-2000
1 (800) 654-3131 (toll free—
reservations
1 (800) 654-2280 (toll free TDD)

Customer Information Center
Hewlett-Packard Company
19310 Prune Ridge Avenue
Cupertino, CA 95014
(408) 973-1919

Mr. Tony Schwartz
Helpline
Highland Superstores Inc.
909 North Sheldon Road
Plymouth, MI 48170
(313) 451-3200

Hilton Hotels Corporation
9336 Civic Center Drive
Beverly Hills, CA 90209-5567
(213) 278-4321

Ms. Casslyn Allen
Vice President, Human Resources
Hit or Miss
100 Campanelli Parkway
Stoughton, MA 02072
(617) 344-0800

Mr. Jim Drummond, Director
Advertising and Sales Promotion
**Hitachi Home Electronics
(America), Inc.**
3890 Steve Reynolds Boulevard
Norcross, GA 30093
(404) 279-5600
1 (800) 241-6558 (toll free)

Mr. Bill Bellican
Holiday Inns
3796 Lamar Avenue
Memphis, TN 38195
(901) 362-4827
1 (800) 621-0555 (toll free)

Mr. Bill Sanders
Director, Consumer Affairs
Home Depot Inc.
2727 Pacs Ferry Road
Atlanta, GA 30339
(404) 433-8211

Ms. Karen McKeever
Director of Marketing
**Home Owners Warranty
Corporation (HOW)**
1110 North Glebe Road
Arlington, VA 22201
(703) 516-4100
1 (800) CALL-HOW (toll free)

Home Shopping Network
P.O. Box 9090
Clearwater, FL 34618-9090
(813) 572-8585
1 (800) 753-5353 (toll free TDD)

Mr. Ray Gwin, Manager
Consumer Affairs
Residential Division
Honeywell, Inc.
1885 Douglas Drive
Golden Valley, MN 55422-4386
(612) 542-7354
1 (800) 468-1502 (toll free)

Mr. Larry Calder
Manager of Consumer Affairs
Hoover Company
101 East Maple
North Canton, OH 44720
(216) 499-9200, ext. 2669

Customer Service Division
The Horchow Collection
13800 Diplomat Drive
Dallas, TX 75234
(214) 484-6600
1 (800) 395-5397 (toll free)

Mr. Allan Krejci
Director, Public Relations
George A. Hormel and Company
501 16th Avenue NE
Austin, MN 55912-9989
(507) 437-5355

**Hostess
see Continental Baking Co.**

Mrs. Joyce Bryant
Vice President, Consumer Affairs
Household International
2700 Sanders Road
Prospect Heights, IL 60070
(708) 564-5000

Ms. Judy McCray, Consumer Relations
Huffy Corporation
P.O. Box 1204
Dayton, OH 45401
(513) 866-6251

Customer Relations
Humana Inc.
500 West Main Street
P.O Box 1438
Louisville, KY 40201-1438
(502) 580-1000

Hunt-Wesson, Inc.
Grocery Division
1645 West Balencia Drive
Fullerton, CA 92634
(714) 680-1430

Ms. Chris Buzanis
Director, Quality Assurance
Hyatt Hotels & Resorts
200 West Madison Street, 39th Floor
Chicago, IL 60606
(312) 750-1234
1 (800) 228-3336 (toll free)

I

Mr. John F. Akers
Chairman of the Board
IBM Corporation
Old Orchard Road
Armonk, NY 10504
(914) 765-5546

Consumer Affairs Department
Illinois Bell
225 West Randolph Street, Room 30-D
Chicago, IL 60606
(312) 727-9411

Mr. Stephen Powell
Community Affairs Manager
Indiana Bell
251 North Illinois Street, Room 1680
Indianapolis, IN 46204
(317) 265-5965
1 (800) 556-4949 (toll free)

Mr. David Steadman
President and CEO
Integra
4441 West Airport Freeway
Irving, TX 75062
(214) 258-8500

Communications Department
International Dairy Queen, Inc.
5701 Green Valley Drive
Minneapolis, MN 55437-1089
(612) 830-0200

J

Mr. James Bennett
Customer Relations Manager
JVC Company of America
41 Slater Drive
Elmwood Park, NJ 07407
(201) 794-3900
1 (800) 252-5722 (toll free)

Mr. Murray Taylor
Manager, Customer Service
Jackson & Perkins Nursery Stock
2518 South Pacific Highway
Medford, OR 97501
(503) 776-2400
1 (800) 872-7673 (toll free)

Ms. Eileen Guernsey
Manager of Consumer Affairs
James River Corporation
Dixie Products
P.O. Box 6000
Norwalk, CT 06856-6000
(203) 854-2469
1 (800) 243-5384 (toll free)

Ms. Rita Topp
Manager of Consumer Affairs
James River Corporation
Towel and Tissue Products
P.O. Box 6000
Norwalk, CT 06856-6000
1 (800) 243-5384 (toll free)

Customer Service
James River Traders
5000 City Lane Road
Hampton, VA 23661
(804) 827-6000

Jenn-Air Company
see Maycor

Jhirmack
see Playtex Family Products Group

Ms. Barbara Short
Consumer Relations
Jockey International, Inc.
2300 60th Street
Kenosha, WI 53140
(414) 658-8111

Consumer Affairs
John Hancock Financial Services
P.O. Box 111
Boston, MA 02117
(617) 572-6272

Johnny Appleseed's, Inc.
30 Tozer Road
Beverly, MA 01915-0720
1 (800) 225-5051 (toll free)

Johnson & Johnson Consumer
Products, Inc.
Information Center
199 Grandview Road
Skillman, NJ 08558
1 (800) 526-2433 (toll free)
1 (800) 526-3967 (toll free)

Complaint Department
Johnson Publishing Company, Inc.
820 South Michigan Avenue
Chicago, IL 60605
(written complaints only)

Mr. Tom Conrardy
Consumer Affairs Director
S.C. Johnson and Sons
1525 Howe Street
Racine, WI 53403
1 (800) 558-5252 (toll free)

Ms. Denise Mori
Manager, Guest Services
Howard Johnson, Inc.
P.O. Box 29004
Phoenix, AZ 85038
(602) 389-5555

Mr. Jerry Taylor, Vice President
Advertising and Marketing
Jordache Enterprises, Inc.
226 West 37th Street
New York, NY 10018
(212) 279-7343
1 (800) 289-5326 (toll free)
1 (800) 442-2056 (toll free)

K _____

Mr. Robert J. Clark
Manager, Customer Service
K mart Corporation
3100 West Big Beaver Road
Troy, MI 48084
(313) 643-1643
1 (800) 63-KMART (toll free)

Ms. Annette Watkins-Habeski
Manager, Consumer Relations
Fieldcrest Cannon Carpet Division
Karastan/Bigelow
725 North Regional Road
Greensboro, NC 27409
(919) 665-4000
1 (800) 476-7113 (toll free)

Mr. Ray Perry
Vice President, Operations
Carl Karcher Enterprises
1200 North Harbor Boulevard
P.O. Box 4349
Anaheim, CA 92803
(714) 774-5796

Consumer Services
**Kawasaki Motor Corporation,
U.S.A.**
P.O. Box 25252
Santa Ana, CA 92799-5252
(714) 770-0400

Ms. Sara C. Maness
Consumer Relations Manager
Kayser-Roth Corporation
612 South Main Street
Burlington, NC 27215
(919) 229-2224

Ms. Paige Riccio, Supervisor
Consumer Communications
Keebler Company, Inc.
One Hollow Tree Lane
Elmhurst, IL 60126
(708) 833-2900

Ms. Linda J. Pell
Manager, Consumer Affairs
Kellogg Company
P.O. Box CAMB
Battle Creek, MI 49016
(616) 961-2277

Mr. Don Diehl, Manager
Product Service
**The Kelly Springfield
Tire Company**
Willowbrook Road
Cumberland, MD 21502-2599
(301) 777-6631
(301) 777-6017

**Kelvinator Appliance Company
see White Consolidated Industries**

Ms. Dee Atkinson
Consumer Relations Manager
**Kemper National Insurance
Company**
Public Affairs and Communications
Long Grove, IL 60049-0001
(708) 540-2122
1 (800) 833-0355 (toll free)

Consumer Affairs
Kenner Products
1014 Vine Street
Cincinnati, OH 45202
(513) 579-4041
1 (800) 347-4613 (toll free)

Ms. Cindy Van Grinsven
Director, Consumer Services
Kimberly-Clark Corporation
P.O. Box 2020
Neenah, WI 54957-2020
(414) 721-5604
1 (800) 544-1847 (toll free)

**Kingsford Products Company
see Clorox Company**

Consumer Assistance Center
KitchenAid
701 Main Street
St. Joseph, MO 49085-1392
(616) 982-4500
1 (800) 422-1230 (toll free)

Mrs. Lori Masters
Assistant to the Senior Vice President
Public Relations and Communications
Calvin Klein Industries, Inc.
205 West 39th Street, 10th Floor
New York, NY 10018
(212) 719-2600
1 (800) 327-8731 (toll free)

Ms. Anita Davis, Director
Customer Relations
Kloster Cruise Ltd.
95 Merrick Way
Miami, FL 33134
(305) 447-9660

**Kodiak Smokeless Tobacco
see Conwood Co., L.P.**

Mr. Paul Scholten, Manager
Service and Technical Publications
Kohler Company
Kohler, WI 53044
(414) 457-4441

Mr. Allen Wilson, Manager
Sales Administration
Kohler Company
Kohler, WI 53044
(414) 457-4441

Mr. Mark Grunow, Manager
Consumer Affairs
**Plumbing Products
Kohler Company**
Kohler, WI 53044
(414) 457-4441

ATTN: Consumer Response Center
Kraft, Inc.
Kraftcourt
Glenview, IL 60025
1 (800) 323-0768 (toll free)

Ms. Judy Ball
Customer Relations Manager
Kroger Company
1014 Vine Street
Cincinnati, OH 45201
(513) 762-1589
1 (800) 632-6900
(toll free—product information)

Mr. Rody Davenport, IV
Vice President Operations
Krystal Company
One Union Square
Chattanooga, TN 37402
(615) 757-1550

L _____

Ms. Danielle King
Consumer Affairs Coordinator
LA Gear
4221 Redwood Avenue
Los Angeles, CA 90066
(213) 822-1995

Mrs. Colleen Fogle
Manager of Consumer Services
La-Z-Boy Chair Company
1284 North Telegraph Road
Monroe, MI 48161-3309
(313) 242-1444

Consumer Relations
L&F Products
225 Summit Avenue
Montvale, NJ 07645
(201) 573-5700

Ms. Marie Holen
Manager, Consumer Affairs
Land O'Lakes, Inc.
P.O. Box 116
Minneapolis, MN 55440-0116
1 (800) 328-4155 (toll free)

Customer Service
Land's End
One Land's End Lane
Dodgeville, WI 53595
1 (800) 356-4444 (toll free)

Mr. Donald Tucker
Manager, Customer Service
Lane Furniture
East Franklin Avenue
P.O. Box 151
Altavista, VA 24517
(804) 369-5641

Mr. John Gray, Director
Customer Services
Lechmere
275 Wildwood Street
Woburn, MA 01801
(617) 935-8340
1 (800) 733-4666 (toll free)

Ms. Barbara Distasi
Manager, Consumer Affairs
**Lederle Consumer Health
Products Division**
697 Route 46
Clifton, NJ 07015
1 (800) 282-8805
(toll free 9 A.M.–4 P.M., M–F)

Ms. Christine Anderson
Customer Service
Lee Company
9001 West 67th Street
Marriam, KS 66202
(913) 384-4000

L'eggs Products, Inc.
Sara Lee Hosiery
Sara Lee Corporation
5660 University Parkway
Winston-Salem, NC 27105
(919) 768-9540

Customer Service
Leichtung, Inc.
4944 Commerce Parkway
Cleveland, OH 44128
(216) 831-7645
1 (800) 654-7817 (toll free)

Lennox Industries
P.O. Box 799900
Dallas, TX 75380-9000
(214) 497-5000

Consumer Service Manager
Lever Brothers Corporation
390 Park Avenue
New York, NY 10022-4698
1 (800) 451-6679 (toll free)

Consumer Affairs
Levi Strauss & Co.
1155 Battery Street
San Francisco, CA 94111
1 (800) USA-LEVI (toll free)

Ms. Eleanor Eckardt
Vice President, Consumer Relations
Levitz Furniture Corporation
6111 Broken Sound Parkway, N.W.
Boca Raton, FL 33487-2799
1 (800) 523-2572
(toll free in FL)
1 (800) 631-4601
(toll free outside FL)

Customer Service
Levolor Corporation
7614 Business Park Drive
Greensboro, NC 27409
1 (800) LEVOLOR (toll free)

Mr. Edward T. Frackiewicz
Manager of Consumer Affairs
Liberty Mutual Insurance Group
175 Berkeley Street
Boston, MA 02117
(617) 357-9500
1 (800) 225-2390 (toll free)

Customer Service
Life Fitness Products
10601 West Belmont
Franklin Park, IL 60131
1 (800) 351-3737 (toll free)

Customer Service
Lillian Vernon Corporation
2600 International Parkway
Virginia Beach, VA 23452
(804) 430-1500

Consumer Technical Services
Eli Lilly & Company
Lilly Corporate Center
Indianapolis, IN 46285
(317) 276-2339 (product information)
(For medical information, contact
your physician)

Mr. Alfred Dietzel
Vice President
Financial and Public Relations
The Limited, Inc.
Two Limited Parkway
P.O. Box 16000
Columbus, OH 43216
(614) 479-7000

Ms. Sharlene Ungar
Manager
Customer Service Center
Little Caeser Enterprises
2211 Woodward Avenue
Detroit, MI 48201
1 (800) 7-CAESAR

**Lone Star Brewing Company
see G. Heileman Brewing**

Long John Silver's
101 Jerrico Drive
P.O. Box 11988
Lexington, KY 40579
(606) 263-6000

**L'Oreal
see Cosmair, Inc.**

Mr. David Hicks
Customer Relations Manager
Lorillard Tobacco Company
2525 East Market Street
P.O. Box 21688
Greensboro, NC 27420-1688
(919) 373-6669

Public Relations Department
Los Angeles Times
Times Mirror Square
Los Angeles, CA 90053
(213) 237-5000

Ms. Judy Decker
Communications Coordinator
Lucky Stores, Inc.
P.O. Box BB
Dublin, CA 94568
(415) 833-6000

M_____

Ms. Marie A. Lentz
Director, Customer Services
MAACO Enterprises, Inc.
381 Brooks Road
King of Prussia, PA 19406
1 (800) 523-1180
(toll free outside PA)

Public Information
MCA, Inc.
100 Universal City Plaza
Universal City, CA 91608-1085
(818) 777-1000

Mr. Roy Gamse
Senior Vice President
Consumer Service
MCI Consumer Markets
1200 South Hayes Street, 12th Floor
Arlington, VA 22202
(703) 415-6726

Consumer Affairs Department
M&M/Mars, Inc.
High Street
Hackettstown, NJ 07840
(201) 852-1000
1 (800) 222-0293 (toll free)

MTV Networks, Inc.
see Viacom International, Inc.

Vice President
Customer Service
R.H. Macy & Company, Inc.
151 West 34th Street
New York, NY 10001
(212) 695-4400

Magic Chef
see Maycor

Magnavox
see Philips Company

Valli Zale, General Manager
I. Magnin
3050 Wilshire Boulevard
Los Angeles, CA 90010
(213) 382-6161

Mr. Ross DeMaris
Consumer Services Manager
Mannington Resilient Floors, Inc.
P.O. Box 30
Salem, NJ 08079
(609) 935-3000
1 (800) 356-6787 (toll free)

Professional Services Department
Manor Care Healthcare
10770 Columbia Pike
Silver Spring, MD 20901
(301) 681-9400
1 (800) 637-1400
(toll free outside MD)

Ms. Marie DeAngelo
Assistant Vice President
**Manufacturers Hanover
Trust Company**
270 Park Avenue
New York, NY 10017
(212) 270-7370

Manville Corporation
P.O. Box 5108
Denver, CO 80217-5108
(303) 978-2000
1 (800) 654-3103
(toll free—product information)

Corporate Customer Relations
Marine Midland Bank, N.A.
One Marine Midland Center
Buffalo, NY 14203
(716) 841-2424

Mr. William Guinty
Manager, Regulatory Services
Marion Merrell Dow
Consumer Products Division
Marion Park Drive
Kansas City, MO 64134
(816) 966-5305

Consumer Affairs
Marriott Corporation
One Marriott Drive
Attn: Department 921-60
Washington, DC 20058
(301) 380-7600

Ms. Norma Vinick
Director of Customer Relations
**Massachusetts Mutual Life
Insurance Company**
1295 State Street
Springfield, MA 01111
(413) 788-8411
1 (800) 828-4902 (toll free)

**MasterCard International
(contact issuing bank)**

Mr. Joseph Dillon, President
Matsushita Servicing Company
50 Meadowlands Parkway
Secaucus, NJ 07094
(201) 348-7000

Ms. Tammy Longworth
Director, Consumer Affairs
Mattel Toys, Inc.
333 Continental Boulevard
El Segundo, CA 90245-5012
(213) 524-2000
1 (800) 421-2887
(toll free outside CA)

Max Factor
see Revlon

Consumer Affairs
Maxicare Health Plans, Inc.
1149 South Broadway
Los Angeles, CA 90015
(213) 742-0900

Maxwell House
see General Foods

Mr. James F. Harner
Senior Vice President
Customer Service and Operations
May Department Stores Co.
611 Olive Street
St. Louis, MO 63101
(314) 342-4336

Maybelline
see Schering-Plough HealthCare
Products, Inc.

Maycor Appliance, Parts, and
Service Company
240 Edwards Street, SE
Cleveland, TN 37311
(615) 472-3333

Customer Service Department
Mayflower Transit, Inc.
P.O. Box 107
Indianapolis, IN 46206
(317) 875-1000
1 (800) 428-1200 (toll free)

Maytag
see Maycor

Ms. Mary Randisi, Director
Consumer Affairs
McCormick & Company, Inc.
211 Schilling Circle
Hunt Valley, MD 21031
(301) 527-6273
1 (800) 632-5847 (toll free)

McCrory Stores, Inc.
2955 East Market Street
York, PA 17402
(717) 757-8181

Ms. Beth Petersohn
Manager, Customer Relations
McDonald's Corporation
McDonald's Plaza
Oak Brook, IL 60521
(708) 575-6198

Ms. Mary Jo Oller
Customer Service
McGraw-Hill Company
Blue Ridge Summit, PA 17294
(717) 794-5461
1 (800) 262-4729 (toll free)

Consumer Services
McKee Baking Company
P.O. Box 750
Collegedale, TN 37315
(615) 238-7111

Vice President Marketing
McKesson Water Products
Company
4500 York Boulevard
Los Angeles, CA 90041
(213) 259-2000

Consumer Affairs
McNeil Consumer Products
Company
Johnson & Johnson
Camp Hill Road
Fort Washington, PA 19034
(215) 233-7000

Mr. Marshall Morton
Senior Vice President
Media General, Inc.
333 East Grace Street
Richmond, VA 23219
(804) 649-6000

Ms. Angela Cureton
Customer Service Representative
Meineke Discount Muffler
128 South Tryon Street, Suite 900
Charlotte, NC 28202
(704) 377-8855

Customer Service Department
Melitta USA, Inc.
1401 Berlin Road
Cherry Hill, NJ 08003
(609) 428-7202
1 (800) 451-1694 (toll free)

Ms. Sandra J. McLaughlin
Senior Vice President
Corporate Affairs
Mellon Bank Corporation
One Mellon Bank Center, 151-1840
Pittsburgh, PA 15258
(412) 234-4003

Ms. Diana Epstein
Consumer Affairs
Melville Corporation
1 Theall Road
Rye, NY 10580
(914) 925-4000

Mr. Otto Schmin
Consumer Relations
Mem Company, Inc.
Union Street
Northvale, NJ 07647
(201) 767-0100

Ms. Mary Ann Molnar
Consumer Relations Administrator
Mennen Company
Hanover Avenue
Morristown, NJ 07962-1928
(201) 631-9000
(collect calls accepted)

Mr. Jim Dickson
Product Manager
Mentholatum Company Inc.
1360 Niagara Street
Buffalo, NY 14213
(716) 882-7660

Consumer Affairs
Mercury Marine
P.O. Box 1939
Fond du Lac, WI 54936-1935
(414) 929-5000

Mr. Dave Smith, Manager
Customer Service
Merillat Industries
5353 West U.S. 223
Adrian, MI 49221
(517) 263-0771

Customer Service Department
**Merrill Lynch Pierce
Fenner & Smith**
265 Davidson Avenue, 4th Floor
Somerset, NJ 08873
(908) 563-8777

Ms. Colleen Dahle-Hong
Consumer Affairs Analyst
Mervyn's
25001 Industrial Boulevard
Hayward, CA 94545
(415) 786-8337

Office of the President
Metromedia Steakhouses, Inc.
P.O. Box 578
Dayton, OH 45401-0578
(513) 454-2400

Mr. Bruce C. Hemer
Director, Consumer Affairs
**Metropolitan Life and
Affiliated Companies**
One Madison Avenue
Area 1-Z
New York, NY 10010-3690
(212) 578-2544

Mr. Martin J. Wertheim, Manager
Corporate Consumer Relations
Michelin Tire Corporation
One Parkway South
Greenville, SC 29615
(803) 458-5000

Mr. David E. Bassett
Senior Director, Community Relations
Michigan Bell Telephone Co.
1365 Cass Avenue, Room 1800
Detroit, MI 48226
(313) 223-7224
1 (800) 482-3141 (toll free TDD)

Ms. Darlene Snape
Customer Service Manager
Michigan Bulb Company
1950 Waldorf, NW
Grand Rapids, MI 49550
(616) 771-9500

Mr. Charles Ayers, Manager
Consumer Relations
Midas International
225 North Michigan Avenue
Chicago, IL 60601
(312) 565-7500
1 (800) 621-8545
(toll free outside IL)

Mid-Michigan Surgical Supply
360 Capitol Avenue, NE
Battlecreek, MI 49017
(616) 962-9541

Ms. Diane Ferri, Manager
Customer Relations
Midway Airlines
5959 South Cicero Avenue
Chicago, IL 60638
(312) 838-4684
1 (800) 866-9000, ext. 4684
(toll free)

Customer Service
Miles Kimball
41 West 8
Oshkosh, WI 54906
(written inquiries only)

Ms. Debra K. Wood
Consumer Service Representative
Milton Bradley Company
443 Shaker Road
East Long Meadow, MA 01028
(413) 525-6411

Mr. George Manning
National Manager
Consumer Relations
Minolta Corporation
100 Williams Drive
Ramsey, NJ 07446
(201) 825-4000

Technical Services
Minwax, Inc.
15 Mercedes Drive
Montvale, NJ 07645
1 (800) 526-0495 (toll free)

Miracle Gro Products, Inc.
P.O. Box 800
Port Washington, NY 11050
(516) 883-6550

Consumer Relations
**Mitsubishi Electric Sales
of America, Inc.**
5757 Plaza Drive
P.O. Box 6007
Cypress, CA 90630
(714) 220-2500

Mr. G.T. Cox, Manager
Customer Relations
Mobil Oil Corporation
3225 Gallows Road
Fairfax, VA 22037
(703) 849-3994

Mr. Al Kedora
Customer Services Manager
Mobil Oil Credit Corporation
210 West Tenth Street
Kansas City, MO 64105
(816) 391-9100

Customer Service
Crystal Brand Jewelry Group
**Monet Crisart and Marvella
Jewelry**
Number Two Lonsdale Avenue
Pawtucket, RI 02860
(401) 728-9800

Mr. Dan R. Bishop, Director
Corporate Communications
Monsanto Company
800 North Lindbergh Boulevard
St. Louis, MO 63167
(314) 694-2883

Mr. W. Andrew Werry
Consumer Affairs Manager
Montgomery Ward
One Montgomery Ward Plaza, 9-S
Chicago, IL 60671
(312) 467-2814

Mr. Kenneth C. Cummins
Vice President and General Counsel
Morse Shoe Company
555 Turnpike Street
Canton, MA 02021
(617) 828-9300
1 (800) 366-6773 (toll free)

Consumer Affairs
Morton International
Morton Salt Division
100 North Riverside Plaza
Chicago, IL 60606
(312) 807-2694

Director of Marketing
Motorola, Inc.
1303 East Algonquin Road
Schaumburg, IL 60196
(708) 576-5000

Mr. Paul Murphy
Vice President, Advertising
Murphy-Phoenix Co.
25800 Science Park Drive, Suite 200
P.O. Box 22930
Beachwood, OH 44122
(216) 831-0404

**Mutual Lite Insurance Company
of New York (MONY)**
Glenpoint Center West
500 Frank W. Burr Boulevard
Teaneck, NJ 07666
(201) 907-6669

Ms. Terry Calek
Second Vice President, Public Affairs
Mutual of Omaha Insurance Co.
Mutual of Omaha Plaza
Omaha, NE 68175
(402) 342-7600

N _____

Audience Services
NBC
30 Rockefeller Plaza
New York, NY 10112
(212) 664-2333

Mr. Greg VanZandt
Consumer Affairs
NEC Technologies Inc.
1255 Michael Drive
Wood Dale, IL 60191-1094
(708) 860-0335

Ms. Alice Gabel, Manager
"800" Toll Free Center
Consumer Affairs
Nabisco Brands, Inc.
100 DeForest Avenue
East Hanover, NJ 07936
(201) 503-2659
1 (800) 932-7800 (toll free)

Mr. Dennis Dotson
Director, Theater Operations
National Amusements Inc.
200 Elm Street
Dedham, MA 02026
(617) 461-1600

Mr. Joel Martin
Divisional Vice President
Customer Services
National Car Rental System, Inc.
7700 France Avenue, South
Minneapolis, MN 55435
(612) 893-6209
1 (800) 627-7777 (toll free)

National Education Corporation
1732 Reynolds Street
Irvine, CA 92714
(714) 261-7606

Mr. Bill Campbell, Vice President
National Media Corporation
4360 Main Street
Philadelphia, PA 19127
(215) 482-9800

Mr. James Jenson, Controller
National Presto Industries, Inc.
3925 North Hastings Way
Eau Claire, WI 54703-3703
(715) 839-2121

Mr. Glenn W. Soden
Customer Relations Officer
Nationwide Insurance Companies
One Nationwide Plaza
Columbus, OH 43216
(614) 249-6985

Customer Relations
Neighborhood Periodical Club, Inc.
One Crowne Point Court, #130
Cincinnati, OH 45241
(513) 771-9400

Customer Service Department
Neiman-Marcus
P.O. Box 64780
Dallas, TX 75206
(214) 761-2600
1 (800) 442-2274
(toll free in TX)
1 (800) 527-1767
(toll free outside TX)

Mrs. Andrea McLean
Manager, Consumer Affairs
Nestle Foods Corporation
100 Manhattanville Road
Purchase, NY 10577
(914) 251-3000
1 (800) NESTLES (toll free)

Mr. Dick L. Curd
Media Affairs Director
Corporate Communications
Nestle USA, Inc.
800 North Brand Boulevard
Glendale, CA 91203
(818) 549-6000

Ms. Alene Lain
Consumer Relations
Neutrogena Corporation
5760 West 96th Street
Los Angeles, CA 90045
(213) 642-1150
1 (800) 421-6857
(toll free outside CA)

Consumer Relations
Nevada Bell
645 East Plumb Lane
Reno, NV 89520
(702) 789-6000

Mr. Edward C. Hall
Executive Vice President
The New England
500 Boylston Street
Boston, MA 02117
(617) 578-2000

Mr. William H. Willett
Chairman, CEO
New Hampton, Inc.
5000 City Line Road
Hampton, VA 23661
(804) 827-7010

Customer Service
News America Publishing, Inc.
Four Radnor Corporate Center
Radnor, PA 19088
(215) 293-8500
1 (800) 625-7300 (toll free)

Ms. Barbara Fagnano
Assistant Vice President
New York Life Insurance Company
51 Madison Avenue
New York, NY 10010
(212) 576-5081
(collect calls accepted)

Mr. Robert P. Smith, Manager
Advertising Acceptability Department
New York Times Company
229 West 43rd Street
New York, NY 10036
(212) 556-7171

Customer Service Representative
Newsweek, Inc.
P.O. Box 403
Livingston, NJ 07039
(212) 350-4000
1 (800) 631-1040
(toll free—subscriber service only)

Customer Service
Nexxus Products
P.O. Box 1274
Santa Barbara, CA 93116-9976
(805) 968-6900

Ms. Nancy L. Testani
Director, Consumer Affairs
**Niagara Mohawk Power
Corporation**
300 Erie Boulevard West
Syracuse, NY 13202
(315) 474-1511

Ms. Jackie Evey, Supervisor
Consumer Services
Nike, Inc.
Nike/World Campus
1 Bowerman Drive
Beaverton, OR 97005
(503) 671-6453
1 (800) 344-6453
(toll free outside OR)

Consumer Affairs
Nintendo of America Inc.
4820 150th Avenue NE
Redmond, WA 98052
1 (800) 255-3700 (toll free)

**No Nonsense
see Kayser-Roth Corporation**

**Norge
see Maycor**

Ms. Amy Grant
Marketing Servicing Manager
**North American Watch
Corporation**
650 Fifth Avenue
New York, NY 10019
(212) 397-7800

Mr. G.C. Strickland
Supervisor, Consumer Affairs
Northern Electric Company
1621 Highway 15 North
P.O. Box 247
Laurel, MS 39441-0247
(601) 649-6170

Customer Relations
Northwest Airlines
A5270 Minneapolis/St. Paul
International Airport
St. Paul, MN 55111-3034
(612) 726-2046
1 (800) 328-2298
(toll free TDD—reservations)

Mr. Thomas W. Towers
Associate Director, Public Relations
**Northwestern Mutual Life
Insurance Company**
720 East Wisconsin Avenue
Milwaukee, WI 53202
(414) 271-1444

**Norwegian Cruise Line
see Kloster Cruise Ltd.**

Ms. Claire Lee, Product Manager
Nostril/Nostrilla
Boehringer Ingelheim
90 East Ridge
P.O. Box 368
Ridgefield, CT 06877
(203) 798-9988

Mr. E.R. Steinmeier
Director, Consumer Services
Noxell Corporation
11050 York Road
Hunt Valley, MD 21030-2098
(301) 785-4411
1 (800) 638-6204 (toll free)

Mr. Ralph Profitt
Director of Consumer Relations
Nu Tone, Inc.
Madison and Red Bank Roads
Cincinnati, OH 45227
(513) 527-5100
1 (800) 582-2030
(toll free in OH)
1 (800) 543-8687
(toll free outside OH)

The NutraSweet Company
1751 Lake Cook Road
Deerfield, IL 60015
1 (800) 321-7254
(toll free—NutraSweet®)
1 (800) 323-5316
(toll free—Equal®)

Ms. Nancy Moskowitz
Customer Relations
Nutri/System Inc.
380 Sentry Parkway
Blue Bell, PA 19422-2332
(215) 940-3000, ext. 3443

President's Help Line
Nynex/New York Telephone
1095 Avenue of the Americas
New York, NY 10036
1 (800) 722-2300 (toll free)
1 (800) 342-4181
(toll free TDD in NY)

O

Mrs. Linda Compton
Supervisor, Consumer Affairs
Ocean Spray Cranberries Inc.
One Ocean Spray Drive
Lakeville/Middleboro, MA 02349
(508) 946-1000

Ms. Gail Holmes, District Manager
Consumer Affairs
Ohio Bell Telephone Company
45 ErieView, Room 870
Cleveland, OH 44114
(216) 822-2124

**O'Keefe & Merit Appliances
see White Consolidated Industries**

Ms. Gay F. Gandrow
Director, Marketing Services
Olan Mills, Inc.
4325 Amnicola Highway
P.O. Box 23456
Chattanooga, TN 37422-3456
(615) 622-5141
1 (800) 251-6323 (toll free)

Mr. Ralph LePore
Manager, Camera Service
Olympus Optical Company, Ltd.
145 Crossways Park
Woodbury, NY 11797
(516) 364-3000

Ms. Bridget Burke
Consumer Relations Representative
Oneida, Ltd.
Kenwood Station
Oneida, NY 13421
(315) 361-3000
1 (800) 877-6667 (toll free)

**Orkin
see Rollins, Inc.**

Mr. Brodrick William Hill
Manager, Consumer Affairs
Ortho Consumer Products
Chevron Chemical Company
P.O. Box 5047
San Ramon, CA 94583-0947
(415) 842-5500

**OSCO Drugs
see American Stores Company**

Mr. Bob Schroer, Manager
Field and Customer Services
Outboard Marine Corporation
100 Sea Horse Drive
Waukegan, IL 60085
(708) 689-6200

**Owens-Corning Fiberglas
Corporation**
Fiberglas Tower
Toledo, OH 43659
(419) 248-8000

P

Customer Appeals Group
Pacific Bell
140 New Montgomery Street
San Francisco, CA 94108
(415) 882-8000
1 (800) 592-6500 (toll free in CA)

Public Affairs
Pacific Enterprises
P.O. Box 60043
Los Angeles, CA 90060-0043
(213) 895-5000

Consumer Relations Department
Pacific Telesis Group
130 Kearny Street
San Francisco, CA 94108
(415) 882-8000

Mr. Frank S. Pluchino
Director and Vice President
Customer Services
PaineWebber, Inc.
Lincoln Harbor
1200 Harbor Boulevard, 10th Floor
Weehawken, NJ 07087
(201) 902-3000

Mr. Alan Vose
Director, Consumer Affairs
Pan American World Airways
Customer Relations
P.O. Box 592055 AMF
Miami International Airport
Miami, FL 33159
1 (800) 428-1100 (toll free)

**Panasonic
see Matsushita Servicing Company**

**Paper Art Company
see Mennen Company**

Mr. Rick Bates
Vice President
Customer Operations
Paramount Communications Inc.
200 Old Tappan Road
Old Tappan, NJ 07675
(201) 767-5000

**Parke-Davis
see Warner-Lambert Company**

**Peidmont Airlines
see USAir**

Ms. Pamela Lumpkin
Consumer Relations Manager
J.C. Penney Company, Inc.
P.O. Box 659000
Dallas, TX 75265-9000
(214) 591-8500

Mr. William E. Place
National Technical Service Manager
Pennzoil Products Company
P.O. Box 2967
Houston, TX 77252-2967
(713) 546-8783 (collect calls accepted)

Ms. Redon Forest
Director of Public Affairs
Peoples Drug Stores, Inc.
6315 Bren Mar Drive
Alexandria, VA 22312
(703) 750-6100
1 (800) 572-0267
(toll free in VA)
1 (800) 336-4990
(toll free outside VA)

Mrs. Ellie Eng
Manager, Consumer Services
Pepperidge Farm, Inc.
595 Westport Avenue
Norwalk, CT 06856
(203) 846-7276

Ms. Christine Jones
Manager, Consumer Affairs
Pepsi-Cola Company
1 Pepsi Way
Somers, NY 10589-2201
(914) 767-6000

Ms. Connie Littleton
Director of Advertising
Perdue Farms
P.O. Box 1537
Salisbury, MD 21802
(301) 543-3000
1 (800) 442-2034
(toll free outside MD)

Ms. Maria Cammarosano
Marketing Division
The Perrier Group
777 West Putnam Avenue
Greenwich CT 06830
(203) 531-4100

Ms. Joyce Hofer
Consumer Affairs Correspondent
**Dry Foods (Except Progresso)
Pet Incorporated**
P.O. Box 66719
St. Louis, MO 63166-6719
(314) 622-6695

Ms. Janice Leidner
Consumer Affairs Correspondent
**Progresso Line
Pet Incorporated**
P.O. Box 66719
St. Louis, MO 63166-6719
(314) 622-6364

Ms. Mary Carich
Consumer Affairs Specialist
**Frozen and Bakery Foods
Pet Incorporated**
P.O. Box 66719
St. Louis, MO 63166-6719
(314) 622-6146

Marketing Department
Pfizer Inc.
235 East 42nd Street
New York, NY 10017
(212) 573-2323

Philco
see Philips Company

Ms. Anne T. Dowling, Director
Corporate Contributions
Philip Morris Companies
Incorporated
120 Park Avenue
New York, NY 10017
(212) 880-3366

Department of Consumer Affairs
Philips Company
Consumer Electronics Division
P.O. Box 555
Jefferson City, TN 37760
(615) 475-0317

Ms. Toni J. Honkisz
Corporate Quality Administrator
Philips Lighting Company
200 Franklin Square Drive
P.O. Box 6800
Somerset, NJ 08875-6800
1 (800) 543-8167 (toll free)

Public Relations
Phillips Petroleum Company
16 Phillips Building
Bartlesville, OK 74004
(918) 661-1215

Piaget
see North American Watch
Corporation

Pillsbury Company
Consumer Response
P.O. Box 550
Minneapolis, MN 55440
1 (800) 767-4466 (toll free)

Mr. Al Segaul, Division Manager
Customer Service
Pioneer Electronics Service, Inc.
P.O. Box 1760
Long Beach, CA 90810
1 (800) 421-1404 (toll free)

Mr. Fred Fuest
Manager, Consumer Affairs
Pirelli Tire
Pirelli/Armstrong Tire Corporation
500 Sargent Drive
New Haven, CT 06536-0201
1 (800) 327-2442 (toll free)

Playskool
see Hasbro, Inc.

Ms. Theresa M. Boutin
Manager, Consumer Affairs
Playtex Apparel, Inc.
P.O. Box 631
MS 1526
Dover, DE 19903-0631
(302) 674-6000
1 (800) 537-9955 (toll free)

Playtex Family Products Corp.
215 College Road
P.O. Box 728
Paramus, NJ 07652
1 (800) 624-0825
(toll free in NJ)
1 (800) 222-0453
(toll free outside NJ)

Customer Service Department
Polaroid Corporation
784 Memorial Drive
Cambridge, MA 02139
(617) 577-2000
(collect calls accepted within MA)
1 (800) 343-5000
(toll free outside MA)

Mr. Richard Lugo
Customer Relations Manager
Polo/Ralph Lauren Corporation
4100 Beechwood Drive
Greensboro, NC 27410
1 (800) 765-6369 (toll free)

Ponderosa
see Metromedia Steakhouses, Inc.

Operations Department
Popeye's/Church's Fried Chicken, Inc.
P.O. Box BH001
San Antonio, TX 78201
(512) 735-9392
1 (800) 222-5857 (toll free)

Premier Beverages
see Dr. Pepper

Prescriptives, Inc.
see Estee Lauder

Princeton Pharmaceutical Products
see Bristol-Myers Squibb Pharmaceutical Group

Ms. Patti Schively
Associate Director, Consumer Services
Procter & Gamble Co.
P.O. Box 599
Cincinnati, OH 45201-0599
(513) 983-2200
(toll-free numbers appear on all
Procter & Gamble product labels)

Mr. Joe Kenney
Associate Counsel and Secretary
Provident Mutual Life Insurance
1600 Market Street
P.O. Box 7378
Philadelphia, PA 19101
(215) 636-5000

Individual Insurance Services
Prudential Insurance Company Of America
Executive Offices
Prudential Plaza, 24th Floor
Newark, NJ 07101
(201) 802-6000

Public Affairs
Prudential Property & Casualty Company
23 Main Street
P.O. Box 419
Holmdel, NJ 07733
(609) 653-3000

Client Relations
Prudential Securities Inc.
One Seaport Plaza
New York, NY 10292
(212) 214-1000

Ms. Patricia Kaufman
Director, Customer Operations
Publishers Clearing House
382 Channel Drive
Port Washington, NY 11050
(516) 883-5432
1 (800) 645-9242
(toll free outside NY)

Ms. Mary Ann Jones
Director of Customer Relations
Publix Super Markets
1936 George Jenkins Boulevard
P.O. Box 407
Lakeland, FL 33802
(813) 688-1188

Q

QVC Network
Goshen Corporate Park
1365 Enterprise Drive
West Chester, PA 19380
(215) 430-1000

Ms. Beverly Kloehn
Director of Consumer Response
Quaker Oats Company
P.O. Box 9003
Chicago, IL 60604-9003
(312) 222-7843

Mr. Benton H. Faulkner
Manager, Public Relations
Quaker State Corporation
P.O. Box 989
Oil City, PA 16301
(814) 676-7676

Quasar
see Matsushita Servicing Company

R

Radio Shack
see Tandy Corporation

Ms. Doris Hewkin, Director
Office of Consumer Affairs
Ralston Purina Company
Checkerboard Square
St. Louis, MO 63164
(314) 982-4566
1 (800) 345-5678 (toll free)

Ms. Judy Crawford
Director, Public Relations
**Ramada International Hotels
and Resorts**
3838 East VanBuren
P.O. Box 29004
Phoenix, AZ 85038
(602) 273-4604

Mrs. Patricia Rosafort
Supervisor, Customer Services
Reader's Digest Association, Inc.
Pleasantville, NY 10570-7000
1 (800) 431-1246 (toll free)
1 (800) 735-4327 (toll free TDD)

Consumer Affairs Department
**Reckitt & Colman Household
Products**
Division of Reckitt & Colman Inc.
P.O. Box 945
Wayne, NJ 07474-0945
(201) 633-6700

**Orville Redenbacher
see Hunt-Wesson, Inc.**

Consumer Relations
Reebok International, Ltd.
100 Technology Center Drive
Stoughton, MA 02072
1 (800) 843-4444 (toll free)

Mr. Richard Jones
Customer Service Manager
The Regina Company
P.O. Box 638
Long Beach, MS 39560
1 (800) 847-8336
(toll free)
1 (800) 321-8293
(toll free—repair location hot line)

Ms. Cass Carroll
Director of Consumer Relations
Reliance Insurance Company
Four Penn Center Plaza
Philadelphia, PA 19103
(215) 864-4445
1 (800) 441-1652 (toll free)

Mr. Mitch Maples, Manager
Consumer Affairs
Remco America, Inc.
P.O. Box 42946
Houston, TX 77242-2946
(713) 977-2288

Customer Relations Department
Remington Products, Inc.
60 Main Street
Bridgeport, CT 06004
(203) 367-4400

**Remington Rifle
see E.I. duPont de Nemours & Co.**

Ms. Natalie Korman
Director, Consumer Relations
Revlon
625 Madison Avenue
New York, NY 10022
(212) 527-5644

Ms. Carol Owen, Director
Consumer Services
Reynolds Metals Company
6603 West Broad Street
Richmond, VA 23230
(804) 281-4073 (collect calls accepted)

**Rhone-Poulenc Rorer
Pharmaceuticals Inc.**
Consumer Affairs Information Center
500 Virginia Drive
Fort Washington, PA 19034
1 (800) 548-3708
(toll free 8:30 A.M.–4:30 P.M. EST)

Ms. Kathleen M. Fitzsimmons
Manager, Consumer Services
Richardson-Vicks, Inc.
One Far Mill Crossing
Shelton, CT 06484-0925
(203) 925-6000

Mr. Marce Seim
Coordinator, Consumer Relations
A.H. Robins Company, Inc.
1405 Cummings Drive
Richmond, VA 23261-6609
(804) 257-2000

Rockport
see Reebok

Mrs. Jean Dorney
Assistant Director of
Fulfillment Services
Rodale Press, Inc.
33 East Minor Street
Emmaus, PA 18049
1 (800) 441-7761 (toll free)

Mr. Patrick Puton
Service Manager
Rolex Watch U.S.A., Inc.
665 Fifth Avenue
New York, NY 10022
(212) 758-7700

Ms. Jan Bell, Director
Customer Service
Rollins, Inc.
2170 Piedmont Road, N.E.
Atlanta, GA 30324
(404) 888-2151

Mr. Leo VanVark, Manager
Customer Service
Rolscreen Company
102 Main Street
Pella, IA 50219
(515) 628-1000

Ms. Joanne Taddeo, Manager
Customer Relations
Ross Laboratories
625 Cleveland Avenue
Columbus, OH 43215
(614) 229-7900

Mr. Paul W. Carter, Director
Franchise Administration
Roto-Rooter Corporation
300 Ashworth Road
West Des Moines, IA 50265
(515) 223-1343

Roundup Lawn and Garden
see Greensweep

Ms. Wynelle Sanders
Marketing Secretary
Royal Oak Enterprises, Inc.
900 Ashwood Parkway, Suite 800
Atlanta, GA 30338
(404) 393-1430
1 (800) 241-3955 (toll free)

Mrs. Denice Kaack, Manager
Customer Service
Royal Silk Ltd.
45 East Madison Avenue
Clifton, NJ 07011
1 (800) 451-7455 (toll free)

Royal Viking Cruise Line
see Kloster Cruise Ltd.

Ms. Ruth A. Chambers
Supervisor, Consumer Services
Rubbermaid, Inc.
1147 Akron Road
Wooster, OH 44691-0800
(216) 264-6464

Rustler Jeans
see Blue Bell, Inc.

Mr. Donald Berryman
Director, Customer Service
Ryder Truck Rental
P.O. Box 020816
Miami, FL 33102-0816
1 (800) 327-7777 (toll free)

Administrative Assistant to the
President
Ryland Building Company
Ryland Group, Inc.
P.O. Box 4000
Columbia, MD 21044
(301) 730-7222

S _____

7 Eleven Food Stores
see The Southland Corporation

SFS Corporation
Customer Information Center
1 (800) 421-5013 (toll free)

Mr. Brian Dowling
Public Affairs Department Manager
Safeway Inc.
Oakland, CA 94660
(415) 891-3267

Ms. Victoria Loesch
Director, Corporate Customer
Relations
Saks & Companies NY
450 West 15th Street
New York, NY 10011
(212) 940-5027

Sandoz Company
Sandoz Pharmaceuticals
59 Route 10
East Hanover, NJ 07936
(201) 503-7500

**Sanyo Electric Inc.
see SFS Corporation**

Sara Lee Corporation
Three First National Plaza
70 West Madison Street
Chicago, IL 60602-4260
(312) 726-2600

Ms. Watson Brooks
Manager, Consumer Relations
**Schering-Plough HealthCare
Products, Inc.**
3030 Jackson Avenue
Memphis, TN 38151-0001
(901) 320-2998

**Scholl
see Schering-Plough HealthCare
Products, Inc.**

Consumer Relations Department
Schwinn Bicycle Company
217 North Jefferson Street
Chicago, IL 60661-1111
1 (800) 633-0231 (toll free)

Ms. Janet Jones, Manager
Consumer Relations Operations
Scott Paper Company
Scott Plaza Two
Philadelphia, PA 19113
(215) 522-6170
1 (800) 835-7268 (toll free outside PA)

Shareholder Services Representative
Scudder Funds Distributor
160 Federal Street
Boston, MA 02110
1 (800) 225-2470 (toll free)

Joseph E. Seagram & Sons, Inc.
375 Park Avenue
New York, NY 10152
(212) 572-7147

Customer Service Representative
**Sealy Mattress Manufacturing
Company**
1228 Euclid Avenue, 10th Floor
Cleveland, OH 44115
(216) 522-1310
(216) 522-1366 (TDD)

Mr. Ken Waldhof
Customer Affairs Manager
Seamans Furniture Company, Inc.
70 Charles Lindbergh Boulevard
Uniondale, NY 11553
(516) 227-1563
1 (800) 445-2503 (toll free)

Customer Service
**G.D. Searle and Company
Pharmaceuticals**
P.O. Box 5110
Chicago, IL 60680
1 (800) 323-1603 (toll free)

Mr. Jerry Hauber
National Consumer Relations Manager
Sears, Roebuck & Co.
Department 731 CR, BSC 39-33
Sears Tower
Chicago, IL 60684
(312) 875-5188

**Sedgefield Jeans
see Blue Bell, Inc.**

Coserv
Seiko Corporation of America
27 McKee Drive
Mahwah, NJ 07430
(201) 529-3311

Ms. Rosemarie Martinez
Customer Relations Department
Serta, Inc.
2800 River Road
Des Plaines, IL 60018
(708) 699-9300

Seventeen Magazine
see News America Publishing, Inc.

Seven-Up
see Dr. Pepper

Mr. Vernon Brisson, General Manager
Customer Relations
Sharp Electronics Corporation
Sharp Plaza
P.O. Box 650
Mahwah, NJ 07430-2135
(201) 529-9140
1 (800) 526-0264 (toll free)

Customer Relations
The Sharper Image
650 Davis Street
San Francisco, CA 94111
1 (800) 344-5555 (toll free)

Mr. T. J. McPhail, Manager
Customer Services
Shell Oil Company
P.O. Box 80
Tulsa, OK 74102
(918) 496-4500
1 (800) 331-3703
(toll free—credit card inquiries)

Mr. Dave Schutz
Wholesale Marketing Administrator
Sherman-Williams Company
101 Prospect Avenue NW
Cleveland, OH 44115-1075
(216) 566-2000

Shoppers Department
Shoney's Inc.
1727 Elm Hill Pike
Nashville, TN 37210
(615) 391-5201

ShowBiz Pizza
see Integra

Showtime Networks, Inc.
see Viacom International, Inc.

Ms. Elaine Deaver, Vice President
Consumer/Marketing Services
Simmons Company
P.O. Box 95465
Atlanta, GA 30347
(404) 321-3030

Consumer Affairs Department
Sewing Products Division
Singer Sewing Company
P.O. Box 1909
Edison, NJ 08818-1909
(908) 287-0707

Mr. Mike Minchin
Executive Vice President
Sizzler International, Inc.
12655 West Jefferson Boulevard
Los Angeles, CA 90066
(213) 827-2300, ext. 3324

Skaggs Company
see American Stores Company

Skoal Chewing Tobacco
see UST

Consumer Services Department
Slim•Fast Foods Company
919 Third Avenue
New York, NY 10022-3898
1 (800) 862-4500 (toll free)

Law and Compliance Department
**Smith Barney, Harris Upham
& Co., Inc.**
333 West 34th Street
New York, NY 10001
(212) 356-2800

Consumer/Public Affairs Department
**SmithKline Beecham Consumer
Brands**
P.O. Box 1467
Pittsburgh, PA 15230-1467
(412) 928-1000
1 (800) 245-1040 (toll free)

Ms. Vickie Limbach
Manager of Communications
J.M. Smucker Company
Strawberry Lane
Orrville, OH 44667-0280
(216) 682-3000

Snapper Power Equipment
McDonough, GA 30253
(404) 957-9141
1 (800) 933-9369 (toll free)

Solar Nutritionals
see Thompson Medical Company

Mr. Paul Sonnabend, President
Sonesta International Hotels
Corporation
200 Clarendon Street
Boston, MA 02116
(617) 421-5413

Ms. Kathryn M. O'Brien
Director, National Customer Relations
Sony Corporation of America
Sony Service Company
Sony Drive
Park Ridge, NJ 07656
(201) 930-7669
(NJ Consumer Information Center)
(714) 821-7669
(CA Consumer Information Center)
(708) 250-7669
(IL Consumer Information Center)

South Central Bell
see BellSouth Telephone
Operations

Southern Bell Corporation
see BellSouth Telephone
Operations

Mr. Jerry Snearly
National Consumer Services Manager
The Southland Corporation
P.O. Box 711
Dallas, TX 75221-0711
(214) 841-6642
1 (800) 255-0711 (toll free)

Mr. Jim Ruppel, Director
Customer Relations
Southwest Airlines
Love Field
P.O. Box 36611
Dallas, TX 75235-1657
(214) 904-4223
1 (800) 533-1305
(toll free TDD—reservations)

Executive Director
Corporate Communications
Southwestern Bell Corporation
1667 K Street, NW, Suite 1000
Washington, DC 20006
(202) 293-8550

Ms. Shirley Brisbois
Manager, Consumer Relations
Spalding & Evenflo, Inc.
425 Meadow Street
P.O. Box 901
Chicopee, MA 01021-0901
(413) 536-1200
1 (800) 225-6601 (toll free)

Mr. Paul Weiske
Customer Service Manager
Speed Queen Company
P.O. Box 990
Ripon, WI 54971-0990
(414) 748-3121
(414) 748-4053 (TDD)

Supervisor
Customer Service Department
Spencer Gifts
MCA, Inc.
1050 Black Horse Pike
Pleasantville, NJ 08232
(609) 645-3300

Customer Service
Spiegel, Inc.
P.O. Box 927
Oak Brook, IL 60522-0927
(708) 954-2772

Springs Industries Inc.
Springmaid Home Fashions
Consumer Fashions Division
787 7th Avenue
New York, NY 10019
(212) 903-2100

Squibb
see Bristol-Myers Squibb
Pharmaceutical Group

Mr. Jack Gauthier, Marketing Manager
Stanley Hardware
Division Stanley Works
480 Myrtle Street
New Britain, CT 06050
(203) 225-5111
1 (800) 622-4393 (toll free)

Mr. Jim Stahly
Public Relations Director
**State Farm Mutual Automobile
Insurance Company**
One State Farm Plaza
Bloomington, IL 61710
(309) 766-2714

Consumer Affairs Section
Sterling Drug Inc.
90 Park Avenue, 8th Floor
New York, NY 10016
(212) 907-2000
1 (800) 331-4536
(toll free—Glenbrook,
Winthrop Consumer Products)

**J.P. Stevens
see WestPoint Pepperell**

Ms. Esther Rasmussen
Director, Consumer Relations
Stokely USA, Inc.
626 East Wisconsin Avenue
P.O. Box 248
Oconomowoc, WI 53066-0248
(414) 567-1731
1 (800) 872-1110 (toll free)

Ms. Christine Filardo
Director, Consumer Affairs
**Stop & Shop Supermarket
Company Inc.**
P.O. Box 1942
Boston, MA 02103
(617) 770-8895

Ms. Frances D. Karpowicz, Manager
Consumer Affairs Department
Stouffer Foods Corporation
5750 Harper Road
Solon, OH 44139-1880
(216) 248-3600

President
Stouffer Restaurant Company
30050 Chagrin Boulevard
Cleveland, OH 44124
(216) 464-6606

Mr. Matthew Cook
Director, Customer Relations
Strawbridge & Clothier
801 Market Street
Philadelphia, PA 19107
(215) 629-6722

Ms. Kathy Hatfield, Coordinator
Quality Assurance Administration
The Stroh Brewery Company
100 River Place
Detroit, MI 48207-4291
(313) 446-2000

Consumer Affairs
Sunbeam/Oster Housewares
8989 North Deerwood Drive
Brown Deer, WI 53223
(written inquiries only)

Ms. Donna Samelson, Manager
Consumer Relations
**Sun-Diamond Growers
of California**
P.O. Box 1727
Stockton, CA 95201
(209) 467-6000

Subscriber Service
Sunset Magazine
Box 2040
Harlan, IA 51593-0003
1 (800) 777-0117 (toll free)

Ms. Noreen MacConchie
Manager, Customer Relations
**Supermarkets General
Corporation**
301 Blair Road
Woodbridge, NJ 07095
(908) 499-3500

Mr. Doug Williams, Customer Service
Swatch Watch USA
1817 William Penn Way
Lancaster, PA 17604
(717) 394-5288
1 (800) 8-SWATCH (toll free)

Swift-Eckrich, Inc.
2001 Butterfield Road
Downers Grove, IL 60515
(708) 512-1000
1 (800) 325-7424 (toll free)

The Swiss Colony
Customer Service
1112 Seventh Avenue
Monroe, WI 53566
(608) 324-4000

Sylvania Television
see Philips Company

T _____

Ms. Deedee Kindy, Supervisor
Consumer Affairs
3M
3M Center, Building 225-5N-04
St. Paul, MN 55144-1000
(612) 733-1871

TJX Companies (T.J. Maxx)
770 Cochituate Rd.
Framingham, MA 01701
(508) 390- 1000
1 (800) 926-6299 (toll free)

National Consumer Assistance Center
TRW Information Services
12606 Greenville Avenue
P.O. Box 749029
Dallas, TX 75374-9029
(214) 699-6111

T.V. Guide
see News America Publishing, Inc.

Customer Service
Talbots
175 Beal Street
Hingham, MA 02043
1 (800) 992-9010 (toll free)
1 (800) 624-9179 (toll tree TDD)

Ms. Cindy Nothe
Manager, Consumer Services
TAMBRANDS, Inc.
P.O. Box 271
Palmer, MA 01069
(413) 283-3431
1 (800) 523-0014 (toll free)

Ms. Lucille Frey, Director
Customer Relations
Tandy Corporation/
Radio Shack
1600 One Tandy Center
Fort Worth, TX 76102
(817) 390-3218

Tappan Company, Inc.
see White Consolidated
Industries

Consumer Relations and
Quality Assurance
Target Stores
33 South 6th Street
P.O. Box 1392
Minneapolis, MN 55440-1392
(612) 370-6056

Technics
see Matsushita Servicing Company

Mr. Richard C. Keller
Director, Consumer Affairs
Teledyne Water Pik
1730 East Prospect Street
Fort Collins, CO 80553-0001
(303) 484-1352
1 (800) 525-2774 (toll free)

Ms. Kathy Laffin, Supervisor
Customer Service
Teleflora
12233 West Olympic, Suite 140
Los Angeles, CA 90064-0780
(213) 826-5253
1 (800) 421-2815 (toll free)

Mr. Charles Funk
Telesphere
6000 Executive Boulevard, Suite 400
Rockville, MD 20852-3902
1 (800) 864-4468 (toll free)

Public Affairs
Tenneco, Inc.
P.O. Box 2511
Houston, TX 77001-2511
(713) 757-2131

Consumer Affairs Department
Tetley Inc.
100 Commerce Drive
P.O. Box 856
Shelton, CT 06484-0856
(203) 929-9342

Mr. W.D. Kistler
Manager, Customer Relations
Texaco Refining and Marketing
P.O. Box 2000
Bellaire, TX 77401-2000
(713) 432-2235
1 (800) 552-7827 (toll free)

Mr. Tom Thomas, Consumer Products
Texas Instruments Incorporated
P.O. Box 53
Lubbock, TX 79408-0053
(806) 741-2000
1 (800) 842-2737 (toll free)

Customer Service Representative
Thom McAn Shoe Co.
67 Millbrook Street
Worcester, MA 01606-2804
(508) 791-3811

Thompson & Formby, Inc.
825 Crossover Lane, Suite 240
Memphis, TN 38117
1 (800) FORMBYS (toll free)

Consumer Services Department
Thompson Medical Company, Inc.
222 Lakeview Avenue
West Palm Beach, FL 33401-6112
(407) 820-9900
1 (800) 521-7857 (toll free)

Ms. Janice Meikle, Vice President
Professional & Public Affairs
Thrift Drug, Inc.
615 Alpha Drive
Pittsburgh, PA 15238
(412) 963-6600
1 (800) 2-THRIFT (toll free)

Customer Service
Time Inc.
1 North Dale Mabry
Tampa, FL 33609
(813) 878-6100
1 (800) 541-1000 (toll free)

Corporate Public Affairs
Time Warner Inc.
75 Rockefeller Plaza
New York, NY 10019
(212) 484-6630

Ms. Letha Watkins
Consumer Correspondent
Timex Corporation
P.O. Box 2740
Little Rock, AR 72203-2740
(501) 372-1111
1 (800) 367-9282 (toll free)

Mr. Jim Percherke and Mr. Jeff Cline
Golf Division
National Consumer Relations
Titleist
P.O. Box B 965
New Bedford, MA 02741
1 (800) 225-8500 (toll free)

Ms. Karen Bramow
Assistant Manager,
Sales Administration
Tonka Products
Interchange North
300 South Highway 169, Suite 500
St. Louis Park, MN 55426
(612) 525-3500
1 (800) 347-3628 (toll free)

Ms. Mary Elliott, Director
Communications and Public Affairs
The Toro Company
8111 Lyndale Avenue South
Minneapolis, MN 55420
(612) 887-8900

Mr. John Newman
Vice President of Service
Mr. Dave Byrnes
Administrative Manager of Service
**Toshiba America Consumer
Products, Inc.**
Consumer Products Business Sector
1420 Toshiba Drive
Lebanon, TN 37087
(615) 449-2360

Ms. Helen Baur
Administrative Assistant
Totes, Incorporated
10078 East Kemper Road
Loveland, OH 45140
(513) 583-2300

Director, Consumer Complaints
Tourneau, Inc.
488 Madison Avenue
New York, NY 10022
(212) 758-3265
1 (800) 223-1288
(toll free outside NY)

Corporate Spokesperson
Toys "R" Us
461 From Road
Paramus, NJ 07652
(201) 599-7897

Ms. Thompson, Manager
Control Center
Trak Auto
3300 75th Avenue
Landover, MD 20785
(301) 731-1200

Trane/CAC, Inc.
see American Standard, Inc.

Trans Union Corporation

Western Region
1561 E. Orangethorpe
Fullerton, CA 92631

Southern Region
222 S. First Street
Louisville, KY 40202

North Eastern Region
1211 Chestnut Street
Philadelphia, PA 19107

Midwest
212 S. Market Street
Wichita, KS 67202

North Eastern Ohio
25249 Country Club Boulevard
N. Olmstead, OH 44070

Ms. Rosemary Aurichio
Director, Customer Relations
Trans World Airlines (TWA)
110 South Bedford Road
Mt. Kisco, NY 10549
(914) 242-3000
1 (800) 421- 8480
(toll free TDD—reservations)

Office Of Consumer Information
The Travelers Companies
One Tower Square
Hartford, CT 06183-1060
1 (800) 243-0191 (toll free)

True Value Hardware Stores
see Cotter & Company

Ms. Chris Clark, Manager
Customer Services Department
Tupperware
P.O. Box 2353
Orlando, FL 32802
(407) 847-3111
1 (800) 858-7221 (toll free)

Ms. Terri Tingle
Director, Public Affairs
Turner Broadcasting System Inc.
One CNN Center
Atlanta, GA 30335
(404) 827-1690

Ms. Karen Hanik
Consumer Correspondence
Representative
Turtle Wax, Inc.
5655 West 73rd Street
Chicago, IL 60638-6211
(708) 563-3600
1 (800) 323-9883 (toll free)

Mr. Jerry Rasor
Manager, Quality Control
Tyco Industries
540 Glenn Avenue
Moorestown, NJ 08057
(609) 234-7714

Mr. Jay Benham
Manager, Consumer Relations
Tyson Foods
P.O. Box 2020
Springdale, AR 72765-2020
(501) 756-4714
1 (800) 233-6332 (toll free)

U _____

Ms. Elaine De Shong, Vice President
Marketing Consumer Service
U-Haul International
2727 North Central Avenue
Phoenix, AZ 85004-1120
(602) 263-6771
1 (800) 528-0463
(toll free outside AZ)

Mr. Alan Kaiser, Director
Corporate Communications
UST
100 West Putnam Avenue
Greenwich, CT 06830
(203) 661-1100

**Union Fidelity Life
Insurance Company
see Aon Corporation**

Mr. Stephen A. Colton
Manager, Consumer Affairs
Uniroyal Goodrich Tire Company
600 South Main Street
Akron, OH 44397-0001
(216) 374-3796
1 (800) 521-9796 (toll free)

UNISYS Corporation
P.O. Box 500
Blue Bell, PA 19424-0001
(215) 986-4011

Mr. Paul Tinebra
Director of Customer Relations
United Airlines
P.O. Box 66100
Chicago, IL 60666
(312) 952-6168
1 (800) 323-0170
(toll free TDD—reservations)

Mr. Dick Porter
National Consumer Relations Manager
**United Parcel Service of
America, Incorporated**
51 Weaver Street, OPS
Greenwich, CT 06831
(203) 862-6000

**United States Fidelity &
Guarantee Corporation**
100 Light Street
Baltimore, MD 21203-1138
(301) 547-3000

Bette Malone® Relocation Service
United Van Lines, Inc.
One United Drive
Fenton, MO 63026
1 (800) 325-3870 (toll free)

Ms. Hattie Amer
Supervisor, Customer Service
Unocal Corporation
Room 1405
P.O. Box 7600
Los Angeles, CA 90051-7600
(213) 977-6728
1 (800) 527-5476 (toll free)

Consumer Products Division
(over-the-counter)
Customer Service Unit (prescriptions)
Upjohn Company
7000 Portage Road
Kalamazoo, MI 49001
1 (800) 253-8600 (toll free)

Mrs. Deborah Thompson
Director, Consumer Affairs
USAir
4001 North Liberty Street
Winston-Salem, NC 27105
(919) 661-8126
(collect calls accepted)

Consumer Services Representative
U.S. Shoe Corporation
One Eastwood Drive
Cincinnati, OH 45227-1197
(513) 527-7590

Mr. Slobodan B. Ajdukovic, Supervisor
Executive Consumer Services
U.S. Sprint
8001 Stemmons Freeway
Dallas, TX 75247
(214) 688-5707
1 (800) 877-4646 (toll free)

U S WEST, Inc.
Orchard Falls Building
7800 E. Orchard Road
Englewood, CO 80111-2533
(303) 793-6500
1 (800) USW-HELP (toll free)
1 (800) 955-5833 (toll free TDD)

V _____

Consumer Relations Department
Valvoline Oil Company
3499 Dabney Drive
P.O. Box 14000
Lexington, KY 40512
(606) 264-7777

Van Heusen Company
281 Centennial Avenue
Piscataway, NJ 08854
(908) 885-5000
1 (800) 631-5809
(toll free outside NJ)

Mr. John McAna
Executive Vice President
Van Munching and Co., Inc.
1270 Avenue of the Americas,
10th Floor
New York, NY 10020
(212) 265-2685

Ms. Jan Still-Lindeman
Vanity Fair
640 Fifth Avenue
New York, NY 10019
(212) 582-6767
1 (800) 832-8662 (toll free)

Ms. Hilary E. Condit
Director, Corporate Relations
Viacom International Inc.
1515 Broadway
New York, NY 10036
(212) 258-6346

Mr. Peter Doane
Vice President/Treasurer
Vicorp Restaurants
400 West 48th Avenue
Denver, CO 80216
(303) 296-2121

Customer Relations
Visa USA, Inc.
P.O. Box 8999
San Francisco, CA 94128-8999
(415) 570-2900

Customer Service
Vons Companies Inc.
P.O. Box 3338
Los Angeles, CA 90054
(818) 821-7000

W_____

Customer Service Representative
Wagner Spray Tech Corporation
1770 Fernbrook Lane
Plymouth, MN 55447
(612) 553-7000
1 (800) 328-8251 (toll free)

Mr. Edward H. King, Director
Government and Corporate Relations
Walgreen Co.
200 Wilmot Road
Deerfield, IL 60015
(708) 940-3500
1 (800) 289-2273 (toll free)

Customer Relations
Wal-Mart Stores, Inc.
702 SW Eighth Street
Bentonville, AR 72716-0117
(501) 273-4000

Ms. Rebecca Pierce
Consumer Affairs Manager
Wamsutta Pacific
1285 Avenue of the Americas
34th Floor
New York, NY 10019
(212) 903-2000
1 (800) 344-2142 (toll free)

Wang Direct
Wang Laboratories Inc.
1001 Pawtucket Boulevard
Lowell, MA 01854
(508) 656-8000

Mr. George A. Silva
Manufacturing Vice President
Warnaco Men's Apparel
10 Water Street
Waterville, ME 04901
(207) 873-4241

Mr. Mitch Rosalsky, Director
Consumer Affairs Division
Warner-Lambert Company
201 Tabor Road
Morris Plains, NJ 07950
(201) 540-2459
1 (800) 223-0182 (toll free)
1 (800) 524-2624 (toll free—Parke
Davis Products/over-the-counter)
1 (800) 742-8377 (toll free—
Schick Razor)
1 (800) 562-0266 (toll free—EPT)
1 (800) 223-0182 (toll free—
Warner-Lambert products)
1 (800) 524-2854 (toll free—Trident)
1 (800) 343-7805 (toll free TDD)

Customer Service
Weider Health and Fitness
615 West Johnson Avenue, Suite 3
Cheshire, CT 06410
1 (800) 423-5713 (toll free)

Ms. Karen Wegmann
Executive Vice President
Corporate Community
Development Group
Wells Fargo & Company
420 Montgomery Street
MAC 0101-111
San Francisco, CA 94163
(415) 396-3832
(916) 322-1700 (TDD)

Ms. Susan Kosling
Consumer Relations Manager
Wendy's International, Inc.
P.O. Box 256
Dublin, OH 43017-0256
(614) 764-6800

Ms. Joanne Turchany
Manager of Consumer Information
West Bend Company
400 Washington Street
West Bend, WI 53095
(414) 334-2311

Mr. Russ A. Phillips
Director, Consumer Affairs
Western Union Financial Services
One Lake Street
Upper Saddle River, NJ 07458
(201) 818-6041

Ms. Jackie McWhorter
Consumer Affairs Coordinator
WestPoint Pepperell
P.O. Box 609
West Point, GA 31833-0609
1 (800) 533-8229 (toll free)

Mr. Don Skinner, Director
Customer Relations Department
Whirlpool Corporation
Administrative Center, 2000 M-63
Benton Harbor, MI 49022
(616) 926-5000
1 (800) 253-1301 (toll free)

Mr. Brian Wooden
Manager, Consumer Relations
White Consolidated Industries
6000 Perimeter Drive
Dublin, OH 43017
(614) 792-4100
1 (800) 451-7007
(toll free—Frigidaire Appliances)
1 (800) 485-1445
(toll free—Gibson Appliances)
1 (800) 323-7773
(toll free—Kelvinator Appliance
Company)
1 (800) 537-5530
(toll free—O'Keefe & Merit Appliances)
1 (800) 537-5530
(toll free—Tappan Company, Inc.)
1 (800) 245-0600
(toll free—White Westinghouse)

White Westinghouse
see White Consolidated Industries

Ms. Terese Kaminskas
Corporate Communicator
Wickes Companies, Inc.
3340 Ocean Park Boulevard,
Suite 2000
Santa Monica, CA 90405
(213) 452-0160

Customer Service
Williams-Sonoma
100 North Point Street
San Francisco, CA 94133
(415) 421-7900

Mr. C.H. McKellar
Executive Vice President
Winn Dixie Stores Inc.
Box B
Jacksonville, FL 32203
(904) 783-5000

Mr. Steven R. Evenson
Owner Relations Manager
Winnebago Industries
P.O. Box 152
Forest City, IA 50436-0152
(515) 582-6939

Winthrop Consumer Products
see Sterling Drug Inc.

Corporate Communications
Wisconsin Bell
722 North Broadway, 13th Floor
Milwaukee, WI 53202-4396
(414) 678-0681
1 (800) 237-8576 (toll free)
1 (800) 242-9393
(toll free TDD in WI)

Wonderbread
see Continental Baking Company

Customer Service
F.W. Woolworth Company
233 Broadway
New York, NY 10279-0001
(212) 553-2000

Customer Service
World Book Educational Products
101 Northwest Point Boulevard
Elk Grove Village, IL 60007-1192
1 (800) 621-8202 (toll free)

Wrangler Jeans
see Blue Bell, Inc.

Ms. Barbara Zibell
Consumer Affairs Coordinator
William Wrigley Jr. Company
410 North Michigan Avenue
Chicago, IL 60611
(312) 645-4076

X _____

Customer Relations
Xerox Corporation
100 Clinton Avenue South
Rochester, NY 14644
(716) 423-5480

Y _____

Ms. Lindsey Bice, Manager
Customer Relations
Yamaha Motor Corporation
6555 Katella Avenue
Cypress, CA 90630-5101
(714) 761-7439

Z _____

Ms. Renee Hoke, Director
Communications
Zale Corporation
901 West Walnut Hill Lane
Irving, TX 75038-1003
(214) 580-5104

Zayre Corporation
see TJX Companies

Mr. Don Knutson
Vice President, Customer Service
Zenith Data Systems
2150 East Lake Cook Road
Buffalo Grove, IL 60089
(708) 808-4697

Vice President, Consumer Affairs
Zenith Electronics Corporation
1000 Milwaukee Avenue
Glenview, IL 60025-2493
(708) 391-8100
1 (800) 488-8129 (toll free)

Appendix B:
Car Manufacturers

If you have a problem with a car purchased from a local dealer, first try to work it out with the dealer. If an agreement cannot be reached, contact the manufacturer's regional or national office. Many of these offices are listed in this section.

If the regional office cannot resolve the problem, you might wish to contact one of the third-party dispute resolution programs. The list of these programs begins on page 205.

All of the toll-free 800 numbers in the following list can be reached from anywhere in the continental United States.

ACURA

Customer Relations Department
ACURA
1919 Torrance Boulevard
Torrance, CA 90501-2746
1 (800) 382-2238 (toll free)

**Alfa-Romeo Distributors of
North America, Inc.**

Customer Service Manager
**Alfa-Romeo Distributors of
North America, Inc.**
8259 Exchange Drive
P.O. Box 598026
Orlando, FL 32859-8026
(407) 856-5000

**American Honda Motor
Company, Inc.**

California
Customer Relations Department
**American Honda Motor
Company, Inc.**
Western Zone
700 Van Ness Boulevard
Torrance, CA 90509-2260
(213) 781-4565

*Utah, Arizona, Colorado,
New Mexico, Nebraska, Kansas,
Oklahoma, Nevada, Texas (El Paso)*
Customer Relations Department
**American Honda Motor
Company, Inc.**
West Central Zone
1600 South Abilene Street, Suite D
Aurora, CO 80012-5815
(303) 696-3935

*Maine, Vermont, New Hampshire,
New York State (excluding NY City,
its five boroughs, Long Island,
Westchester County), Connecticut
(excluding Fairfield County),
Massachusetts, Rhode Island*
Customer Relations Department
**American Honda Motor
Company, Inc.**
New England Zone
555 Old County Road
Windsor Locks, CT 06096-0465
(203) 623-3310

*Tennessee, Alabama, Georgia,
Florida*
Customer Relations Department
**American Honda Motor
Company, Inc.**
Southeastern Zone
1500 Morrison Parkway
Alpharetta, GA 30201-2199
(404) 442-2045
(collect calls accepted)

*Minnesota, Iowa, Missouri,
Wisconsin, Illinois, Michigan
(Upper Peninsula)*
Customer Relations Department
**American Honda Motor
Company, Inc.**
North Central Zone
601 Campus Drive, Suite A-9
Arlington Heights, IL 60004-1407
(708) 870-5600

*West Virginia, Maryland, Virginia,
North Carolina, South Carolina,
District of Columbia*
Customer Relations Department
**American Honda Motor
Company, Inc.**
Mid-Atlantic Zone Office
902 Wind River Lane, Suite 200
Gaithersburg, MD 20878-1974
(301) 990-2020

Ohio (Steubenville), West Virginia (Wheeling), Pennsylvania, New Jersey, Delaware, New York (NY City, its five boroughs, Long Island, Westchester County), Connecticut (Fairfield County)
Customer Relations Department
American Honda Motor Company, Inc.
Northeast Zone
115 Gaither Drive
Moorestown, NJ 08057-0337
(609) 235-5533

Michigan (except for Upper Peninsula), Indiana, Ohio, Kentucky
Customer Relations Department
American Honda Motor Company, Inc.
Central Zone
101 South Stanfield Road
Troy, OH 45373-8010
(513) 332-6250

Washington, Oregon, Idaho, Montana, Wyoming, North Dakota, South Dakota, Hawaii, Alaska
Customer Relations Department
American Honda Motor Company, Inc.
Northwest Zone
12439 NE Airport Way
Portland, OR 97220-0186
(503) 256-0943

Texas (excluding El Paso), Arkansas (excluding Fayetteville, Bentonville, Fort Smith, Jonesboro), Oklahoma (Lawton, Ardmore), Louisiana, Mississippi
Customer Relations Department
American Honda Motor Company, Inc.
South Central Zone
4529 Royal Lane
Irving, TX 75063-2583
(214) 929-5481

Corporate Office:
American Honda Motor Company, Inc.
Consumer Affairs Department
1919 Torrance Boulevard
Torrance, CA 90501-2746
(213) 783-3260

American Isuzu Motors, Inc.

California
Mr. Neil Wiggins
Regional Customer Relations Manager
American Isuzu Motors, Inc.
One Autry Street
Irvine, CA 92718-2785
(714) 770-2626

Alabama, Florida, Georgia, Mississippi, North Carolina, South Carolina
Regional Customer Relations Manager
American Isuzu Motors, Inc.
Southeast Region
205 Hembree Park Drive
P.O. Box 6250
Roswell, GA 30076
(404) 475-1995

Illinois, Indiana, Iowa, Michigan, Minnesota, Missouri, North Dakota, Ohio, Wisconsin
Regional Customer Relations Manager
American Isuzu Motors, Inc.
Central Region
1830 Jarvis Avenue
Elk Grove Village, IL 60007
(708) 952-8111

Connecticut, Maine, Massachusetts, New Hampshire, New Jersey (north of Toms River), New York, Rhode Island, Vermont
Regional Customer Relations Manager
American Isuzu Motors, Inc.
Northeast Region
156 Ludlow Avenue
P.O. Box 965
Northvale, NJ 07647-0965
(201) 784-1414

Arizona, Arkansas, Kansas,
Louisiana, Nevada (southern),
New Mexico, Oklahoma, Texas
Regional Customer Relations Manager
American Isuzu Motors, Inc.
Southwest Region
1150 Isuzu Parkway
Grand Prairie, TX 75050
(214) 647-2911

Alaska, Hawaii, Idaho, Montana,
Nevada (northern), Oregon, Utah,
Washington, Wyoming, Colorado,
Nebraska, South Dakota
Regional Customer Relations Manager
American Isuzu Motors, Inc.
Northwest Region
8727 148th Avenue NE
Redmond, WA 98052
(206) 881-0203

New Jersey (south of Toms River),
Pennsylvania, Maryland, Delaware,
Kentucky, Tennessee, Virginia,
West Virginia
Regional Customer Relations Manager
American Isuzu Motors, Inc.
1 Isuzu Way
Glen Burnie, MD 21061
(301) 761-2121

Headquarters:
American Isuzu Motors, Inc.
13181 Crossroads Parkway North
P.O. Box 2480
City of Industry, CA 91746-0480
(213) 699-0500
1 (800) 255-6727 (toll free)

American Motors Corporation
see Jeep/Eagle Division of
Chrysler Motors Corporation

American Suzuki Motor
Corporation
3251 E. Imperial Highway
Brea, CA 92621-6722
Attn: Customer Relations Department
Automobiles
1 (800) 877-6900, ext. 445 (toll free)
Motorcycles
(714) 996-7040, ext. 380

Audi of America, Inc.

Connecticut, New Jersey, New York
Director, Corporate Service
World-Wide Volkswagen Corp.
Greenbush Road
Orangeburg, NY 10962
(914) 578-5000

Corporate Office
(and all other states):
Consumer Relations Manager
Audi of America, Inc.
888 West Big Beaver Road
Troy, MI 48007-3951
1 (800) 822-AUDI (toll free)

BMW of North America, Inc.

Arizona, California, Nevada, Oregon,
Washington, Montana, Idaho,
Arizona, Alaska, Hawaii, Colorado,
Utah, New Mexico, Wyoming, Texas
(El Paso)
Customer Relations Manager
BMW of North America, Inc.
Western Region
12541 Beatrice Street
P.O. Box 66916
Los Angeles, CA 90066
(213) 574-7300

Tennessee, North Carolina,
Virginia (except northern),
Mississippi, Alabama, Georgia,
Florida, South Carolina, Louisiana,
Oklahoma, Arkansas, Texas
(except El Paso)
Customer Relations Manager
BMW of North America, Inc.
Southern Region
1280 Hightower Trail
Atlanta, GA 30350-2977
(404) 552-3800

*North Dakota, South Dakota,
Minnesota, Wisconsin, Iowa, Illinois,
Michigan, Indiana, Ohio, Kentucky,
Kansas, Missouri, Nebraska*
Customer Relations Manager
**BMW of North America, Inc.
Central Region**
498 East Commerce Drive
Schaumburg, IL 60173
(708) 310-2700

*Connecticut, Maine, Massachusetts,
New Hampshire, New Jersey,
New York, Rhode Island, Vermont,
Washington, DC, Virginia (northern),
West Virginia, Delaware, Maryland,
Pennsylvania*
Customer Relations Manager
**BMW of North America, Inc.
Eastern Region**
BMW Plaza
Montvale, NJ 07645
(201) 573-2100

Corporate Office:
National Customer Relations Manager
BMW of North America, Inc.
P.O. Box 1227
Westwood, NJ 07675-1227
(201) 307-4000

Chrysler Motors Corporation

Phoenix Zone Office
Customer Relations Manager
Chrysler Motors Corporation
11811 N. Tatum Boulevard, Suite 4025
Phoenix, AZ 85028
(602) 953-6899

Los Angeles Zone Office
Customer Relations Manager
Chrysler Motors Corporation
P.O. Box 14112
Orange, CA 92668-4600
(714) 565-5111

San Francisco Zone Office
Customer Relations Manager
Chrysler Motors Corporation
P.O. Box 5009
Pleasanton, CA 94566-0509
(415) 463-1770

Denver Zone Office
Customer Relations Manager
Chrysler Motors Corporation
P.O. Box 39006
Denver, CO 80239
(303) 373-8888

Orlando Zone Office
Customer Relations Manager
Chrysler Motors Corporation
8000 South Orange Blossom Trail
Orlando, FL 32809
(407) 352-7402

Atlanta Zone Office
Customer Relations Manager
Chrysler Motors Corporation
900 Circle 75 Parkway, Suite 1600
Atlanta, GA 30339
(404) 953-8880

Chicago Zone Office
Customer Relations Manager
Chrysler Motors Corporation
650 Warrenville Road, Suite 502
Lisle, IL 60532
(708) 515-2450

Kansas City Zone Office
Customer Relations Manager
Chrysler Motors Corporation
P.O. Box 25668
Overland Park, KS 66225-5668
(913) 469-3090

New Orleans Zone Office
Customer Relations Manager
Chrysler Motors Corporation
P.O. Box 157
Metairie, LA 70004
(504) 838-8788

Washington, D.C. Zone Office
Customer Relations Manager
Chrysler Motors Corporation
P.O. Box 1900
Bowie, MD 20716
(301) 464-4040

Boston Zone Office
Customer Relations Manager
Chrysler Motors Corporation
550 Forbes Boulevard
Mansfield, MA 02048-2038
(508) 261-2299

Detroit Zone Office
Customer Relations Manager
Chrysler Motors Corporation
P.O. Box 3000
Troy, MI 48007-3000
(313) 952-1300

Minneapolis Zone Office
Customer Relations Manager
Chrysler Motors Corporation
P.O. Box 1231
Minneapolis, MN 55440
(612) 553-2546

St. Louis Zone Office
Customer Relations Manager
Chrysler Motors Corporation
P.O. Box 278
Hazelwood, MO 63042
(314) 895-0731

Syracuse Zone Office
Customer Relations Manager
Chrysler Motors Corporation
P.O. Box 603
Dewitt, NY 13214-0603
(315) 445-6941

New York Zone Office
Customer Relations Manager
Chrysler Motors Corporation
500 Route 303
Tappan, NY 10983-1592
(914) 359-0110

Charlotte Zone Office
Customer Relations Manager
Chrysler Motors Corporation
4944 Parkway Plaza Boulevard
Suite 470
Charlotte, NC 28217
(704) 357-7065

Cincinnati Zone Office
Customer Relations Manager
Chrysler Motors Corporation
P.O. Box 41902
Cincinnati, OH 45241
(513) 530- 1500

Portland Zone Office
Customer Relations Manager
Chrysler Motors Corporation
P.O. Box 744
Beaverton, OR 97075
(503) 526-5555

Philadelphia Zone Office
Customer Relations Manager
Chrysler Motors Corporation
Valley Brook Corporate Center
101 Linden Wood Drive, Suite 320
Malvern, PA 19355
(215) 251-2990

Pittsburgh Zone Office
Customer Relations Manager
Chrysler Motors Corporation
Penn Center West 3, Suite 420
Pittsburgh, PA 15276
(412) 788-6622

Memphis Zone Office
Customer Relations Manager
Chrysler Motors Corporation
P.O. Box 18008
Memphis, TN 38181-0008
(901) 797-3870

Dallas Zone Office
Customer Relations Manager
Chrysler Motors Corporation
P.O. Box 110162
Carrollton, TX 75011-0162
(214) 242-8462

Houston Zone Office
Customer Relations Manager
Chrysler Motors Corporation
363 North Sam Houston Parkway East
Suite 590
Houston, TX 77060-2405
(713) 820-7062

Milwaukee Zone Office
Customer Relations Manager
Chrysler Motors Corporation
445 South Moorland Road, Suite 470
Brookfield, WI 53005
(414) 797-3750

Corporate Office:
Mr. R.T. Smith
National Owner Relations Manager
Chrysler Motors Corporation
P.O. Box 1086
Detroit, MI 48288-1086
1 (800) 992-1997 (toll free)

Ferrari North America, Inc.

Corporate Office:
Mr. Kenneth McCay
Director of Service and Parts
Ferrari North America, Inc.
250 Sylvan Avenue
Englewood Cliffs, NJ 07632
(201) 816-2650

Ford Motor Company
Customer Relations Manager
Ford Motor Company
300 Renaissance Center
P.O. Box 43360
Detroit, MI 48243
1 (800) 392-3673
(toll free—all makes)
1 (800) 521-4140
(toll free—Lincoln and Merkur only)
1 (800) 241-3673
(toll free—towing and dealer
location service)
1 (800) 232-5952
(toll free TDD)

General Motors Corporation

Customer Assistance Center
Chevrolet/Geo Motor Division
General Motors Corporation
P.O. Box 7047
Troy, MI 48007-7047
1 (800) 222-1020 (toll free)
1 (800) TDD-CHEV (toll free TDD)

Customer Assistance Center
Pontiac Division
General Motors Corporation
One Pontiac Plaza
Pontiac, MI 48340-2952
1 (800) 762-2737 (toll free)
1 (800) TDD-PONT (toll free TDD)

Customer Assistance Network
Oldsmobile Division
General Motors Corporation
P.O. Box 30095
Lansing, MI 48909-7595
1 (800) 442-6537 (toll free)
1 (800) TDD-OLDS (toll free TDD)

Customer Assistance Center
Buick Motor Division
General Motors Corporation
902 East Hamilton Avenue
Flint, MI 48550
1 (800) 521-7300 (toll free)
1 (800) TD-BUICK (toll free TDD)

Consumer Relations Center
Cadillac Motor Car Division
General Motors Corporation
2860 Clark Street
Detroit, MI 48232
1 (800) 458-8006 (toll free)
1 (800) TDD-CMCC (toll free TDD)

Customer Service Department
GMC Truck Division
General Motors Corporation
Mail Code 1607-07
31 Judson Street
Pontiac, MI 48342
(313) 456-4547
1 (800) TDD-TKTD (toll free TDD)

Saturn Assistance Center
Saturn Corporation
General Motors Corporation
100 Saturn Parkway
Spring Hill, TN 37174
1 (800) 553-6000 (toll free)
1 (800) TDD-6000 (toll free TDD)

Mr. Duane E. Poole
Director, Public Relations
GM Service Parts Operations
6060 West Bristol Road
Flint, MI 48554-2110
(313) 635-5412

**Honda
see American Honda Motor
Company, Inc.**

Hyundai Motor America

Customer Service
Hyundai Motor America
10550 Talbert Avenue
P.O. Box 20850
Fountain Valley, CA 92728-0850
1 (800) 633-5151 (toll free)

**Isuzu
see American Isuzu**

Jaguar Cars, Inc.

*Alaska, Arizona, California,
Colorado, Hawaii, Idaho, Montana,
Nevada, New Mexico, Oregon, Utah,
Washington, Wyoming, Texas
(El Paso)*
Western Zone
Customer Relations Manager
Jaguar Cars, Inc.
422 Valley Drive
Brisbane, CA 94005
(415) 467-9402

Eastern Zone *(all other states)*
Customer Relations Manager
Jaguar Cars, Inc.
555 MacArthur Boulevard
Mahwah, NJ 07430-2327
(201) 818-8500

**Jeep/Eagle Division of Chrysler
Motors Corporation
see Chrysler Zone and
National Offices**

Mazda Motor of America, Inc.

Corporate Headquarters:
Customer Relations Manager
Mazda Motor of America, Inc.
P.O. Box 19734
Irvine, CA 92718
1 (800) 222-5500 (toll free)

**Mercedes-Benz of
North America, Inc.**

National Headquarters:
Mercedes-Benz of North America
1 Mercedes Drive
Montvale, NJ 07645-0350
(201) 573-0600 (Owner Service)

North Central Region Office
3333 Charles Street
Franklin Park, IL 60131-1469

Northeast Region Office
Baltimore Commons Business Park
1300 Mercedes Drive (2nd Floor)
Hanover, MD 21076-0348

Southern Region Office
8813 Western Way
Jacksonville, FL 32245-7604

Western Region Office
6357 Sunset Boulevard
Hollywood, CA 90093-0637

**Mitsubishi Motor Sales of
America, Inc.**

Corporate Office:
National Consumer Relations Manager
**Mitsubishi Motor Sales of
America, Inc.**
6400 West Katella Avenue
Cypress, CA 90630-0064
1 (800) 222-0037 (toll free)

Nissan Motor Corporation in USA

P.O. Box 191
Gardena, CA 90248-0191
1 (800) 647-7261
(toll free—all consumer inquiries)

Peugeot Motors of America, Inc.

Mr. William J. Atanasio
National Customer Relations Manager
Peugeot Motors of America, Inc.
P.O. Box 607
One Peugeot Plaza
Lyndhurst, NJ 07071-3498
(201) 935-8400
1 (800) 345-5549 (toll free)

Porsche Cars North America, Inc.

Customer Relations Manager
Porsche Cars North America, Inc.
100 West Liberty Street
P.O. Box 30911
Reno, NV 89520-3911
(702) 348-3154

Saab Cars USA, Inc.

National Consumer Relations
P.O. Box 697
Orange, CT 06477
(203) 795-5671
1 (800) 955-9007 (toll free)

Subaru of America

Arizona, California, Nevada
Owner Service Manager
**Subaru of America,
Western Region**
12 Whatney Drive
Irvine, CA 92718-2895
(714) 951-6592

*Alabama, Georgia, North Carolina,
South Carolina, Florida, Tennessee,
West Virginia, Virginia, Maryland,
Washington, DC*
Owner Service Manager
Southeast Region Subaru
220 The Bluffs
Austell, GA 30001
(404) 732-3200

*Illinois, Indiana, Iowa, Kentucky,
Michigan, Minnesota, Missouri,
Ohio, Wisconsin*
Owner Service Manager
Subaru Mid-America Region
301 Mitchell Court
Addison, IL 60101
(708) 953-1188

*Maine, Vermont, New Hampshire,
Massachusetts, Rhode Island,
Connecticut*
Customer Relations Manager
Subaru of New England, Inc.
95 Morse Street
Norwood, MA 02062
(617) 769-5100

*Southern New Jersey, Pennsylvania,
Delaware*
Customer Relations Manager
Penn Jersey Region
1504 Glen Avenue
Moorestown, NJ 08057
(609) 234-7600

New York, Northern New Jersey
Customer Relations Manager
Subaru Distributors Corporation
6 Ramland Road
Orangeburg, NY 10962
(914) 359-2500

Hawaii
Schuman-Carriage Co. Inc.
1234 South Beretania Street
P.O. Box 2420
Honolulu, HI 96804
(808) 533-6211

*Alaska, Idaho, Montana, Nebraska,
Oregon, Utah, Washington, North
Dakota, South Dakota, Wyoming*
Owner Service Manager
**Subaru of America
Northwest Region**
8040 East 33rd Drive
Portland, OR 97211
1 (800) 878-6677 (toll free)

*Arkansas, Colorado, Kansas,
New Mexico, Mississippi,
Oklahoma, Texas*
Owner Service Manager
**Subaru of America
Southwest Region**
1500 East 39th Avenue
Aurora, CO 80011
(303) 373-8895

Corporate Office:
Owner Service Department
Subaru of America
P.O. Box 6000
Cherry Hill, NJ 08034-6000
(609) 488-3278

Toyota Motor Sales, Inc.
Customer Assistance Center
Toyota Motor Sales USA, Inc.
Department A404
19001 South Western Avenue
Torrance, CA 90509
1 (800) 331-4331 (toll free)

Volkswagen United States, Inc.

Connecticut, New Jersey, New York
Director of Corporation Service
World-Wide Volkswagen, Inc.
Greenbush Road
Orangeburg, NY 10962
(914) 578-5000
1 (800) 822-8987 (toll free)

For all other locations:
Consumer Relations
Volkswagen United States, Inc.
888 West Big Beaver
Troy, MI 48007
General assistance and customer relations
1 (800) 822-8987 (toll free)
Replacement and repurchase assistance
1 (800) 955-5100 (toll free)

Volvo Cars of North America

Corporate Office:
Operations Manager
Volvo Cars of North America
15 Volvo Drive, Building D
P.O. Box 914
Rockleigh, NJ 07647-0914
(201) 767-4737

Yugo America, Inc.

Director, Customer Services
Yugo America, Inc.
120 Pleasant Avenue
P.O. Box 730
Upper Saddle River, NJ 07458-0730
(201) 825-4600
1 (800) 872-9846 (toll free)

Appendix C:
Trade Association and
Other Resolution Programs

Companies that manufacture similar products or offer similar services often belong to industry associations. These associations help resolve problems between their member companies and consumers. Depending on the industry, you might have to contact an association, service council, or consumer action program.

If you have a problem with a company and cannot get it resolved with the company, ask if the company is a member of an association. Then check this list to see if the association is shown. If the name of the association is not included on this list, check with a local library.

This list includes the names and addresses of the association and other dispute resolution programs that handle consumer complaints for their members. In some cases, the national organizations listed here can refer you to dispute-resolution programs near you.

These programs are usually called alternative dispute-resolution programs. Generally, there are three types of programs: arbitration, conciliation, and mediation. All three methods of dispute resolution vary. Ask for a copy of the rules of the program before you file your case. Generally, the decisions of the arbitrators are binding and must be accepted by both the customer and the business. However, in other forms of dispute resolution, only the business is required to accept the decision. In some programs, decisions are not binding on either party.

Remember, before contacting one of these programs, try to resolve the complaint by contacting the company.

Ms. Ann Lawrence, Director
Education and Conventions
American Apparel Manufacturers Association
2500 Wilson Boulevard, Suite 301
Arlington, VA 22201
(703) 524-1864
Membership: Manufacturers of clothing.

Ms. Donna Silberberg
Public Relations Director
American Arbitration Association
140 West 51st Street
New York, NY 10020-1203
(212) 484-4006
Private, nonprofit organization with 35 regional offices across the country. Provides consumer information on request. Check local telephone directory for listing. If there is no office in your area, write or call the office listed above.

American Automobile Association AUTOSOLVE
1000 AAA Drive
Heathrow, FL 32746-5064
1 (800) 477-6583 (toll free)
Third-party dispute-resolution program for Toyota, Lexus, Hyundai, and Subaru in selected areas of the United States.

American Bar Association
Standing Committee on Dispute Resolution
1800 M Street NW, Suite 790
Washington, DC 20036
(202) 331-2258
Publishes a directory of state and local alternative dispute-resolution programs. Provides consumer information on request.

Mr. John W. Johnson
Executive Vice President
American Collectors Association
4040 West 70th Street
P.O. Box 39106
Minneapolis, MN 55439-0106
(612) 926-6547
Membership: Collection services handling overdue accounts for retail, professional, and commercial credit grantors.

Information Department
American Council of Life Insurance
1001 Pennsylvania Avenue NW
Washington, DC 20004-2599
1 (800) 942-4242
(toll free—8 A.M.–8 P.M. EST, M–F)
Membership: Life insurance companies authorized to do business in the United States.

Ms. Jane Marden, Director
Consumer Affairs
Ms. Linda Wood, Associate Director
Community Affairs
American Gas Association
1515 Wilson Boulevard
Arlington, VA 22209
(703) 841-8583
Membership: Distributors and transporters of natural gas.

American Health Care Association
1201 L Street, N.W.
Washington, DC 20005-4014
(202) 842-4444
1 (800) 321-0343
(toll free—publications only)
Membership: State associations of long-term health care facilities.

American Hotel and Motel Association
1201 New York Avenue NW, Suite 600
Washington, DC 20005-3931
(written inquiries only)
Membership: State and regional hotel associations.

Mr. Herbert A. Finkston, Director
Professional Ethics Division
**American Institute of Certified
Public Accountants**
1211 Avenue of the Americas
New York, NY 10036-8775
(212) 575-6209
Membership: Professional society
of accountants certified by the states
and territories.

**American Newspaper
Publishers Assn.
Credit Bureau Inc.**
P.O. Box 17022
Dulles International Airport
Washington, DC 20041
(703) 648-1038
Investigates fraudulent advertising
published in newspapers.

**American Orthotic and
Prosthetic Association**
1650 King Street, Suite 500
Alexandria, VA 22314-1885
(703) 836-7116
Represents member companies that
custom fit or manufacture components for patients with prostheses
or orthoses.

Mr. Ray Greenly, Vice President
Consumer Affairs
**American Society of
Travel Agents, Inc.**
P.O. Box 23992
Washington, DC 20026-3992
(703) 739-2782
Membership: Travel agents.

Mr. James A. Morrissey, Director
Communications Division
**American Textile Manufacturers
Institute**
1801 K Street NW, Suite 900
Washington, DC 20006
(202) 862-0552
Membership: Textile mills which
produce a variety of textile products,
e.g., clothing using natural and syn-
thetic fibers.

Manager, Consumer Affairs
**Automotive Consumer Action
Program (AUTOCAP)**
8400 Westpark Drive
McLean, VA 22102
(703) 821-7144
Third-party dispute-resolution
program administered through
the National Automobile Dealers
Association. Consumer information
available on request.

BBB AUTO LINE
Council of Better Business Bureaus, Inc.
4200 Wilson Boulevard, Suite 800
Arlington, VA 22203-1804
(703) 276-0100
Third-party dispute-resolution pro-
gram for AMC, Audi, General Motors
and its divisions, Honda, Jeep, Nissan,
Peugeot, Porsche, Renault, SAAB, and
Volkswagen.

Better Hearing Institute
P.O. Box 1840
Washington, DC 20013
(703) 642-0580
1 (800) EAR-WELL (toll free)
Membership: Professionals and others
who help persons with impaired hearing. Provides voluntary mediation
between consumers and hearing aid
dispensers.

Consumer Affairs
**Blue Cross and Blue Shield
Association**
Metro Square—Phase II
655 15th Street NW, Suite 350F
Washington, DC 20005
(202) 626-4780
Membership: Local Blue Cross and
Blue Shield plans in the United States,
Canada, and Jamaica.

Ms. Caroline C. Ortado
Administrator, Consumer
Protection Bureau
**Boat Owners Association of the
United States (BOAT/U.S.)**
880 South Pickett Street
Alexandria, VA 22304-0730
(703) 823-9550
Consumer Protection Bureau serves
as a mediator in disputes between
boat owners and the marine industry.
BOAT/U.S. also works closely with the
U.S. Coast Guard to monitor safety
defect problems.

Mr. Richard N. "Ned" Hopper
Director of Governmental Affairs
Carpet and Rug Institute
1155 Connecticut Avenue NW
Suite 500
Washington, DC 20036
(written inquiries only)
Membership: Manufacturers of car-
pets, rugs, bath mats, and bedspreads;
suppliers of raw materials and services
to the industry.

Mr. Robert M. Fells, Assistant Secretary
**Cemetery Consumer
Service Council**
P.O. Box 3574
Washington, DC 20007
(703) 379-6426
Industry-sponsored dispute-resolution
program. Other consumer information
about cemetery practices and rules
available on request.

**Children's Advertising Review
Unit (CARU)**
Council of Better Business
Bureaus, Inc.
845 Third Avenue
New York, NY 10022
(212) 754-1354
Handles consumer complaints about
fraudulent and deceptive advertising
related to children.

**Chrysler Motors
Customer Relations**
National Office
26311 Lawrence Avenue
Center Line, MI 48288
1 (800) 992-1997 (toll free)

Department of Defense
Office of National Ombudsman
National Committee for Employer
Support of the Guard and Reserve
1555 Wilson Boulevard, Suite 200
Arlington, VA 22209-2405
(703) 696-1391
1 (800) 336-4590
(toll free outside DC)
Provides assistance with employer/
employee problems for members of
the Guard and Reserve and their
employers.

Ms. Lorna Christie, Director
Ethics and Consumer Affairs
**Direct Marketing Association
(DMA)**
6 East 43rd Street
New York, NY 10017-4646
(written complaints only)
Membership: Members who market
goods and services directly to consumers using direct mail, catalogs,
telemarketing, magazine and newspaper ads, and broadcast advertising.

DMA operates the Mail Order Action
Line, Mail Preference Service, and
Telephone Preference Service.

For problems with a mail order
company, write:
Mail Order Action Line
6 East 43rd Street
New York, NY 10017

To remove your name from a
direct mail list, write:
Mail Preference Service
P.O. Box 3861
Grand Central Station
New York, NY 10163

To remove your name from a telephone solicitation list, write:
Telephone Preference Service
6 East 43rd Street
New York, NY 10017

Mr. William Rogal
Code Administrator
Direct Selling Association
1776 K Street NW, Suite 600
Washington, DC 20006-2387
(202) 293-5760
Membership: Manufacturers and distributors selling consumer products door-to-door and through home-party plans.

Ms. Sally Browne, Executive Director
Consumer Affairs
Electronic Industries Association
2001 Pennsylvania Avenue NW
10th Floor
Washington, DC 20006
(202) 457-4977
Complaint assistance program, consumer education, etc. concerning televisions, videocassette recorders, and other video systems, audio products, personal computers, and communication electronic products.

Ford Consumer Appeals Board
P.O. Box 5120
Southfield, MI 48086-5120
1 (800) 392-3673 (toll free)

Funeral Service Consumer Arbitration Program (FSCAP)
1614 Central Street
Evanston, IL 60201
1 (800) 662-7666 (toll free)
Third-party dispute-resolution program sponsored by the National Funeral Directors Association.

Ms. Carole M. Rogin, President
Market Development
Hearing Industries Association
1255 23rd Street NW
Washington, DC 20037-1174
(202) 833-1411
Membership: Companies engaged in the manufacture and/or sale of electronic hearing aids, their components, parts, and related products and services on a national basis.

Home Owners Warranty Corporation
(HOW) Operation Center
P.O. Box 152087
Irving, TX 75015-2087
1 (800) 433-7657 (toll free)
Third-party dispute-resolution program for new homes built by HOW-member home builders.

Ms. Jill A. Wolper, Manager
Consumer Affairs and Education
Insurance Information Institute
110 William Street
New York, NY 10038
1 (800) 942-4242 (toll free)
National Insurance Consumer Helpline is a resource for consumers with automobile and home insurance questions. The Helpline is open Monday through Friday from 8 A.M. to 8 P.M.

National Headquarters
International Association for Financial Planning
2 Concourse Parkway, Suite 800
Atlanta, GA 30328
(404) 395-1605
Membership: Individuals involved in financial planning.

Major Appliance Consumer Action Panel (MACAP)
20 North Wacker Drive
Chicago, IL 60606
(312) 984-5858
1 (800) 621-0477 (toll free)
Third-party dispute-resolution program of the major appliance industry.

Mr. John E. Dianis
Executive Vice President
**Monument Builders of
North America**
1740 Ridge Avenue
Evanston, IL 60201
(708) 869-2031
Membership: Cemetery monument
retailers, manufacturers, and whole-
salers; bronze manufacturers and suppliers. Consumer brochures available
on request.

Ms. Sharon McHale
Media Relations Coordinator/
Consumer Affairs
**Mortgage Bankers Association
of America**
1125 15th Street NW, 7th Floor
Washington, DC 20005
(202) 861-1929
Membership: Mortgage banking firms,
commercial banks, life insurance companies, title companies, and savings
and loan associations.

**National Advertising Division
(NAD)**
A Division of the Council of
Better Business Bureaus, Inc.
845 Third Avenue
New York, NY 10022
(212) 754-1320
Program: Handles consumer com-
plaints about the truth and accuracy
of national advertising.

Mr. William Young, Director
Consumer Affairs/Public Liaison
**National Association of
Home Builders**
15th and M Streets NW
Washington, DC 20005
(202) 822-0409
1 (800) 368-5242
(toll free outside DC)
Membership: Single and multifamily
home builders, commercial builders,
and others associated with the building industry.

**National Association of
Personnel Consultants**
3133 Mt. Vernon Avenue
Alexandria, VA 22305
(703) 684-0180
Membership: Private employment
agencies.

Consumer Arbitration Center
**National Association of
Securities Dealers, Inc.**
33 Whitehall Street, 10th Floor
New York, NY 10004
(212) 858-4000
Third-party dispute-resolution for
complaints about over-the-counter
stocks and corporate bonds.

Accrediting Commission
**National Association of Trade
and Technical Schools**
2251 Wisconsin Avenue NW
Washington, DC 20007-4181
(202) 333-1021
(written inquiries only)
Membership: Private schools providing job training.

Mrs. Juanita Duggan
Government Affairs
**National Food Processors
Association**
1401 New York Avenue NW
Washington, DC 20005
(202) 639-5939
Membership: Commercial packers
of such food products as fruit, vegetables, meat, poultry, seafood, and
canned, frozen, dehydrated, pickled,
and other preserved food items.

Ms. Deb Deutsch
Manager, Compliance
National Futures Association
200 West Madison Street
Chicago, IL 60606-3447
(312) 781-1410
1 (800) 621-3570 (toll free outside IL)
Membership: Futures commission
merchants; commodity trading
advisers; commodity pool operators;
introducing brokers; and brokers and
associated individuals.

Ms. Cindy Donahue
Assistant to Executive Director
National Home Study Council
1601 18th Street NW
Washington, DC 20009
(written inquiries only)
Membership: Home study
(correspondence) schools.

**National Tire Dealers and
Retreaders Association**
1250 Eye Street NW, Suite 400
Washington, DC 20005
(202) 789-2300
1 (800) 876-8372 (toll free)
Membership: Independent tire
dealers and retreaders.

Department of Consumer Affairs
National Turkey Federation
11319 Sunset Hills Road
Reston, VA 22090-5205
(written inquiries only)
Membership: Turkey growers, turkey
hatcheries, turkey breeders, processors, marketers, and allied industry
firms and poultry distributors.

Mr. Craig Halverson
Assistant Executive Director
Photo Marketing Association
3000 Picture Place
Jackson, MI 49201
(written complaints only)
Membership: Retailers of photo
equipment, film, and supplies; firms
developing and printing film.

Mrs. Jane Meyer
Director of Consumer Affairs
**The Soap and Detergent
Association**
475 Park Avenue South
New York, NY 10016
(212) 725-1262
Membership: Manufacturers of soap,
detergents, fatty acids, and glycerine;
raw materials suppliers.

Tele-Consumer Hotline
1910 K Street NW, Suite 610
Washington, DC 20006
(202) 223-4371 (voice/TDD)
Provides information on special telephone products and services for persons with disabilities, selecting a long
distance company, money-saving tips
for people on low income, reducing
unsolicited phone calls, telemarketing
fraud, dealing with the phone company, and other issues. All telephone
assistance and publications are free of
charge, and Spanish-speaking coun-
selors are available.

Ms. Diane Cardinale
Assistant Communications Director
Toy Manufacturers of America
200 Fifth Avenue, Room 740
New York, NY 10010
(212) 675-1141
Membership: American toy
manufacturers

Mr. Robert E. Whitley, President
**U.S. Tour Operators Association
(USTOA)**
211 East 51st Street, Suite 12-B
New York, NY 10022
(212) 944-5727
Membership: Wholesale tour operators, common carriers, suppliers, and
providers of travel services.

Appendix D:
State, County, and City Government Consumer Protection Offices

City and county consumer offices can be helpful because they are easy to contact and are familiar with local businesses and laws. Some will investigate and help resolve consumer complaints. If there is no local consumer office in your area, contact a state consumer office. State consumer offices are set up differently across the nation. Some states have a separate department of consumer affairs, while others have a consumer affairs office as part of the governor's or attorney general's office. These offices will help or refer you to the proper agency.

If you have a consumer problem with a business outside the state where you live, you should contact the consumer office in the state where you made the purchase. When you contact any local or state consumer office, be sure to have handy copies of your sales receipts, other sales documents, and all correspondence with the company.

To save time, try to contact the office by telephone before sending a written complaint. Most consumer affairs offices that handle complaints have special forms or other requirements for filing complaints.

This list is arranged in alphabetical order by state name. The state name, city name, and any toll-free 800 and TDD numbers are printed in bold type.

Alabama

State Office
Mr. Dennis Wright, Director
Consumer Protection Division
Office of Attorney General
11 South Union Street
Montgomery, AL 36130
(205) 242-7334
1 (800) 392-5658 (toll free in AL)

Alaska
The Consumer Protection Section in
the Office of the Attorney General has
been closed. Consumers with complaints are being referred to the Better
Business Bureau (see page 243), small
claims court, and private attorneys.

American Samoa
Mr. Tauivi Tuinei
Assistant Attorney General
Consumer Protection Bureau
P.O. Box 7
Pago Pago, AS 96799
011 (684) 633-4163
011 (684) 633-4164

Arizona

State Offices
Ms. H. Leslie Hall, Chief Counsel
Consumer Protection
Office of the Attorney General
1275 West Washington Street,
Room 259
Phoenix, AZ 85007
(602) 542-3702
(602) 542-5763
(consumer information and
complaints)
1 (800) 352-8431 (toll free in AZ)

Ms. Noreen Matts
Assistant Attorney General
Consumer Protection
Office of the Attorney General
402 West Congress Street, Suite 315
Tucson, AZ 85701
(602) 628-6504

County Offices
Mr. Stephen Udall, County Attorney
Apache County Attorney's Office
P.O. Box 637
St. Johns, AZ 85936
(602) 337-4364, ext. 240

Mr. Alan Polley, County Attorney
Cochise County Attorney's Office
P.O. Drawer CA
Bisbee, AZ 85603
(602) 432-9377

Mr. John Verkamp, County Attorney
Coconino County Attorney's Office
Coconino County Courthouse
100 East Birch
Flagstaff, AZ 86001
(602) 779-6518

Mr. Joe Albo, Jr., County Attorney
Gila County Attorney's Office
1400 East Ash Street
Globe, AZ 85501
(602) 425-3231

Mr. Paul H. McCullar, County Attorney
Graham County Attorney's Office
Graham County Courthouse
800 West Main
Safford, AZ 85546
(602) 428-3620

Mr. Charles E. Fletcher
County Attorney
Greenlee County Attorney's Office
P.O. Box 1387
Clifton, AZ 85533
(602) 865-3842

Mr. Steven P. Suskin, County Attorney
La Paz County Attorney's Office
1200 Arizona Avenue
P.O. Box 709
Parker, AZ 85344
(602) 669-6118

Mr. William Ekstrom, County Attorney
Mohave County Attorney's Office
315 North 4th Street
Kingman, AZ 86401
(602) 753-0719

Mr. Melvin Bowers, County Attorney
Navajo County Attorney's Office
Governmental Complex
Holbrook, AZ 86025
(602) 524-6161

Mr. Stephen D. Neely
County Attorney
Pima County Attorney's Office
1400 Great American Tower
32 North Stone
Tucson, AZ 85701
(602) 740-5733

Mr. Roy Mendoza, County Attorney
Pinal County Attorney's Office
P.O. Box 887
Florence, AZ 85232
(602) 868-5801

Mr. Jose L. Machado, County Attorney
Santa Cruz County Attorney's Office
2100 N. Congress Drive, Suite 201
Nogales, AZ 85621
(602) 281-4966

Mr. Charles Hastings, County Attorney
Yavapai County Attorney's Office
Yavapai County Courthouse
Prescott, AZ 86301
(602) 771-3344

Mr. David S. Ellsworth
County Attorney
Yuma County Attorney's Office
168 South Second Avenue
Yuma, AZ 85364
(602) 329-2270

City Office
Mr. Ronald M. Detrick
Supervising Attorney
Consumer Affairs Division
Tucson City Attorney's Office
110 East Pennington Street, 2nd Floor
P.O. Box 27210
Tucson, AZ 85726-7210
(602) 791-4886

Arkansas

State Office
Mr. Royce Griffin, Director
Consumer Protection Division
Office of Attorney General
200 Tower Building
323 Center Street
Little Rock, AR 72201
(501) 682-2341 (voice/TDD)
1 (800) 482-8982
(toll free voice/TDD in AR)

California

State Offices
Mr. James Conran, Director
California Department of
Consumer Affairs
400 R Street, Suite 1040
Sacramento, CA 95814
(916) 445-0660
(complaint assistance)
(916) 445-1254
(consumer information)
(916) 522-1700 (TDD)
1 (800) 344-9940
(toll free in CA)

Office of Attorney General
Public Inquiry Unit
P.O. Box 944255
Sacramento, CA 94244-2550
(916) 322-3360
1 (800) 952-5225
(toll free in CA)
1 (800) 952-5548
(toll free TDD in CA)

Bureau of Automotive Repair
California Department of
Consumer Affairs
10240 Systems Parkway
Sacramento, CA 95827
(916) 366-5100
1 (800) 952-5210
(toll free in CA—auto repair only)

County Offices
Ms. Lorraine K. Provost
Coordinator
Alameda County Consumer Affairs
Commission
4400 MacArthur Boulevard
Oakland, CA 94619
(415) 530-8682

Mr. Gary Yancey, District Attorney
Contra Costa County
District Attorney's Office
725 Court Street, 4th Floor
P.O. Box 670
Martinez, CA 94553
(415) 646-4500

Mr. Alan Yengoyan
Senior Deputy District Attorney
Business Affairs
Fresno County District
Attorney's Office
2220 Tulare Street, Suite 1000
Fresno, CA 93721
(209) 488-3156

Mr. Edward R. Jagels, District Attorney
Consumer and Major Business
Fraud Section
Kern County District Attorney's Office
1215 Truxtun Avenue
Bakersville, CA 93301
(805) 861-2421

Mr. Pastor Herrera, Jr., Director
Los Angeles County Department
of Consumer Affairs
500 West Temple Street, Room B-96
Los Angeles, CA 90012
(213) 974-1452

Ms. Betty Times, Director
Citizens Service Office
Marin County Mediation Services
Marin County Civic Center, Room 412
San Rafael, CA 94903
(415) 499-6190

Mr. Jerry Herman, District Attorney
Marin County District
Attorney's Office
Marin County Civic Center, Room 155
San Rafael, CA 94903
(415) 499-6482

Mr. Robert Nichols
Deputy District Attorney
Consumer Protection Division
Marin County District
Attorney's Office
Hall of Justice, Room 183
San Rafael, CA 94903
(415) 499-6450

Ms. Susan Massini, District Attorney
Mendocino County District
Attorney's Office
P.O. Box 1000
Ukiah, CA 95482
(707) 463-4211

Ms. Candice Chin, Coordinator
Monterey County Office of
Consumer Affairs
P.O. Box 1369
Salinas, CA 93902
(408) 755-5073

Mr. Daryl A. Roberts
Deputy District Attorney
Consumer Affairs Division
Napa County District Attorney's Office
931 Parkway Mall
P.O. Box 720
Napa, CA 94559
(707) 253-4059

Mr. Guy Ormes
Deputy District Attorney in Charge
Major Fraud Unit
Orange County District
Attorney's Office
801 Civic Center Drive West, Suite 120
Santa Ana, CA 92701
(714) 541-7600

Mr. Christopher P. Kralick
Deputy District Attorney in Charge
Consumer and Environmental
Protection Unit
Orange County District
Attorney's Office
801 Civic Center Drive West, Suite 120
Santa Ana, CA 92702-0808
(714) 541-7600

Mr. Paul Zellerbach
Deputy District Attorney
Economic Crime Division
Riverside County District
Attorney's Office
4075 Main Street
Riverside, CA 92501
(714) 275-5400

Mr. M. Scott Prentice
Supervising Deputy District Attorney
Consumer and Environmental
Protection Division
Sacramento County District
Attorney's Office
P.O. Box 749
Sacramento, CA 95812-0749
(916) 440-6174

Mr. Anthony Samson, Director
Consumer Fraud Division
San Diego County District
Attorney's Office
P.O. Box X-1011
San Diego, CA 92112
(619) 531-3507 (fraud complaint line)
(8:30 A.M.–11:30 A.M.; leave message
at other times)

Mr. Robert H. Perez, Attorney
Consumer and Environmental
Protection Unit
San Francisco County District
Attorney's Office
732 Brannan Street
San Francisco, CA 94103
(415) 552-6400 (public inquiries)
(415) 553-1814 (complaints)

Mr. Stephen Taylor, Deputy
District Attorney
Consumer and Business Affairs
Division
San Joaquin County District
Attorney's Office
222 East Weber, Room 202
P.O. Box 990
Stockton, CA 95202
(209) 468-2419

Ms. Leigh Lawrence
Director, Economic Crime Unit
Consumer Fraud Department
County Government Center
1050 Monterey Street, Room 235
San Luis Obispo, CA 93408
(805) 549-5800

Mr. John E. Wilson, Deputy in Charge
Consumer Fraud and Environmental
Protection Unit
San Mateo County District
Attorney's Office
401 Marshall Street
Hall of Justice and Records
Redwood City, CA 94063
(415) 363-4656

Mr. Alan Kaplan
Deputy District Attorney
Consumer Protection Unit
Santa Barbara County District
Attorney's Office
1105 Santa Barbara Street
Santa Barbara, CA 93101
(805) 568-2300

Mr. Albert C. Bender
Deputy District Attorney
Consumer Fraud Unit
Santa Clara County District
Attorney's Office
70 West Hedding Street, West Wing
San Jose, CA 95110
(408) 299-7400

Mr. Lawrence R. Sheahan, Director
Santa Clara County Department
of Consumer Affairs
2175 The Alameda
San Jose, CA 95126
(408) 299-4211

Ms. Robin McFarland Gysin
Ms. Gloria Lorenzo
Coordinators, Division of
Consumer Affairs
Santa Cruz County District
Attorney's Office
701 Ocean Street, Room 200
Santa Cruz, CA 95060
(408) 425-2054

Mr. William Atkinson
Deputy District Attorney
Consumer Affairs Unit
Solano County District
Attorney's Office
600 Union Avenue
Fairfield, CA 94533
(707) 421-6860

Mr. Thomas Quinlan
Deputy District Attorney
Consumer Fraud Unit
Stanislaus County District
Attorney's Office
P.O. Box 442
Modesto, CA 95353
(209) 571-5550

Mr. Greg Brose
Deputy District Attorney
Consumer and Environmental
Protection Division
Ventura County District
Attorney's Office
800 South Victoria Avenue
Ventura, CA 93009
(805) 654-3110

Mr. Mark Jerome Jones
Supervising Deputy District Attorney
Special Services Unit—
Consumer/Environmental
Yolo County District Attorney's Office
P.O. Box 245
Woodland, CA 95695
(916) 666-8424

City Offices
Ms. Sue Frauens
Supervising Deputy City Attorney
Consumer Protection Division
Los Angeles City Attorney's Office
200 North Main Street
1600 City Hall East
Los Angeles, CA 90012
(213) 485-4515

Ms. Teresa Bransfield
Consumer Affairs Specialist
Consumer Division
Santa Monica City Attorney's Office
1685 Main Street, Room 310
Santa Monica, CA 90401
(213) 458-8336

Colorado

State Offices
Consumer Protection Unit
Office of Attorney General
110 16th Street, 10th Floor
Denver, CO 80202
(303) 620-4500

Ms. Helen Davis
Consumer and Food Specialist
Department of Agriculture
700 Kipling Street, Suite 4000
Lakewood, CO 80215-5894
(303) 239-4114

County Offices
Mr. Victor Reichman, District Attorney
Archuleta, LaPlata, and San Juan
Counties
District Attorney's Office
P.O. Drawer 3455
Durango, CO 81302
(303) 247-8850

Mr. Alex Hunter, District Attorney
Boulder County District
Attorney's Office
P.O. Box 471
Boulder, CO 80306
(303) 441-3700

Ms. Clair Villano, Executive Director
Denver County District Attorney's
Consumer Fraud Office
303 West Colfax Avenue, Suite 1300
Denver, CO 80204
(303) 640-3555 (inquiries)
(303) 640-3557 (complaints)

Mr. David Zook
Chief Deputy District Attorney
Economic Crime Division
El Paso and Teller Counties District
Attorney's Office
326 South Tejon
Colorado Springs, CO 80903-2083
(719) 520-6002

Mr. Gus Sandstrom, District Attorney
Pueblo County District
Attorney's Office
Courthouse
215 West Tenth Street
Pueblo, CO 81003
(719) 546-6030

Mr. A.M. Dominguez, Jr.
District Attorney
Mr. Tony Molocznik
Consumer Fraud Investigator
Weld County District Attorney's
Consumer Office
P.O. Box 1167
Greeley, CO 80632
(303) 356-4000 ext. 4735

Connecticut

State Offices
Ms. Gloria Schaffer, Commissioner
Department of Consumer Protection
State Office Building
165 Capitol Avenue
Hartford, CT 06106
(203) 566-4999
1 (800) 842-2649 (toll free in CT)

Mr. Robert M. Langer
Assistant Attorney General
Antitrust/Consumer Protection
Office of Attorney General
110 Sherman Street
Hartford, CT 06105
(203) 566-5374

City Office
Mr. Guy Tommasi, Director
Middletown Office of
Consumer Protection
City Hall
Middletown, CT 06457
(203) 344-3492

Delaware

State Offices
Mr. Donald E. Williams, Director
Division of Consumer Affairs
Department of Community Affairs
820 North French Street, 4th Floor
Wilmington, DE 19801
(302) 577-3250

Mr. Stuart Drowos, Deputy Attorney
General for Economic Crime and
Consumer Protection
Office of Attorney General
820 North French Street
Wilmington, DE 19801
(302) 577-3250

District of Columbia
Mr. Aubrey Edwards, Director
Department of Consumer and
Regulatory Affairs
614 H Street NW
Washington, DC 20001
(202) 727-7000

Florida

State Offices

Ms. Barbara Edwards, Assistant
Department of Agriculture and
Consumer Services
Division of Consumer Services
218 Mayo Building
Tallahassee, FL 32399
(904) 488-2226
1 (800) 342-2176
(toll free TDD in FL)
1 (800) 327-3382
(toll free information and
education in FL)
1 (800) 321-5366
(toll free lemon law in FL)

Mr. Jack A. Norris, Jr., Chief
Consumer Litigation Section
The Capitol
Tallahassee, FL 32399-1050
(904) 488-9105

Mr. Richard Scott, Chief
Consumer Division
Office of Attorney General
4000 Hollywood Boulevard
Suite 505 South
Hollywood, FL 33021
(305) 985-4780

County Offices

Mr. Stanley A. Kaufman, Director
Broward County Consumer
Affairs Division
115 South Andrews Avenue, Room 119
Fort Lauderdale, FL 33301
(305) 357-6030

Mr. Leonard Elias, Consumer Advocate
Metropolitan Dade County
Consumer Protection Division
140 West Flagler Street, Suite 902
Miami, FL 33130
(305) 375-4222

Mr. Frederic A. Kerstein, Chief
Dade County Economic Crime Unit
Office of State Attorney
1469 NW 13th Terrace, Room 600
Miami, FL 33125
(305) 324-3030

Mr. Henry Huerta, Manager
Hillsborough County Department
of Consumer Affairs
412 East Madison Street, Room 1001
Tampa, FL 33602
(813) 272-6750

Mr. Larry F. Blalock, Chief
Orange County Consumer Fraud Unit
250 North Orange Avenue
P.O. Box 1673
Orlando, FL 32802
(407) 836-2490

Citizens Intake
Palm Beach County
Office of State Attorney
P.O. Drawer 2905
West Palm Beach, FL 33402
(407) 355-3560

Mr. Lawrence Breeden, Director
Palm Beach County Department
of Consumer Affairs
3111 S. Dixie Highway, Suite 128
West Palm Beach, FL 33405
(407) 355-2670

Mr. Alfred J. Cortis, Administrator
Pasco County Consumer
Affairs Division
7530 Little Road
New Port Richey, FL 34654
(813) 847-8110

Mr. William H. Richards, Director
Pinellas County Office of
Consumer Affairs
P.O. Box 17268
Clearwater, FL 34622-0268
(813) 530-6200

Ms. Beth Rutberg, Coordinator
Seminole Economic Crime Unit
Office of State Attorney
100 East First Street
Sanford, FL 32771
(407) 322-7534

State Attorney
Consumer Fraud Unit
700 South Park Avenue
Titusville, FL 32780
(407) 264-5230

City Offices

Ms. Rachel Marcus-Hendry
Chief of Consumer Affairs
City of Jacksonville
Division of Consumer Affairs
421 W. Church Street, Suite 404
Jacksonville, FL 32202
(904) 630-3667

Mr. Al Dezure, Chairman
Lauderhill Consumer Protection Board
1176 NW 42nd Way
Lauderhill, FL 33313
(305) 321-2450

Mr. Irving Lopatey, Chairman
Tamarac Board of Consumer Affairs
7525 NW 88th Avenue
Tamarac, FL 33321
(305) 722-5900, ext. 389
(Tuesday, Wednesday, and Thursday—
10 A.M. to Noon)

Georgia

State Office

Mr. Barry W. Reid, Administrator
Governor's Office of Consumer Affairs
2 Martin Luther King, Jr. Drive, S.E.
Plaza Level—East Tower
Atlanta, GA 30334
(404) 651-8600
(404) 656-3790
1 (800) 869-1123 (toll free in GA)

Hawaii

State Offices

Mr. Philip Doi, Director
Office of Consumer Protection
Department of Commerce and
Consumer Affairs
828 Fort Street Mall, Suite 600B
P.O. Box 3767
Honolulu, HI 96812-3767
(808) 586-2630

Mr. Gene Murayama, Investigator
Office of Consumer Protection
Department of Commerce and
Consumer Affairs
75 Aupuni Street
Hilo, HI 96720
(808) 933-4433

Mr. Glenn Ikemoto, Investigator
Office of Consumer Protection
Department of Commerce and
Consumer Affairs
3060 Eiwa Street
Lihue, HI 96766
(808) 241-3365

Mr. James E. Radford, Investigator
Office of Consumer Protection
Department of Commerce and
Consumer Affairs
54 High Street
P.O. Box 3767
Honolulu, HI 96812
(808) 586-2630

Idaho

State Office

Mr. Brett De Lange
Deputy Attorney General
Office of the Attorney General
Consumer Protection Unit
Statehouse, Room 113A
Boise, ID 83720-1000
(208) 334-2424
1 (800) 432-3545 (toll free in ID)

Illinois

State Offices

Ms. Drinda L. O'Connor, Director
Governor's Office of
Citizens Assistance
222 South College
Springfield, IL 62706
(217) 782-0244
1 (800) 642-3112 (toll free in IL)

Ms. Sally Saltzberg, Chief
Consumer Protection Division
Office of Attorney General
100 West Randolph, 12th Floor
Chicago, IL 60601
(312) 814-3580
(312) 793-2852 (TDD)

Ms. Elaine Hirsch, Director
Department of Citizen Rights
100 West Randolph, 13th Floor
Chicago, IL 60601
(312) 814-3289
(312) 814-7123 (TDD)

Regional Offices

Mr. Anthony Dyhrkopp
Assistant Attorney General
Carbondale Regional Office
Office of Attorney General
626A East Walnut Street
Carbondale, IL 62901
(618) 457-3505
(618) 457-4421 (TDD)

Ms. Regina Haasis
Assistant Attorney General
Champaign Regional Office
34 East Main Street
Champaign, IL 61820
(217) 333-7691 (voice/TDD)

Ms. Agatha McKeel
Assistant Attorney General
East St. Louis Regional Office
Office of Attorney General
8712 State Street
East St. Louis, IL 62203
(618) 398-1006
(618) 398-1009 (TDD)

Mr. Dennis Orsey
Assistant Attorney General
Granite City Regional Office
Office of Attorney General
1314 Niedringhaus
Granite City, IL 62040
(618) 877-0404

Mr. Tony L. Brasel
Assistant Attorney General
Kankakee Regional Office
Office of Attorney General
1012 North 5th Avenue
Kankakee, IL 60901
(815) 935-8500

Ms. Cynthia Tracy
Assistant Attorney General
LaSalle Regional Office
Office of Attorney General
1222 Shooting Park Rd., Suite 106
Peru, IL 61354
(815) 224-4861
(815) 224-4864 (TDD)

Mt. Vernon Regional Office
Office of Attorney General
3405 Broadway
Mt. Vernon, IL 62864
(618) 242-8200 (voice/TDD)

Ms. Dianna Zimmerman
Assistant Attorney General
Peoria Regional Office
Office of Attorney General
323 Main Street
Peoria, IL 61602
(309) 671-3191
(309) 671-3089 (TDD)

Quincy Regional Office
Office of Attorney General
523 Main Street
Quincy, IL 62301
(217) 223-2221 (voice/TDD)

Mr. Joseph Bruscato
Assistant Attorney General
Rockford Regional Office
Office of Attorney General
119 North Church Street
Rockford, IL 61101
(815) 987-7580
(815) 987-7579 (TDD)

Mr. Herbert S. Schultz, Jr.
Assistant Attorney General
Rock Island Regional Office
Office of Attorney General
1614 2nd Avenue
Rock Island, IL 61201
(309) 793-0950
(309) 793-0956 (TDD)

Ms. Deborah Hagan
Assistant Attorney General and Chief
Consumer Protection Division
Office of Attorney General
500 South Second Street
Springfield, IL 62706
(217) 782-9011
1 (800) 252-8666 (toll free in IL)

Ms. Elizabeth Foran
Assistant Attorney General
Waukegan Regional Office
Office of Attorney General
12 South County Street
Waukegan, IL 60085
(708) 336-2207
(708) 336-2374 (TDD)

Mr. Michael Pasko
Assistant Attorney General
West Frankfort Regional Office
Office of Attorney General
222 East Main Street
West Frankfort, IL 62896
(618) 937-6453

Ms. Colleen McLaughlin
Assistant Attorney General
West Chicago Regional Office
Office of Attorney General
122A County Farm Road
Wheaton, IL 60187
(708) 653-5060 (voice/TDD)

County Offices
Mr. Allen Reissman, Supervisor
Consumer Fraud Division—303
Cook County Office of
State's Attorney
303 Daley Center
Chicago, IL 60602
(312) 443-4600

Mr. William Haine, State's Attorney
Madison County Office
of State's Attorney
325 East Vandalia
Edwardsville, IL 62025
(618) 692-6280

Mr. Floyd Atkinson, Director
Consumer Protection Division
Rock Island County
State's Attorney's Office
County Courthouse
Rock Island, IL 61201
(309) 786-4451, ext. 229

City Offices
Ms. Mary Runion, Consumer Fraud
Wheeling Township
1616 North Arlington Heights Road
Arlington Heights, IL 60004
(708) 259-7730 (Wednesdays only)

Ms. Caroline O. Shoenberger
Commissioner
Chicago Department of
Consumer Services
121 North LaSalle Street, Room 808
Chicago, IL 60602
(312) 744-4090
(312) 744-9385 (TDD)

Mr. Robert E. Hinde, Administrator
Des Plaines Consumer Protection
Commission
1420 Miner Street
Des Plaines, IL 60016
(708) 391-5363

Indiana

State Office
Mr. David A. Miller
Chief Counsel and Director
Consumer Protection Division
Office of Attorney General
219 State House
Indianapolis, IN 46204
(317) 232-6330
1 (800) 382-5516 (toll free in IN)

County Offices
Ms. Gail Barus, Director
Consumer Protection Division
Lake County Prosecutors Office
2293 North Main Street
Crown Point, IN 46307
(219) 755-3720

Mr. Jeffrey Modisett
Marion County Prosecuting Attorney
560 City-County Building
200 East Washington Street
Indianapolis, IN 46204-3363
(317) 236-3522

Mr. Stanley Levco
Vanderburgh County
Prosecuting Attorney
108 Administration Building
Civic Center Complex
Evansville, IN 47708
(812) 426-5150

City Office
Mr. Robert McCrady, Director
Gary Office of Consumer Affairs
Annex East
1100 Massachusetts Street
Gary, IN 46407
(219) 886-0145

Iowa

State Office
Mr. Steve St. Clair
Assistant Attorney General
Consumer Protection Division
Office of Attorney General
1300 East Walnut Street, 2nd Floor
Des Moines, IA 50319
(515) 281-5926

Kansas

State Office
Mr. Daniel P. Kolditz
Deputy Attorney General
Consumer Protection Division
Office of Attorney General
301 West 10th
Kansas Judicial Center
Topeka, KS 66612-1597
(913) 296-3751
1 (800) 432-2310 (toll free in KS)

County Offices
Mr. Roger A. Nordeen, Head
Consumer Fraud Division
Johnson County District
Attorney's Office
Johnson County Courthouse
P.O. Box 728
Olathe, KS 66061
(913) 782-5000

Mr. Richard L. Schodorf
Chief Attorney
Consumer Fraud and Economic
Crime Division
Sedgwick County District
Attorney's Office
Sedgwick County Courthouse
Wichita, KS 67203
(316) 268-7921

Mr. James J. Welch
Assistant District Attorney
Shawnee County District
Attorney's Office
Shawnee County Courthouse,
Room 212
Topeka, KS 66603-3922
(913) 291-4330

City Office
Mr. Brenden Long
Assistant City Attorney
Topeka Consumer Protection Division
City Attorney's Office
215 East Seventh Street
Topeka, KS 66603
(913) 295-3883

Kentucky

State Offices

Ms. Nora K. McCormick, Director
Consumer Protection Division
Office of Attorney General
209 Saint Clair Street
Frankfort, KY 40601-1875
(502) 564-2200
1 (800) 432-9257 (toll free in KY)

Mr. Robert L. Winlock, Administrator
Consumer Protection Division
Office of Attorney General
107 South 4th Street
Louisville, KY 40202
(502) 588-3262
1 (800) 432-9257 (toll free in KY)

Louisiana

State Office

Ms. Mary H. Travis, Chief
Consumer Protection Section
Office of Attorney General
State Capitol Building
P.O. Box 94005
Baton Rouge, LA 70804-9005
(504) 342-7373

County Office

Sgt. Albert H. Olsen, Chief
Consumer Protection Division
Jefferson Parish District
Attorney's Office
200 Huey P. Long Avenue
Gretna, LA 70053
(504) 364-3644

Maine

State Offices

Mr. William N. Lund
Superintendent
Bureau of Consumer Credit Protection
State House Station No. 35
Augusta, ME 04333-0035
(207) 582-8718
1 (800) 332-8529 (toll free)

Mr. Stephen Wessler, Chief
Consumer and Antitrust Division
Office of Attorney General
State House Station No. 6
Augusta, ME 04333
(207) 289-3716 (9 A.M.–1 P.M.)

Maryland

State Offices

Mr. William Leibovici, Chief
Consumer Protection Division
Office of Attorney General
200 St. Paul Place
Baltimore, MD 21202-2021
(301) 528-8662 (9 A.M.–3 P.M.)
(301) 576-6372
(TDD in Baltimore area)
(301) 565-0451
(TDD in DC metro area)
1 (800) 969-5766 (toll free)

Mr. Ronald E. Forbes, Director
Licensing & Consumer Services
Motor Vehicle Administration
6601 Ritchie Highway NE
Glen Burnie, MD 21062
(301) 768-7420

Ms. Emalu Myer
Consumer Affairs Specialist
Eastern Shore Branch Office
Consumer Protection Division
Office of Attorney General
Salisbury District Court/
Multi-service Center
201 Baptist Street, Suite 30
Salisbury, MD 21801-4976
(301) 543-6620

Mr. Larry Munson, Director
Western Maryland Branch Office
Consumer Protection Division
Office of Attorney General
138 East Antietam Street, Suite 210
Hagerstown, MD 21740-5684
(301) 791-4780

County Offices
Mr. Stephen D. Hannan, Administrator
Howard County Office
of Consumer Affairs
9250 Rumsey Road
Columbia, MD 21045
(301) 313-7220
(301) 313-7201, 2323 (TDD)

Ms. Barbara B. Gregg
Executive Director
Montgomery County Office
of Consumer Affairs
100 Maryland Avenue, 3rd Floor
Rockville, MD 20850
(301) 217-7373

Ms. Michelle Tucker Rozner
Executive Director
Prince Georges County
Consumer Protection Commission
9201 Basil Court
Landover, MD 20785
(301) 925-5100
(301) 925-5167 (TDD)

Massachusetts

State Offices
Mr. Robert Sherman, Chief
Consumer Protection Division
Department of Attorney General
131 Tremont Street
Boston, MA 02111
(617) 727-8400
(information and referral to local
consumer offices that work in conjunction with the Department of
Attorney General)

Ms. Gloria Cordes Larson, Secretary
Executive Office of Consumer Affairs
and Business Regulation
One Ashburton Place, Room 1411
Boston, MA 02108
(617) 727-7780
(information and referral only)

Mr. Carmen Picknally
Managing Attorney
Western Massachusetts Consumer
Protection Division
Department of Attorney General
436 Dwight Street
Springfield, MA 01103
(413) 784-1240

County Offices
Ms. Margaret Platek
Complaint Supervisor
Consumer Fraud Prevention
Franklin County District
Attorney's Office
238 Main Street
Greenfield MA 01301
(413) 774-5102

Ms. Susan Grant, Director
Consumer Fraud Prevention
Hampshire County District
Attorney's Office
1 Court Square
Northhampton, MA 01060
(413) 586-9225

Project Coordinator
Worcester County Consumer
Rights Project
340 Main Street, Room 370
Worcester, MA 01608
(508) 754-7420 (9:30 A.M.–4 P.M.)

City Offices
Ms. Diane J. Modica, Commissioner
Mayor's Office of Consumer Affairs
and Licensing
Boston City Hall, Room 613
Boston, MA 02201
(617) 725-3320

Ms. Jean Courtney, Director
Consumer Information Center
Springfield Action Commission
P.O. Box 1449 Main Office
Springfield, MA 01101
(413) 737-4376
(Hampton and Hampshire Counties)

Michigan

State Offices

Mr. Frederick H. Hoffecker
Assistant in Charge Consumer
Protection Division
Office of Attorney General
P.O. Box 30213
Lansing, MI 48909
(517) 373-1140

Mr. Kent Wilcox, Executive Director
Michigan Consumers Council
414 Hollister Building
106 West Allegan Street
Lansing, MI 48933
(517) 373-0947
(517) 373-0701 (TDD)

Mr. Rodger James, Acting Director
Bureau of Automotive Regulation
Michigan Department of State
Lansing, MI 48918
(517) 373-7858
1 (800) 292-4204 (toll free in MI)

County Offices

Mr. George Mullison
Prosecuting Attorney
Bay County Consumer Protection Unit
Bay County Building
Bay City, MI 48708-5994
(517) 893-3594

Ms. Margaret DeMuynck, Director
Consumer Protection Department
Macomb County
Office of the Prosecuting Attorney
Macomb Court Building, 6th Floor
Mt. Clemens, MI 48043
(313) 469-5350

Ms. Charleen Berels, Director
Washtenaw County
Consumer Services
4133 Washtenaw Street
P.O. Box 8645
Ann Arbor, MI 48107-8645
(313) 971-6054

City Office

Ms. Esther K. Shapiro, Director
City of Detroit
Department of Consumer Affairs
1600 Cadillac Tower
Detroit, MI 48226
(313) 224-3508

Minnesota

State Offices

Mr. Curt Loewe, Director
Office of Consumer Services
Office of Attorney General
117 University Avenue
St. Paul, MN 55155
(612) 296-2331

Consumer Services Division
Office of Attorney General
320 West Second Street
Duluth, MN 55802
(218) 723-4891

County Office
Ms. Kate McPherson
Citizen Protection Unit
Hennepin County Attorney's Office
C2000 County Government Center
Minneapolis, MN 55487
(612) 348-4528

City Office

Mr. James Moncur, Director
Consumer Affairs Division
Minneapolis Department of
Licenses & Consumer Services
One C City Hall
Minneapolis, MN 55415
(612) 348-2080

Mississippi

State Offices

Mr. Trey Bobinger
Special Assistant Attorney General
Chief, Consumer Protection Division
Office of Attorney General
P.O. Box 22947
Jackson, MS 39225-2947
(601) 354-6018

Mr. Joe B. Hardy, Director
Regulatory Services
Department of Agriculture and
Commerce
500 Greymont Avenue
P.O. Box 1609
Jackson, MS 39215
(601) 354-7063

Ms. Mattie T. Stevens
Consumer Counselor
Gulf Coast Regional Office
of the Attorney General
P.O. Box 1411
Biloxi, MS 39533
(601) 436-6000

Missouri

State Offices
Office of the Attorney General
Consumer Complaints or Problems
P.O. Box 899
Jefferson City, MO 65102
(314) 751-3321
1 (800) 392-8222 (toll free in MO)

Mr. Henry Herschel, Chief Counsel
Trade Offense Division
Office of Attorney General
P.O. Box 899
Jefferson City, MO 65102
(314) 751-3321
1 (800) 392-8222 (toll free in MO)

Montana

State Office
Consumer Affairs Unit
Department of Commerce
1424 Ninth Avenue
Helena, MT 59620
(406) 444-4312

Nebraska

State Office
Mr. Paul N. Potadle
Assistant Attorney General
Consumer Protection Division
Department of Justice
2115 State Capitol
P.O. Box 98920
Lincoln, NE 68509
(402) 471-2682

County Office
Mr. James Jansen
Douglas County Attorney
County Attorney's Office
428 Hall of Justice
17th and Farnam
Omaha, NE 68183
(402) 444-7040

Nevada

State Offices
Mr. Myram Borders
Commissioner of Consumer Affairs
Department of Commerce
State Mail Room Complex
Las Vegas, NV 89158
(702) 486-7355
1 (800) 992-0900 (toll free in NV)

Mr. Ray Trease
Consumer Services Officer
Consumer Affairs Division
Department of Commerce
4600 Kietzke Lane, M-245
Reno, NV 89502
(702) 688-1800
1 (800) 992-0900 (toll free in NV)

County Office
Mr. John Long, Investigator
Consumer Fraud Division
Washoe County District
Attorney's Office
P.O. Box 11130
Reno, NV 89520
(702) 328-3456

New Hampshire

State Office
Chief
Consumer Protection and
Antitrust Bureau
Office of Attorney General
State House Annex
Concord, NH 03301
(603) 271-3641

New Jersey

State Offices
Ms. Patricia A. Royer, Director
Division of Consumer Affairs
P.O. Box 45027
Newark, NJ 07101
(201) 648-4010

Mr. Wilfredo Caraballo, Commissioner
Department of the Public Advocate
CN 850, Justice Complex
Trenton, NJ 08625
(609) 292-7087
1 (800) 792-8600 (toll free in NJ)

Ms. Cindy K. Miller
Deputy Attorney General
New Jersey Division of Law
1207 Raymond Boulevard
P.O. Box 45029
Newark, NJ 07101
(201) 648-7579

County Offices
Mr. William H. Ross III, Director
Atlantic County Consumer Affairs
1333 Atlantic Avenue, 8th Floor
Atlantic City, NJ 08401
(609) 345-6700

Mary E. Courtney, Director
Bergen County Division of
Consumer Affairs
21 Main Street, Room 101-E
Hackensack, NJ 07601-7000
(201) 646-2650

Mrs. Renee L. Borstad, Director
Burlington County Office of
Consumer Affairs
49 Rancocas Road
Mount Holly, NJ 08060
(609) 265-5054

Ms. Patricia M. Tuck, Director
Camden County Office
of Consumer Affairs
1800 Pavilion West
2101 Ferry Avenue, Suite 609
Camden, NJ 08104
(609) 757-8397

Mr. Mark Diederich, Director
Cape May County Consumer Affairs
DN-310, Central Mail Room
Cape May Court House
Cape May Court House, NJ 08210
(609) 465-1076

Mr. Louis G. Moreno, Director
Cumberland County Department
of Consumer Affairs and Weights
and Measures
788 East Commerce Street
Bridgeton, NJ 08302
(609) 453-2202

Director
Essex County Consumer Services
15 Southmunn Avenue, 2nd Floor
East Orange, NJ 07018
(201) 678-8071
(201) 678-8928

Mr. Edward McGoldrick, Director
Gloucester County Consumer Affairs
152 North Broad Street
Woodbury, NJ 08096
(609) 853-3349
(609) 848-6616 (TDD)

Ms. Barbara Donnelly, Director
Hudson County Division
of Consumer Affairs
595 Newark Avenue
Jersey City, NJ 07306
(201) 795-6295

Ms. Helen Mataka, Director
Hunterdon County Consumer Affairs
P.O. Box 283
Lebanon, NJ 08833
(908) 236-2249

Ms. Donna Giovannetti, Division Chief
Mercer County Consumer Affairs
640 South Broad Street, Room 229
Trenton, NJ 08650-0068
(609) 989-6671

Mr. Lawrence Cimmino, Director
Middlesex County Consumer Affairs
149 Kearny Avenue
Perth Amboy, NJ 08861
(201) 324-4600

Ms. Dorothy H. Avallone, Director
Monmouth County Consumer Affairs
1 East Main Street
P.O. Box 1255
Freehold, NJ 07728-1255
(908) 431-7900

Ms. Janet Opiekun, Director
Morris County Consumer Affairs
P.O. Box 900
Morristown, NJ 07963-0900
(201) 285-6070
(201) 584-9189 (TDD)

Mr. Kenneth J. Leake, Director
Ocean County Consumer Affairs
P.O. Box 2191
County Administration Building
Room 130-1
Toms River, NJ 08754-2191
(908) 929-2105

Ms. Mary Ann Maloney, Director
Passaic County Consumer Affairs
County Administration Building
309 Pennsylvania Avenue
Paterson, NJ 07503
(201) 881-4547, 4499

Ms. Ruth A. Hotz
Somerset County Consumer Affairs
County Administration Building
P.O. Box 3000
Somerville, NJ 08876
(908) 231-7000, ext. 7400

Mrs. Ollie Jones, Office Manager
Union County Consumer Affairs
300 North Avenue East
P.O. Box 186
Westfield, NJ 07091
(201) 654-9840

Ms. Barbara McHenry, Director
Warren County Consumer Affairs
Dumont Administration Building
Route 519
Belvedere, NJ 07823
(908) 475-6500

City Offices
Ms. Lorraine Sudia, Director
Brick Consumer Affairs
Municipal Building
401 Chambers Bridge Road
Brick, NJ 08723
(908) 477-3000, ext. 296

Mr. Lawrence A. Eleuteri, Director
Cinnaminson Consumer Affairs
Municipal Building
1621 Riverton Road
Cinnaminson, NJ 08077
(609) 829-6000

Ms. Theresa Ward, Director
Clark Consumer Affairs
430 Westfield Avenue
Clark, NJ 07066
(908) 388-3600

Ms. Mary Ann Pizzello, Director
Elizabeth Consumer Affairs
City Hall
60 West Scott Plaza
Elizabeth, NJ 07203
(908) 820-4183

Mr. H. Gerald Niemira, Director
Fort Lee Consumer Protection Board
Bourough Hall
309 Main Street
Fort Lee, NJ 07024
(201) 592-3579

Ms. Libby Saltzman, Director
Glen Rock Consumer Affairs
Municipal Building, Harding Plaza
Glen Rock, NJ 07452-2100
(201) 670-3956

Mr. Robert King
Consumer Advocate
City Hall
94 Washington Street
Hoboken, NJ 07030
(201) 420-2038

Ms. Bernadine Jacobs, Director
Livingston Consumer Affairs
357 South Livingston Avenue
Livingston, NJ 07039
(201) 535-7976

Ms. Genevieve Ross, Director
Middlesex Borough Consumer Affairs
1200 Mountain Avenue
Middlesex, NJ 08846
(908) 356-8090

Ms. Mildred Pastore, Director
Mountainside Consumer Affairs
1455 Coles Avenue
Mountainside, NJ 07092
(908) 232-6600

Mr. Max Moses
Department of Community Services
Municipal Building
North Bergen, NJ 07047
(201) 330-7292, 91

Ms. Annmarie Nicolette, Director
Nutley Consumer Affairs
City Hall
228 Chestnut Street
Nutley, NJ 07110
(201) 284-4936

Ms. Beth Jenkins, Director
Parsippany Consumer Affairs
Municipal Building, Room 101
1001 Parsippany Boulevard
Parsippany, NJ 07054
(201) 263-7011

Ms. Maria Jimenez, Director
Perth Amboy Consumer Affairs
City Hall
260 High Street
Perth Amboy, NJ 08861
(908) 826-0290, ext. 61, 62

Ms. Priscilla Castles, Director
Plainfield Action Services
510 Watchung Avenue
Plainfield, NJ 07060
(908) 753-3519

Michael B. Bukatman, Director
Secaucus Department of
Consumer Affairs
Municipal Government Center
Secaucus, NJ 07094
(201) 330-2019

Ms. Marion Cramer, Director
Union Township Consumer Affairs
Municipal Building
1976 Morris Avenue
Union, NJ 07083
(908) 688-6763

Mr. Charles A. Stern, Director
Wayne Township Consumer Affairs
475 Valley Road
Wayne, NJ 07470
(201) 694-1800, ext. 290

Mr. John Weitzel, Director
Weehawken Consumer Affairs
400 Park Avenue
Weehawken, NJ 07087
(201) 319-6005

Mr. John Busuttil, Director
West New York Consumer Affairs
428 60th Street
West New York, NJ 07093
(201) 861-2522

New Mexico

State Office
Consumer Protection Division
Office of Attorney General
P.O. Drawer 1508
Santa Fe, NM 87504
(505) 827-6060
1 (800) 432-2070 (toll free in NM)

New York

State Offices
Mr. Richard M. Kessel
Chairperson and Executive Director
New York State Consumer
Protection Board
99 Washington Avenue
Albany, NY 12210-2891
(518) 474-8583

Ms. Rachael Kretser
Assistant Attorney General
Bureau of Consumer Frauds
and Protection
Office of Attorney General
State Capitol
Albany, NY 12224
(518) 474-5481

Mr. Richard M. Kessel
Chairperson and Executive Director
New York State Consumer
Protection Board
250 Broadway, 17th Floor
New York, NY 10007-2593
(212) 417-4908 (complaints)
(212) 417-4482 (main office)

Mr. John Corwin
Assistant Attorney General
Bureau of Consumer Frauds
and Protection
Office of Attorney General
120 Broadway
New York, NY 10271
(212) 341-2345

Regional Offices
Mr. John R. Marshall, Jr.
Assistant Attorney General in Charge
Binghamton Regional Office
Office of Attorney General
59-61 Court Street, 7th Floor
Binghamton, NY 13901
(607) 773-7877

Mr. Peter B. Sullivan
Assistant Attorney General in Charge
Buffalo Regional Office
Office of Attorney General
65 Court Street
Buffalo, NY 14202
(716) 847-7184

Mr. Alan J. Burczak
Assistant Attorney General in Charge
Plattsburgh Regional Office
Office of Attorney General
70 Clinton Street
Plattsburgh, NY 12901
(518) 563-8012

Mr. Kent L. Mardon
Assistant Attorney General in Charge
Poughkeepsie Regional Office
Office of Attorney General
235 Main Street
Poughkeepsie, NY 12601
(914) 485-3920

Mr. Eugene Welch
Assistant Attorney General in Charge
Rochester Regional Office
Office of Attorney General
144 Exchange Boulevard
Rochester, NY 14614
(716) 546-7430

Ms. Susan B. Blum
Assistant Attorney General in Charge
Suffolk Regional Office
Office of Attorney General
300 Motor Parkway
Hauppauge, NY 11788
(516) 231-2400

Mr. John R. Voninski
Assistant Attorney General in Charge
Syracuse Regional Office
Office of Attorney General
615 Erie Boulevard West
Syracuse, NY 13204-2465
(315) 448-4848

Ms. Aniela J. Carl
Assistant Attorney General in Charge
Utica Regional Office
Office of Attorney General
207 Genesee Street
Utica, NY 13501
(315) 793-2225

County Offices

Mr. Thomas M. Jablonowski
Deputy Director of General Services
Broome County Bureau of
Consumer Affairs
Governmental Plaza, P.O. Box 1766
Binghamton, NY 13902
(607) 778-2168

Mr. Nelson Kranker, Director
Dutchess County Department
of Consumer Affairs
38-A Dutchess Turnpike
Poughkeepsie, NY 12603
(914) 471-6322

Ms. Candace K. Vogel
Assistant District Attorney
Consumer Fraud Bureau
Erie County District Attorney's Office
25 Delaware Avenue
Buffalo, NY 14202
(716) 858-2424

Mr. James E. Picken, Commissioner
Nassau County Office of
Consumer Affairs
160 Old Country Road
Mineola, NY 11501
(516) 535-2600

Mr. John McCullough
Executive Director
New Justice Conflict
Resolution Services Inc.
210 East Fayette Street, Suite 700
Syracuse, NY 13202
(315) 471-4676

Mr. Edward J. Brown, Commissioner
Orange County Department
of Consumer Affairs and Weights
and Measures
99 Main Street
Goshen, NY 10924
(914) 294-5151, ext. 1762

Mr. Francis D. Phillips II
District Attorney
Orange County District
Attorney's Office
255 Main Street
County Government Center
Goshen, NY 10924
(914) 294-5471

Mr. Joseph LaBarbera
Putnam County Office Facility
Department of Consumer Affairs
Myrtle Avenue
Mahopac Falls, NY 10542-0368
(914) 621-2317

Mr. Alfred J. Stelzl, Director/
Coordinator
Rockland County Office of
Consumer Protection
County Office Building
18 New Hempstead Road
New City, NY 10956
(914) 638-5282

Mr. Dennis S. Abbey, Director
Steuben County Department
of Weights, Measures, and
Consumer Affairs
3 East Pulteney Square
Bath, NY 14810
(607) 776-9631
(607) 776-9631 ext. 2101
(voice/TDD)

Ms. Jane Devine, Commissioner
Suffolk County Department
of Consumer Affairs
Suffolk County Center
Hauppauge, NY 11788
(516) 360-4600

Mr. Jon Van Vlack, Director
Ulster County Consumer Fraud Bureau
285 Wall Street
Kingston, NY 12401
(914) 339-5680, ext. 240

Mr. Frank D. Castaldi, Jr.
Chief, Frauds Bureau
Westchester County
District Attorney's Office
111 Grove Street
White Plains, NY 10601
(914) 285-3303

Mr. Jeffrey A. Conte, Acting Director
Westchester County Department
of Consumer Affairs
Room 104, Michaelian Office Building
White Plains, NY 10601
(914) 285-2155

City Offices

Mr. Steven M. Nagel, Director
Babylon Consumer Protection Board
Town Hall Office Annex
281 Phelps Lane
North Babylon, NY 11703
(516) 422-7636

Town of Colonie Consumer
Protection
Memorial Town Hall
Newtonville, NY 12128
(518) 783-2790

Mr. Stephen Pedone, Commissioner
Mt. Vernon Office of Consumer Affairs
City Hall
Mt. Vernon, NY 10550
(914) 665-2433

Mr. Mark Green, Commissioner
New York City Department
of Consumer Affairs
42 Broadway
New York, NY 10004
(212) 487-4444

Bronx Neighborhood Office
New York City Department of
Consumer Affairs
1932 Arthur Avenue, Room 104-A
Bronx, NY 10457
(212) 579-6766

Brooklyn Neighborhood Office
New York City Department
of Consumer Affairs
1360 Fulton Street, Room 320
Brooklyn, NY 11216
(718) 636-7092

Ms. Isabel Butler, Director
Queens Neighborhood Office
New York City Department
of Consumer Affairs
120-55 Queens Boulevard,
Room 301A
Kew Gardens, NY 11424
(718) 261-2922

Ms. Johanna Kepley, Director
Staten Island Neighborhood Office
New York City Department of
Consumer Affairs
Staten Island Borough Hall, Room 422
Staten Island, NY 10301
(718) 390-5154

Mr. Joseph Kapuscinski, Director
City of Oswego Office of
Consumer Affairs
City Hall
West Oneida Street
Oswego, NY 13126
(315) 342-8150

Ms. Cathie Dworkin, Chairwoman
Ramapo Consumer Protection Board
Ramapo Town Hall
237 Route 59
Suffern, NY 10901-5399
(914) 357-5100

Schenectady Bureau of Consumer
Protection
City Hall, Room 22
Jay Street
Schenectady, NY 12305
(518) 382-5061

Mr. Jack Casey, Director
White Plains Department
of Weights and Measures
77 South Lexington Avenue
White Plains, NY 10601-2512
(914) 422-6359

Mr. Ralph A. Capozzi, Director
Yonkers Office of Consumer
Protection, Weights, and Measures
201 Palisade Avenue
Yonkers, NY 10703
(914) 377-6807

North Carolina

State Office
Mr. James C. Gulick
Special Deputy Attorney General
Consumer Protection Section
Office of Attorney General
Raney Building
P.O. Box 629
Raleigh, NC 27602
(919) 733-7741

North Dakota

State Offices
Mr. Nicholas J. Spaeth
Office of Attorney General
600 East Boulevard
Bismarck, ND 58505
(701) 224-2210
1 (800) 472-2600 (toll free in ND)

Mr. Tom Engelhardt, Director
Consumer Fraud Section
Office of Attorney General
600 East Boulevard
Bismarck, ND 58505
(701) 224-3404
1 (800) 472-2600 (toll free in ND)

County Office
Mr. Kent Keys, Executive Director
Quad County Community
Action Agency
27½ South Third Street
Grand Forks, ND 58201
(701) 746-5431

Ohio

State Offices
Ms. Dianne Goss Paynter
Consumer Frauds and Crimes Section
Office of Attorney General
30 East Broad Street
State Office Tower, 25th Floor
Columbus, OH 43266-0410
(614) 466-4986 (complaints)
(614) 466-1393 (TDD)
1 (800) 282-0515 (toll free in OH)

Mr. William A. Spratley
Office of Consumers' Counsel
77 South High Street, 15th Floor
Columbus, OH 43266-0550
(614) 466-9605 (voice/TDD)
1 (800) 282-9448 (toll free in OH)

County Offices
Mr. Richard Whitehouse, Director
Economic Crime Division
Franklin County Office of
Prosecuting Attorney
369 South High Street
Columbus, OH 43215
(614) 462-3555

Mr. Steven C. LaTourette
County Prosecutor
Consumer Protection Division
Lake County Office of
Prosecuting Attorney
Lake County Court House
Painesville, OH 44077
(216) 357-2683
1 (800) 899-5253 (toll free in OH)

Mr. Robert A. Skinner
Assistant Prosecuting Attorney
Montgomery County Fraud Section
301 West 3rd Street
Dayton Montgomery
County Courts Building
Dayton, OH 45402
(513) 225-5757

Mr. David Norris
Prosecuting Attorney
Portage County Office
of Prosecuting Attorney
466 South Chestnut Street
Ravenna, OH 44266-0671
(216) 296-4593

Mr. Lynn C. Slaby
Prosecuting Attorney
Summit County Office
of Prosecuting Attorney
53 University Avenue
Akron, OH 44308-1680
(216) 379-2800

City Offices
Mr. Steven Kurtz, Chief
Cincinnati Office of
Consumer Services
Division of Human Services
City Hall, Room 126
Cincinnati, OH 45202
(513) 352-3971

Mr. Anthony C. Julian, Director
Youngstown Office of Consumer
Affairs and Weights and Measures
26 South Phelps Street
City Hall
Youngstown, OH 44503-1318
(216) 742-8884

Oklahoma
State Offices
Ms. Jane Wheeler
Assistant Attorney General
Office of Attorney General
420 West Main, Suite 550
Oklahoma City, OK 73102
(405) 521-4274

Mr. Prescott H. Cowley, Administrator
Department of Consumer Credit
4545 Lincoln Boulevard, Suite 104
Oklahoma City, OK 73105-3408
(405) 521-3653

Oregon
State Office
Mr. Timothy Wood
Attorney in Charge
Financial Fraud Section
Department of Justice
Justice Building
Salem, OR 97310
(503) 378-4320

Pennsylvania
State Offices
Mr. Renardo Hicks, Director
Bureau of Consumer Protection
Office of Attorney General
Strawberry Square, 14th Floor
Harrisburg, PA 17120
(717) 787-9707
1 (800) 441-2555 (toll free in PA)

Mr. Irwin A. Popowsky
Consumer Advocate
Office of Consumer Advocate-Utilities
Office of Attorney General
1425 Strawberry Square
Harrisburg, PA 17120
(717) 783-5048 (utilities only)

Mr. Michael Butler
Deputy Attorney General
Bureau of Consumer Protection
Office of Attorney General
27 North Seventh Street
Allentown, PA 18101
(215) 821-6690

Mr. Joseph Farrell, Director
Bureau of Consumer Services
Pennsylvania Public Utility
Commission
203 North Office Building
Harrisburg, PA 17120
(717) 787-4970 (out-of-state calls only)
1 (800) 782-1110 (toll free in PA)

Mr. Daniel R. Goodemote
Deputy Attorney General
Bureau of Consumer Protection
Office of Attorney General
919 State Street, Room 203
Erie, PA 16501
(814) 871-4371

Mr. Robin David Bleecher
Attorney in Charge
Bureau of Consumer Protection
Office of Attorney General
132 Kline Village
Harrisburg, PA 17104
(717) 787-7109
1 (800) 441-2555 (toll free in PA)

Mr. Barry Creany
Deputy Attorney General
Bureau of Consumer Protection
Office of the Attorney General
IGA Building, Route 219 North
PO. Box 716
Ebensburg, PA 15931
(814) 949-7900

Mr. John E. Kelly
Deputy Attorney General
Bureau of Consumer Protection
Office of Attorney General
21 South 12th Street, 2nd Floor
Philadelphia PA 19107
(215) 560-2414
1 (800) 441-2555 (toll free in PA)

Ms. Caren L. Mariani
Deputy Attorney General
Bureau of Consumer Protection
Office of Attorney General
Manor Complex, 5th Floor
564 Forbes Avenue
Pittsburgh, PA 15219
(412) 565-5394

Mr. J.P. McGowan
Deputy Attorney General
Bureau of Consumer Protection
Office of Attorney General
State Office Building, Room 358
100 Lackawanna Avenue
Scranton, PA 18503
(717) 963-4913

County Offices
Mr. Sidney Elkin, Director
Beaver County Alliance for
Consumer Protection
699 Fifth Street
Beaver, PA 15009-1997
(412) 728-7267

Mr. A. Courtney Yelle
Director/Chief Sealer
Bucks County Consumer Protection,
Weights, and Measures
50 North Main
Doylestown, PA 18901
(215) 348-7442

Mr. Robert Taylor, Director
Chester County Bureau of Consumer
Protection, Weights, and Measures
Courthouse, 5th Floor, North Wing
High and Market Streets
West Chester, PA 19380
(215) 344-6150

Ms. Karen A. Koblish
Consumer Mediator
Cumberland County Consumer Affairs
One Courthouse Square
Carlisle, PA 17013-3387
(717) 240-6180

Ms. Evelyn Yancoskie, Director
Delaware County Office of Consumer
Affairs, Weights, and Measures
Government Center Building
Second and Olive Streets
Media, PA 19063
(215) 891-4865

Mrs. Helen Dunigan, Director
Montgomery County Consumer
Affairs Department
County Courthouse
Norristown, PA 19404
(215) 278-3565

City Office
Mr. James Fitzpatrick, Chief
Economic Crime Unit
Philadelphia District Attorney's Office
1421 Arch Street
Philadelphia, PA 19102
(215) 686-8750

Puerto Rico
Mr. Luis Roberto Pinero, Secretary
Department of Consumer Affairs
(DACO)
Minillas Station, P.O. Box 41059
Santurce, PR 00940
(809) 721-0940

Mr. Hector Rivera Cruz, Secretary
Department of Justice
P.O. Box 192
San Juan, PR 00902
(809) 721-2900

Rhode Island

State Offices
Ms. Lee Baker, Director
Consumer Protection Division
Department of Attorney General
72 Pine Street
Providence, RI 02903
(401) 277-2104
(401) 274-4400 ext. 354
(voice/TDD)
1 (800) 852-7776 (toll free in RI)

Mr. Edwin P. Palumbo
Executive Director
Rhode Island Consumers' Council
365 Broadway
Providence, RI 02909
(401) 277-2764

South Carolina

State Offices
Mr. Ken Moore
Assistant Attorney General
Consumer Fraud and Antitrust Section
Office of Attorney General
P.O. Box 11549
Columbia, SC 29211
(803) 734-3970

Mr. Steve Hamm, Administrator
Department of Consumer Affairs
P.O. Box 5757
Columbia, SC 29250-5757
(803) 734-9452
(803) 734-9455 (TDD)
1 (800) 922-1594 (toll free in SC)

Mr. W. Jefferson Bryson, Jr.
State Ombudsman
Office of Executive Policy
and Program
1205 Pendleton Street, Room 308
Columbia, SC 29201
(803) 734-0457
(803) 734-1147 (TDD)

South Dakota

State Office
Mr. Jeff Hallem
Assistant Attorney General
Division of Consumer Affairs
Office of Attorney General
500 East Capitol
State Capitol Building
Pierre, SD 57501-5070
(605) 773-4400

Tennessee

State Offices
Mr. Perry A. Craft
Deputy Attorney General
Antitrust and Consumer
Protection Division
Office of Attorney General
450 James Robertson Parkway
Nashville, TN 37243-0485
(615) 741-2672

Ms. Elizabeth Owen, Director
Division of Consumer Affairs
Department of Commerce
and Insurance
500 James Robertson Parkway,
5th Floor
Nashville, TN 37243-0600
(615) 741-4737
1 (800) 342-8385
(toll free in TN)
1 (800) 422-CLUB
(toll-free health club hot line in TN)

Texas

State Offices
Mr. Joe Crews
Assistant Attorney General and Chief
Consumer Protection Division
Office of Attorney General
P.O. Box 12548
Austin, TX 78711
(512) 463-2070

Mr. Stephen Gardner
Assistant Attorney General
Consumer Protection Division
Office of Attorney General
714 Jackson Street, Suite 700
Dallas, TX 75202-4506
(214) 742-8944

Ms. Viviana Patino
Assistant Attorney General
Consumer Protection Division
Office of Attorney General
6090 Surety Drive, Room 260
El Paso, TX 79905
(915) 772-9476

Mr. Richard Tomlinson
Assistant Attorney General
Consumer Protection Division
Office of Attorney General
1019 Congress Street, Suite 1550
Houston, TX 77002-1702
(713) 223-5886

Mr. Robert E. Reyna
Assistant Attorney General
Consumer Protection Division
Office of Attorney General
1208 14th Street, Suite 900
Lubbock, TX 79401-3997
(806) 747-5238

Mr. Thomas M. Bernstein
Assistant Attorney General
Consumer Protection Division
Office of Attorney General
3600 North 23rd Street, Suite 305
McAllen, TX 78501-1685
(512) 682-4547

Mr. Aaron Valenzuela
Assistant Attorney General
Consumer Protection Division
Office of Attorney General
115 East Travis Street, Suite 925
San Antonio, TX 78205-1607
(512) 225-4191

Office of Consumer Protection
State Board of Insurance
816 Congress Avenue, Suite 1400
Austin, TX 78701-2430
(512) 322-4143

County Offices
Mr. Ted Steinke
Assistant District Attorney and
Chief of Dallas County District
Attorney's Office
Specialized Crime Division
133 North Industrial Boulevard, LB 19
Dallas, TX 75207-4313
(214) 653-3820

Mr. Russel Turbeville
Assistant District Attorney and
Chief Harris County Consumer
Fraud Division
Office of District Attorney
201 Fannin, Suite 200
Houston, TX 77002-1901
(713) 221-5836

City Office
Ms. Adela Gonzalez, Director
Dallas Consumer Protection Division
Health and Human Services
Department
320 East Jefferson Boulevard,
Suite 312
Dallas, TX 75203
(214) 948-4400

Utah

State Offices
Mr. Gary R. Hansen, Director
Division of Consumer Protection
Department of Commerce
160 East 3rd South
P.O. Box 45802
Salt Lake City, UT 84145-0802
(801) 530-6601

Ms. Sheila Page
Assistant Attorney General for
Consumer Affairs
Office of Attorney General
115 State Capitol
Salt Lake City, UT 84114
(801) 538-1331

Vermont

State Offices
Mr. J. Wallace Malley
Assistant Attorney General and
Chief, Public Protection Division
Office of Attorney General
109 State Street
Montpelier, VT 05609-1001
(802) 828-3171

Mr. Bruce Martell, Supervisor
Consumer Assurance Section
Department of Agriculture,
Food, and Market
120 State Street
Montpelier, VT 05620-2901
(802) 828-2436

Virgin Islands
Mr. Clement Magras, Commissioner
Department of Licensing and
Consumer Affairs
Property and Procurement Building
Subbase #1, Room 205
St. Thomas, VI 00802
(809) 774-3130

Virginia

State Offices
Mr. Frank Seales, Jr., Chief
Antitrust and Consumer
Litigation Section
Office of Attorney General
Supreme Court Building
101 North Eighth Street
Richmond, VA 23219
(804) 786-2116
1 (800) 451-1525 (toll free in VA)

Ms. Betty Blakemore, Director
Division of Consumer Affairs
Department of Agriculture and
Consumer Services
Room 101, Washington Building
1100 Bank Street
P.O. Box 1163
Richmond, VA 23219
(804) 786-2042

Mr. Robert Minnich, Investigator
Northern Virginia Branch
Office of Consumer Affairs
Department of Agriculture and
Consumer Services
100 North Washington St., Suite 412
Falls Church, VA 22046
(703) 532-1613

County Offices
Ms. Diane Jemmott, Section Chief
Office of Citizen and Consumer Affairs
#1 Court House Plaza, Suite 314
2100 Clarendon Boulevard
Arlington, VA 22201
(703) 358-3260

Mr. Ronald B. Mallard, Director
Fairfax County Department of
Consumer Affairs
3959 Pender Drive, Suite 200
Fairfax, VA 22030-6093
(703) 246-5949
(703) 591-3260 (TDD)

Mr. Hubert King, Administrator
Prince William County Office
of Consumer Affairs
4370 Ridgewood Center Drive
Prince William, VA 22192-9201
(703) 792-7370

City Offices
Ms. Rose Boyd, Director
Alexandria Office of Citizens Assistance
City Hall
P.O. Box 178
Alexandria, VA 22313
(703) 838-4350
(703) 838-5056 (TDD)

Mr. Robert L. Gill, Coordinator
Division of Consumer Affairs
City Hall
Norfolk, VA 23501
(804) 441-2821
(804) 441-2000 (TDD)

Ms. Dolores Daniels
Assistant to the City Manager
Roanoke Consumer
Protection Division
364 Municipal Building
215 Church Avenue SW
Roanoke, VA 24011
(703) 981-2583

Mr. J. N. McClanan
Director, Consumer Affairs Division
Office of the Commonwealth's
Attorney
3500 Virginia Beach Boulevard,
Suite 304
Virginia Beach, VA 23452
(804) 431-4610

Washington

State Offices
Ms. Renee Olbricht, Investigator
Consumer and Business
Fair Practices Division
Office of the Attorney General
111 Olympia Avenue NE
Olympia, WA 98501
(206) 753-6210

Ms. Sally Sterling
Director of Consumer Services
Consumer and Business
Fair Practices Division
Office of the Attorney General
900 Fourth Avenue, Suite 2000
Seattle, WA 98164
(206) 464-6431
1 (800) 551-4636 (toll free in WA)

Mr. Owen Clarke, Chief
Consumer and Business
Fair Practices Division
Office of the Attorney General
West 1116 Riverside Avenue
Spokane, WA 99201
(509) 456-3123

Ms. Cynthia Lanphear, Contact Person
Consumer and Business
Fair Practices Division
Office of the Attorney General
1019 Pacific Avenue, 3rd Floor
Tacoma, WA 98402-4411
(206) 593-2904

City Offices
Ms. Kristie Anderson, Director
Department of Weights and Measures
3200 Cedar Street
Everett, WA 98201
(206) 259-8810

Mr. C. Patrick Sainsbury
Chief Deputy Prosecuting Attorney
Fraud Division
1002 Bank of California
900 4th Avenue
Seattle, WA 98164
(206) 296-9010

Mr. Dale H. Tiffany, Director
Seattle Department of Licenses
and Consumer Affairs
102 Municipal Building
600 4th Avenue
Seattle, WA 98104-1893
(206) 684-8484

West Virginia

State Offices
Mr. Robert J. Lamont, Director
Consumer Protection Division
Office of Attorney General
812 Quarrier Street, 6th Floor
Charleston, WV 25301
(304) 348-8986
1 (800) 368-8808 (toll free in WV)

Mr. Stephen Casto, Director
Division of Weights and Measures
Department of Labor
1800 Washington Street East
Building #3, Room 319
Charleston, WV 25305
(304) 348-7890

City Office
Mrs. Carolyn Lawler, Director
Department of Consumer Protection
P.O. Box 2749
Charleston, WV 25330
(304) 348-8172

Wisconsin

State Offices
Mr. John Alberts, Administrator
Division of Trade and Consumer
Protection
Department of Agriculture, Trade,
and Consumer Protection
801 West Badger Road
P.O. Box 8911
Madison, WI 53708
(608) 266-9836
1 (800) 422-7128 (toll free in WI)

Ms. Margaret Quaid
Regional Supervisor
Division of Trade and
Consumer Protection
Department of Agriculture, Trade,
and Consumer Protection
927 Loring Street
Altoona, WI 54720
(715) 839-3848
1 (800) 422-7128 (toll free in WI)

Mr. Eugene E. Lindauer
Regional Supervisor
Division of Trade and
Consumer Protection
Department of Agriculture, Trade,
and Consumer Protection
200 North Jefferson Street, Suite 146A
Green Bay, WI 54301
(414) 448-5111
1 (800) 422-7128 (toll free in WI)

Regional Supervisor
Consumer Protection Regional Office
Department of Agriculture, Trade,
and Consumer Protection
3333 N. Mayfair Road, Suite 114
Milwaukee, WI 53222-3288
(414) 257-8956

Mr. James D. Jeffries
Assistant Attorney General
Office of Consumer Protection
and Citizen Advocacy
Department of Justice
P.O. Box 7856
Madison, WI 53707-7856
(608) 266-1852
1 (800) 362-8189 (toll free)

Mr. Nadim Sahar
Assistant Attorney General
Office of Consumer Protection
Department of Justice
Milwaukee State Office Building
819 North 6th Street, Room 520
Milwaukee, WI 53203-1678
(414) 227-4948
1 (800) 362-8189 (toll free)

County Offices
Mr. Gregory Grau, District Attorney
Marathon County District
Attorney's Office
Marathon County Courthouse
Wausau, WI 54401
(715) 847-5555

Mr. Darryl Nevers
Assistant District Attorney
Milwaukee County District
Attorney's Office
Consumer Fraud Unit
821 West State Street, Room 412
Milwaukee, WI 53233-1485
(414) 278-4792

Mr. James A. Dehne
Consumer Fraud Investigator
Racine County Sheriff's Department
717 Wisconsin Avenue
Racine, WI 53403
(414) 636-3125

Wyoming

State Office
Mr. Mark Moran
Assistant Attorney General
Office of Attorney General
123 State Capitol Building
Cheyenne, WY 82002
(307) 777-7874

Appendix E:
Better Business Bureaus

Better Business Bureaus (BBBs) are nonprofit organizations sponsored by local businesses. BBBs offer a variety of consumer services. For example, they can provide consumer education materials, answer consumer questions, mediate and arbitrate complaints, and provide general information on companies' consumer complaint records.

Each BBB has its own policy about reporting information. It might or might not tell you the nature of the complaint against a business, but all will tell you if a complaint has been registered. Many of the BBBs accept written complaints and will contact a firm on your behalf. BBBs do not judge or rate individual products or brands, handle complaints concerning the prices of goods or services, or give legal advice. However, many bureaus do offer binding arbitration, a form of dispute resolution, to those who ask for it. If you need help with a consumer question or complaint, call your local BBB to ask about their services.

This list includes the local BBBs in the United States. The Council of Better Business Bureaus can give you the addresses for BBBs in Canada.

National Headquarters

Council of Better Business
Bureaus, Inc.
4200 Wilson Boulevard
Arlington, VA 22203
(703) 276-0100

Local Bureaus

Alabama

P.O. Box 55268
Birmingham, AL 35255-5268
(205) 558-2222

118 Woodburn Street
Dothan, AL 36301
(205) 792-3804

P.O. Box 383
Huntsville, AL 35801
(205) 533-1640

707 Van Antwerp Building
Mobile, AL 36602
(205) 433-5494, 5495

Commerce Street, Suite 806
Montgomery, AL 36104
(205) 262-5606

Alaska

3380 C Street, Suite 103
Anchorage, AK 99503
(907) 562-0704

Arizona

4428 North 12th Street
Phoenix, AZ 85014-4585
(602) 264-1721

50 West Drachman Street
Suite 103
Tucson, AZ 85705
(602) 622-7651 (inquiries)
(602) 622-7654 (complaints)

Arkansas

1415 South University
Little Rock, AR 72204
(501) 664-7274

California

705 Eighteenth Street
Bakersfield, CA 93301-4882
(805) 322-2074

P.O. Box 970
Colton, CA 92324-0522
(714) 825-7280

6101 Ball Road, Suite 309
Cypress, CA 90630
(714) 527-0680

1398 West Indianapolis
Suite 102
Fresno, CA 93705
(209) 222-8111

494 Alvarado Street, Suite C
Monterey, CA 93940
(408) 372-3149

510 16th Street
Oakland, CA 94612
(415) 839-5900

400 S Street
Sacramento, CA 95814
(916) 443-6843

3111 Camino del Rio North
Suite 600
San Diego, CA 92108-1729
(619) 281-6422

33 New Montgomery St. Tower
San Francisco, CA 94105
(415) 243-9999

1505 Meridian Avenue
San Jose, CA 95125
(408) 978-8700

P.O. Box 294
San Mateo, CA 94401
(415) 696-1240

P.O. Box 746
Santa Barbara, CA 93102
(805) 963-8657

300 B Street
Santa Rosa, CA 95401
(707) 577-0300

1111 North Center Street
Stockton, CA 95202-1383
(209) 948-4880, 4881

Colorado

P.O. Box 7970
Colorado Springs, CO 80933
(719) 636-1155

1780 South Bellaire, Suite 700
Denver, CO 80222
(303) 758-2100 (inquiries)
(303) 758-2212 (complaints)

1730 S. College Ave., Suite 303
Fort Collins, CO 80525
(303) 484-1348

119 West 6th Street, Suite 203
Pueblo, CO 81003-3119
(719) 542-6464

Connecticut

2345 Black Rock Turnpike
Fairfield, CT 06430
(203) 374-6161

2080 Silas Deane Highway
Rocky Hill, CT 06067-2311
(203) 529-3575

100 South Turnpike Road
Wallingford, CT 06492-4395
(203) 269-2700 (inquiries)
(203) 269-4457 (complaints)

Delaware

2055 Limestone Road
Suite 200
Wilmington, DE 19808
(302) 996-9200

District of Columbia

1012 14th Street NW
14th Floor
Washington, DC 20005-3410
(202) 393-8000

Florida

In addition to the Better Business Bureaus, Florida has a number of Better Business Councils which are affiliated with local Chambers of Commerce throughout the state. The Better Business Councils are listed following the Better Business Bureaus.

Better Business Bureaus

P.O. Box 7950
Clearwater, FL 34618-7950
(813) 535-5522

2976-E Cleveland Avenue
Fort Myers, FL 33901
(813) 334-7331

3100 University Blvd., South
Suite 239
Jacksonville, FL 32216
(904) 721-2288

2605 Maitland Center Parkway
Maitland, FL 32751-7147
(407) 660-9500

16291 Northwest 57th Avenue
Miami, FL 33014-6709
(305) 625-0307
(inquiries for Dade County)
(305) 625-1302
(complaints for Dade County)
(305) 524-2803
(inquiries for Broward County)
(305) 527-1643
(complaints for Broward County)

P.O. Box 1511
Pensacola, FL 32597-1511
(904) 433-6111

1950 SE Port St. Lucie Blvd.
Suite 211
Port St. Lucie, FL 34952
(407) 878-2010
(407) 337-2083 (Martin County)

2247 Palm Beach Lakes Blvd.
Suite 211
West Palm Beach, FL 33409
(407) 686-2200

Better Business Councils

P.O. Box 3607
Lakeland, FL 33802-3607
(813) 680-1030 (Polk County)

P.O. Box 492426
Leesburg, FL 32749-2426
(904) 326-0770 (Lake County)

400 Fortenberry Road
Merritt Island, FL 32952
(407) 452-8869
(Central Brevard County)

13000 South Tamiami Trail
Suite 111
North Port, FL 34287
(813) 426-8744

4100 Dixie Highway NE
Palm Bay, FL 32905
(407) 984-8454
(South Brevard County)

1819 Main Street, Suite 240
Sarasota, FL 34236
(813) 366-3144

P.O. Drawer 2767
Titusville, FL 32781-2767
(407) 268-2822
(North Brevard County)

257 Tamiami Trail North
Venice, FL 34285-1534
(813) 485-3510

Georgia

1319-B Dawson Road
Albany, GA 31707
(912) 883-0744
1 (800) 868-4222 (toll free)

100 Edgewood Avenue
Suite 1012
Atlanta, GA 30303
(404) 688-4910

P.O. Box 2085
Augusta, GA 30903
(404) 722-1574

P.O. Box 2587
Columbus, GA 31902
(404) 324-0712

1765 Shurling Drive
Macon, GA 31211
(912) 742-7999

P.O. Box 13956
Savannah, GA 31416-0956
(912) 354-7521

Hawaii

1600 Kapiolani Boulevard
Suite 714
Honolulu, HI 96814
(808) 942-2355

Idaho

1333 West Jefferson
Boise, ID 83702
(208) 342-4649
(208) 467-5547
(Canyon County)

545 Shoup Avenue, Suite 210
Idaho Falls, ID 83402
(208) 523-9754

Illinois

211 West Wacker Drive
Chicago, IL 60606
(312) 444-1188 (inquiries)
(312) 346-3313 (complaints)

3024 West Lake
Peoria, IL 61615
(309) 688-3741

810 East State Street, 3rd Floor
Rockford, IL 61104
(815) 968-2222

Indiana

P.O. Box 405
Elkhart, IN 46515-0405
(219) 262-8996

4004 Morgan Avenue, Suite 201
Evansville, IN 47715
(812) 473-0202

1203 Webster Street
Fort Wayne, IN 46802
(219) 423-4433

4231 Cleveland Street
Gary, IN 46408
(219) 980-1511

Victoria Centre
22 East Washington Street
Suite 200
Indianapolis, IN 46204
(317) 637-0197

Marion, IN
1 (800) 552-4631 (toll free in IN)

Consumer Education Council
(non-BBB)
BSW WB 150
Muncie, IN 47306
(317) 285-5668

52303 Emmons Road, Suite 9
South Bend, IN 46637
(219) 277-9121

Iowa

852 Middle Road, Suite 290
Bettendorf, IA 52722-4100
(319) 355-6344

615 Insurance Exchange
Building
Des Moines, IA 50309
(515) 243-8137

318 Badgerow Building
Sioux City, IA 51101
(712) 252-4501

Kansas

501 Jefferson, Suite 24
Topeka, KS 66607-1190
(913) 232-0454

300 Kaufman Building
Wichita, KS 67202
(316) 263-3146

Kentucky

311 West Short Street
Lexington, KY 40507
(606) 259-1008

844 South 4th Street
Louisville, KY 40203-2186
(502) 583-6546

Louisiana

1605 Murray Street, Suite 117
Alexandria, LA 71301
(318) 473-4494

2055 Wooddale Boulevard
Baton Rouge, LA 70806-1519
(504) 926-3010

501 East Main Street
Houma, LA 70360
(504) 868-3456

P.O. Box 30297
Lafayette, LA 70593-0297
(318) 981-3497

P.O. Box 1681
Lake Charles, LA 70602
(318) 433-1633

141 De Siard Street, Suite 808
Monroe, LA 71201-7380
(318) 387-4600, 8421

1539 Jackson Avenue
New Orleans, LA 70130-3400
(504) 581-6222

1401 North Market Street
Shreveport, LA 71107-6525
(318) 221-8352

Maine

812 Stevens Avenue
Portland, ME 04103
(207) 878-2715

Maryland

2100 Huntingdon Avenue
Baltimore, MD 21211-3215
(301) 347-3990

Massachusetts

20 Park Plaza, Suite 820
Boston, MA 02116-4404
(617) 426-9000

Framingham, MA
1 (800) 422-2811 (toll free in MA)

78 North Street, Suite 1
Hyannis, MA 02601-3808
(508) 771-3022

Lawrence, MA
1 (800) 422-2811 (toll free in MA)

293 Bridge Street, Suite 320
Springfield, MA 01103
(413) 734-3114

P.O. Box 379
Worcester, MA 01601
(508) 755-2548

Michigan

620 Trust Building
Grand Rapids, MI 49503
(616) 774-8236

30555 Southfield Road
Suite 200
Southfield, MI 48076-7751
(313) 644-1012 (inquiries)
(313) 644-9136 (complaints)
(313) 644-9152 (Auto Line)
1 (800) 955-5100
(toll free nationwide auto line)

Minnesota

2706 Gannon Road
St. Paul, MN 55116
(612) 699-1111

Mississippi

460 Briarwood Drive, Suite 340
Jackson, MS 39206-3088
(601) 956-8282
1 (800) 274-7222
(toll free in MS)
(601) 957-2886
(automotive complaints only)

Missouri

306 East 12th Street,
Suite 1024
Kansas City, MO 64106-2418
(816) 421-7800

5100 Oakland Avenue
Suite 200
St. Louis, MO 63110
(314) 531-3300

205 Park Central East
Suite 509
Springfield, MO 65806
(417) 862-9231

Nebraska

719 North 48th Street
Lincoln, NE 68504-3491
(402) 467-5261

1613 Farnam Street, Room 417
Omaha, NE 68102-2158
(402) 346-3033

Nevada

1022 East Sahara Avenue
Las Vegas, NV 89104-1515
(702) 735-6900, 1969

P.O. Box 21269
Reno, NV 89515-1269
(702) 322-0657

New Hampshire

410 South Main Street
Concord, NH 03301
(603) 224-1991

New Jersey

494 Broad Street
Newark, NJ 07102
(201) 642-INFO

2 Forest Avenue
Paramus, NJ 07652
(201) 845-4044

1721 Route 37, East
Toms River, NJ 08753-8239
(201) 270-5577

1700 Whitehorse
Hamilton Square, Suite D-5
Trenton, NJ 08690
(609) 588-0808 (Mercer County)

P.O. Box 303
Westmont, NJ 08108-0303
(609) 854-8467

New Mexico

4600-A Montgomery NE
Suite 200
Albuquerque, NM 87109
(505) 884-0500
1 (800) 445-1461 (toll free in NM)

308 North Locke
Farmington, NM 87401
(505) 326-6501

2407 West Picacho, Suite B-2
Las Cruces, NM 88005
(505) 524-3130

New York

346 Delaware Avenue
Buffalo, NY 14202
(716) 856-7180

266 Main Street
Farmingdale, NY 11735
(516) 420-0500
1 (800) 955-5100
(toll free—Auto Line)

257 Park Avenue South
New York, NY 10010
(900) 463-6222
($0.85 per minute)

1122 Sibley Tower
Rochester, NY 14604-1084
(716) 546-6776

847 James Street, Suite 200
Syracuse, NY 13203
(315) 479-6635

1211 Route 9
Wappingers Falls, NY 12590
(914) 297-6550
1 (800) 955-5100
(toll free—Auto Line)

30 Glenn Street
White Plains, NY 10603
(914) 428-1230, 1231
1 (800) 955-5100
(toll free—Auto Line)

North Carolina

801 BB&T Building
Asheville, NC 28801
(704) 253-2392

1130 East Third Street
Suite 400
Charlotte, NC 28204-2626
(704) 332-7151

3608 West Friendly Avenue
Greensboro, NC 27410
(919) 852-4240, 4241, 4242

P.O. Box 1882
Hickory, NC 28603
(704) 464-0372

3120 Poplarwood Court
Suite 101
Raleigh, NC 27604-1080
(919) 872-9240

2110 Cloverdale Avenue
Suite 2-B
Winston-Salem, NC 27103
(919) 725-8348

Ohio

222 West Market Street
Akron, OH 44303-2111
(216) 253-4590

1434 Cleveland Avenue NW
Canton, OH 44703
(216) 454-9401

898 Walnut Street
Cincinnati, OH 45202
(513) 421-3015

2217 East 9th St., Suite 200
Cleveland, OH 44115-1299
(216) 241-7678

527 South High Street
Columbus, OH 43215
(614) 221-6336

40 West Fourth Street
Suite 1250
Dayton, OH 45402
(513) 222-5825
1 (800) 521-8357 (toll free in OH)

P.O. Box 269
Lima, OH 45802
(419) 223-7010

130 West 2nd Street
Mansfield, OH 44902-1915
(419) 522-1700

425 Jefferson Avenue
Suite 909
Toledo, OH 43604-1055
(419) 241-6276

345 North Market, Suite 202
Wooster, OH 44691
(216) 263-6444

P.O. Box 1495
Youngstown, OH 44501-1495
(216) 744-3111

Oklahoma

17 South Dewey
Oklahoma City, OK 73102
(405) 239-6860 (inquiries)
(405) 239-6081 (inquiries)
(405) 239-6083 (complaints)
6711 South Yale, Suite 230
Tulsa, OK 74136-3327
(918) 492-1266

Oregon

610 SW Alder St., Suite 615
Portland, OR 97205
(503) 226-3981
1 (800) 488-4166 (toll free in OR)

Pennsylvania

528 North New Street
Bethlehem, PA 18018
(215) 866-8780

6 Marion Court
Lancaster, PA 17602
(717) 291-1151
(717) 232-2800 (Harrisburg)
(717) 846-2700 (York County)
(717) 394-9318 (Auto Line)

P.O. Box 2297
Philadelphia, PA 19103-0297
(215) 496-1000

610 Smithfield Street
Pittsburgh, PA 15222
(412) 456-2700

P.O. Box 993
Scranton, PA 18501
(717) 342-9129, 655-0445

Puerto Rico

Condominium Olimpo Plaza
Suite 208
1002 Munoz Rivera Avenue
Rio Piedras, PR 00927
(809) 756-5400
(809) 767-0446

Rhode Island

Bureau Park
P.O. Box 1300
Warwick, RI 02887-1300
(401) 785-1212 (inquiries)
(401) 785-1213 (complaints)

South Carolina

1830 Bull Street
Columbia, SC 29201
(803) 254-2525

311 Pettigru Street
Greenville, SC 29601
(803) 242-5052

1310-G Azalea Court
Myrtle Beach, SC 29577
(803) 497-8667

Tennessee

P.O. Box 1178 TCAS
Blountville, TN 37617
(615) 323-6311

1010 Market Street, Suite 200
Chattanooga, TN 37402-2614
(615) 266-6144
(also serves Whitfield and Murray
counties in GA)
(615) 479-6096
(Bradley County only)

900 East Hill Avenue, Suite 165
Knoxville, TN 37915-2525
(615) 522-2552

P.O. Box 750704
Memphis, TN 38175-0704
(901) 795-8771

Sovran Plaza, Suite 1830
Nashville, TN 37239
(615) 254-5872

Texas

3300 S. 14th Street, Suite 307
Abilene, TX 79605
(915) 691-1533

P.O. Box 1905
Amarillo, TX 79105-1905
(806) 379-6222

708 Colorado, Suite 720
Austin, TX 78701-3028
(512) 476-1616

P.O. Box 2988
Beaumont, TX 77704-2988
(409) 835-5348

202 Varisco Building
Bryan, TX 77803
(409) 823-8148, 8149

4535 S. Padre Island Drive
Suite 28
Corpus Christi, TX 78411
(512) 854-2892

2001 Bryan Street, Suite 850
Dallas, TX 75201
(214) 220-2000
1 (800) 442-1456 (toll free in TX)

5160 Montana, Lower Level
El Paso, TX 79903
(915) 772-2727

512 Main Street, Suite 807
Fort Worth, TX 76102
(817) 332-7585

2707 North Loop West
Suite 900
Houston, TX 77008
(713) 868-9500

P.O. Box 1178
Lubbock, TX 79408-1178
(806) 763-0459

P.O. Box 60206
Midland, TX 79711-0206
(915) 563-1880
1 (800) 592-4433
(toll free in 915 area code)

P.O. Box 3366
San Angelo, TX 76902-3366
(915) 949-2989

1800 Northeast Loop 410
Suite 400
San Antonio, TX 78217
(512) 828-9441

P.O. Box 6652
Tyler, TX 75711-6652
(903) 581-5704

P.O. Box 7203
Waco, TX 76714-7203
(817) 772-7530

P.O. Box 69
Weslaco, TX 78596-0069
(512) 968-3678

1106 Brook Street
Wichita Falls, TX 76301-5079
(817) 723-5526

Utah

1588 South Main Street
Salt Lake City, UT 84115
(801) 487-4656

Virginia

4022B Plank Road
Fredericksburg, VA 22407
(703) 786-8397

3608 Tidewater Drive
Norfolk, VA 23509-1499
(804) 627-5651

701 East Franklin Street
Suite 712
Richmond, VA 23219
(804) 648-0016

31 West Campbell Avenue
Roanoke, VA 24011-1301
(703) 342-3455

Washington

127 West Canal Drive
Kennewick, WA 99336-3819
(509) 582-0222

2200 Sixth Avenue, Suite 828
Seattle, WA 98121-1857
(206) 448-8888
(206) 448-6222
(24-hour business reporting system)

South 176 Stevens
Spokane, WA 99204-1393
(509) 747-1155

P.O. Box 1274
Tacoma, WA 98401-1274
(206) 383-5561

P.O. Box 1584
Yakima, WA 98907-1584
(509) 248-1326

Wisconsin

740 North Plankinton Avenue
Milwaukee, WI 53203
(414) 273-1600 (inquiries)
(414) 273-0123 (complaints)

Wyoming

BBB/Idaho Falls
(serves Teton, Park, and Lincoln
counties in Wyoming)
545 Shoup Avenue, Suite 210
Idaho Falls, ID 83402
(208) 523-9754

BBB/Fort Collins
(serves all other Wyoming Counties)
1730 South College Avenue
Suite 303
Fort Collins, CO 80525
1 (800) 873-3222 (toll free in WY)

Appendix F:
Federal Information Center

The Federal Information Center (FIC), administered by the General Services Administration, can help you find information about federal government services, programs and regulations. The FIC also can tell you which federal agency to contact for help with problems.

Simply call the telephone number listed for your metropolitan area or state. All the 800 numbers on this list are toll free. These 800 numbers can be called only from within the states and cities listed. If your area is not listed, please call (301) 722-9098. If you would prefer to write, please mail your inquiry to the Federal Information Center, P.O. Box 600, Cumberland, MD 21502.

Users of Telecommunications Devices for the Deaf (TDD/TTY) may call toll free from any point in the United States by dialing 1 (800) 326-2996.

Alabama
Birmingham, Mobile
1 (800) 366-2998

Alaska
Anchorage
1 (800) 729-8003

Arizona
Phoenix
1 (800) 359-3997

Arkansas
Little Rock
1 (800) 366-2998

California
Los Angeles, San Diego,
San Francisco, Santa Ana
1 (800) 726-4995
Sacramento
(916) 973-1695

Colorado
Colorado Springs, Denver, Pueblo
1 (800) 359-3997

Connecticut
Hartford, New Haven
1 (800) 347-1997

Florida
Ft. Lauderdale, Jacksonville, Miami,
Orlando, St. Petersburg, Tampa,
West Palm Beach
1 (800) 347-1997

Georgia
Atlanta
1 (800) 347-1997

Hawaii
Honolulu
1 (800) 733-5996

Illinois
Chicago
1 (800) 366-2998

Indiana
Gary
1 (800) 366-2998
Indianapolis
1 (800) 347-1997

Iowa
All locations
1 (800) 735-8004

Kansas
All locations
1 (800) 735-8004

Kentucky
Louisville
1 (800) 347-1997

Louisiana
New Orleans
1 (800) 366-2998

Maryland
Baltimore
1 (800) 347-1997

Massachusetts
Boston
1 (800) 347-1997

Michigan
Detroit, Grand Rapids
1 (800) 347-1997

Minnesota
Minneapolis
1 (800) 366-2998

Missouri
St. Louis,
1 (800) 366-2998
All other locations
1 (800) 735-8004

Nebraska
Omaha
1 (800) 366-2998
All other locations
1 (800) 735-8004

New Jersey
Newark, Trenton
1 (800) 347-1997

New Mexico
Albuquerque
1 (800) 359-3997

New York
Albany, Buffalo, New York,
Rochester, Syracuse
1 (800) 347-1997

North Carolina
Charlotte
1 (800) 347-1997

Ohio
Akron, Cincinnati, Cleveland,
Columbus, Dayton, Toledo
1 (800) 347-1997

Oklahoma
Oklahoma City, Tulsa
1 (800) 366-2998

Oregon
Portland
1 (800) 726-4995

Pennsylvania
Philadelphia, Pittsburgh
1 (800) 347-1997

Rhode Island
Providence
1 (800) 347-1997

Tennessee
Chattanooga
1 (800) 347-1997
Memphis, Nashville
1 (800) 366-2998

Texas
Austin, Dallas, Fort Worth,
Houston, San Antonio
1 (800) 366-2998

Utah
Salt Lake City
1 (800) 359-3997

Virginia
Norfolk, Richmond, Roanoke
1 (800) 347-1997

Washington
Seattle, Tacoma
1 (800) 726-4995

Wisconsin
Milwaukee
1 (800) 366-2998

Appendix G:
Selected Federal Agencies

Many federal agencies have enforcement and/or complaint-handling duties for products and services used by the general public. Others act for the benefit of the public, but do not resolve individual consumer problems.

Agencies also have fact sheets, booklets, and other information which might be helpful in making purchase decisions and dealing with consumer problems. If you need help in deciding where to go with your consumer problem, check the index at the end of this book or call the nearest Federal Information Center listed on page 253. The Federal agencies listed in this appendix respond to consumer complaints and inquiries.

Commission on Civil Rights

Look in your telephone directory under "U.S. Government, Civil Rights Commission." If it does not appear, call the appropriate FIC number (see page 253), or contact:

Commission on Civil Rights
1121 Vermont Avenue NW, Suite 800
Washington, DC 20425
1 (800) 552-6843
(toll free—complaint referral outside DC)
(202) 376-8512
(complaint referral in DC)
(202) 376-8116
(TDD—nationwide complaint referral)
(202) 376-8105 (publications)
(202) 376-8312 (public affairs)

Commodity Futures Trading Commission (CFTC)
2033 K Street NW
Washington, DC 20581
(202) 254-3067 (complaints only)
(202) 254-8630 (information)

Consumer Information Center (CIC)
Pueblo, CO 81009
You can obtain a free *Consumer Information Catalog* by writing to the above address or by calling (719) 948-4000.

Department of Agriculture (USDA)

Agricultural Marketing Service
Department of Agriculture
Washington, DC 20250
(202) 447-8998

Animal and Plant Health Inspection Service
Public Information
Department of Agriculture
Federal Building, Room 700
6505 Belcrest Road
Hyattsville, MD 20782
(301) 436-7799

Cooperative Extension Service
Department of Agriculture
Washington, DC 20250
(202) 447-3029
(202) 755-2799 (TDD)
Or consult county or city government listings in your local telephone directory for the number of your local Cooperative Extension Service office.

Farmers Home Administration
Department of Agriculture
Washington, DC 20250
(202) 447-4323

Food and Nutrition Service
Department of Agriculture
3101 Park Center Drive
Alexandria, VA 22302
(703) 756-3276

Human Nutrition Information Service
Department of Agriculture
Federal Building
Rooms 360 and 364
6505 Belcrest Road
Hyattsville, MD 20782
(301) 436-8617, 7725

Inspector General's Hotline
Office of the Inspector General
Department of Agriculture
P.O. Box 23399
Washington, DC 20026
1 (800) 424-9121 (toll free)

Meat and Poultry Hotline
Food Safety and Inspection Service
Department of Agriculture
Washington, DC 20250
(202) 447-3333
(voice/TDD)
1 (800) 535-4555
(toll free voice/TDD outside DC)

Office of the Consumer Advisor
Department of Agriculture
Washington, DC 20250
(202) 382-9681

Office of Public Affairs
Visitor Information Center
Department of Agriculture
Washington, DC 20250
(202) 447-2791

Department of Commerce

Bureau of the Census
Customer Services
Data User Services Division
Department of Commerce
Washington, DC 20233
(301) 763-4100

Office of Consumer Affairs
Department of Commerce
Room 5718
Washington, DC 20230
(202) 377-5001

National Institute of Standards and Technology
Office of Weights and Measures
Department of Commerce
Washington, DC 20234
(301) 975-4004

National Marine Fisheries Service
Office of Trade and Industry Services
Department of Commerce
1335 East-West Highway
Silver Spring, MD 20910
(301) 427-2355
(inspection and safety)
(301) 427-2358
(nutrition information)

Constituent Affairs
National Weather Service
Department of Commerce
Washington, DC 20901
(301) 427-7258

Metric Program Office
Department of Commerce
Room H4845
Washington, DC 20230
(202) 377-0944

Patent and Trademark Office
Department of Commerce
Washington, DC 20231
(703) 557-3341

Department of Defense

Office of National Ombudsman
National Committee for Employer
Support of the Guard and Reserve
1555 Wilson Boulevard, Suite 200
Arlington, VA 22209-2405
(703) 696-1400
1 (800) 336-4590 (toll free outside
DC metropolitan area)
Provides assistance with employer/
employee problems for members of
the Guard and Reserve and their
employers.

Department of Education

Clearinghouse on Disability Information
OSERS
Department of Education
Room 330, C Street SW
Washington, DC 20202-2524
(202) 732-1241
(202) 732-1265 (TDD)

Consumer Affairs Staff
OIIA
Department of Education
Room 3061
Washington, DC 20202
(202) 401-3679

Federal Student Financial Aid Programs
Public Documents
Distribution Center
31451 United Avenue
Pueblo, CO 81009-8109
(202) 708-8391

National Clearinghouse on Bilingual Education Hotline
Department of Education
1118 22nd Street NW
Washington, DC 20037
(202) 467-0867
1 (800) 321-NCBE
(toll free outside DC)

Office of Public Affairs
Department of Education
400 Maryland Avenue SW
Washington, DC 20202
(202) 401-3020

Center for Choices in Education
400 Maryland Avenue, S.W.
Room 3077
Washington, DC 20202
1 (800) 442-PICK (toll free)

Department of Energy

For information about conservation
and renewable energy:
**National Appropriate Technology
Assistance Service**
Department of Energy
P.O. Box 2525
Butte, MT 59702-2525
1 (800) 428-1718
(toll free in MT)
1 (800) 428-2525
(toll free outside MT)

**Conservation and Renewable
Energy Inquiry and Referral
Service**
Department of Energy
P.O. Box 8900
Silver Spring, MD 20907
1 (800) 523-2929 (toll free)

**Office of Scientific and Technical
Information**
Department of Energy
P.O. Box 62
Oak Ridge, TN 37831
(written inquiries only)

**Office of Consumer and
Public Liaison**
Department of Energy
Washington, DC 20585
(202) 586-5373

**Office of Conservation and
Renewable Energy**
Weatherization Assistance Inquiries:
Department of Energy
Washington, DC 20585
(202) 586-2204

**Department of Health and
Human Services (HHS)**

**AIDS Hotline
Acquired Immune Deficiency
Syndrome**
1 (800) 342-AIDS (toll free)

Cancer Hotline
1 (800) 4-CANCER (toll free)
During daytime hours, callers in
California, Florida, Georgia, Illinois,
Northern New Jersey, New York, and
Texas may ask for Spanish-speaking
staff members.

**Food and Drug
Administration (FDA)**
Look in your telephone directory
under "U.S. Government, Health and
Human Services Department, Food
and Drug Administration." If it does
not appear, call the appropriate FIC
number (see page 253) or contact:
**Consumer Affairs and
Information Staff**
Food and Drug Administration
(HFE-88)
Department of Health and
Human Services
5600 Fishers Lane
Room 16-85
Rockville, MD 20857
(301) 443-3170

**Division of Beneficiary Services
Health Care Financing
Administration (HCFA)**
Department of Health and
Human Services
6325 Security Boulevard
Baltimore, MD 21207
1 (800) 638-6833 (toll free)
(This is a taped answering service; a
specialist will return your call.)

**Hill-Burton Free Hospital Care
Hotline**
1 (800) 492-0359
(toll free in MD)
1 (800) 638-0742
(toll free outside MD)

**Inspector General's Hotline
HHS/OIG/Hotline**
P.O. Box 17303
Baltimore, MD 21203-7303
1 (800) 368-5779 (toll free)

**National Center on Child Abuse
and Neglect**
Department of Health and
Human Services
330 C Street SW
Washington, DC 20201
(202) 245-0586

**National Health Information
Center**
Department of Health and
Human Services
P.O. Box 1133
Washington, DC 20013-1133
(301) 565-4167
(Washington Metro Area)
1 (800) 336-4797 (toll free)

National Runaway Switchboard
1 (800) 621-4000 (toll free)

**Office of Child Support
Enforcement**
Department of Health and
Human Services
Washington, DC 20201
(202) 401-9387

Office for Civil Rights
Department of Health and
Human Services
Washington, DC 20201
(202) 245-6671
1 (800) 863-0100
(toll free outside DC)
(202) 368-1019 (TDD)

Office of Prepaid Health Care
Operations and Oversight HCFA
Department of Health and
Human Services
Washington, DC 20201
(202) 619-3555

**President's Council on Physical
Fitness and Sports**
Department of Health and
Human Services
450 5th Street NW
Suite 7103
Washington, DC 20001
(202) 272-3430

Second Surgical Opinion Program
Department of Health and
Human Services
Washington, DC 20201
1 (800) 838-6833
(toll free outside DC)

Social Security Administration
1 (800) SSA-1213 (toll free)

**Department of Housing and
Urban Development (HUD)**

HUD Fraud Hotline
(202) 708-4200
1 (800) 347-3735
(toll free outside DC)

**Interstate Land Sales
Registration Division**
Department of Housing and
Urban Development
Room 6278
Washington, DC 20410
(202) 708-0502

**Manufactured Housing and
Construction Standards Division**
Department of Housing and
Urban Development
Room 9158
Washington, DC 20410
(202) 708-2210

**Office of Fair Housing and
Equal Opportunity**
Department of Housing and
Urban Development
Room 5100
Washington, DC 20410
(202) 708-4252
1 (800) 424-8590
(toll free outside DC)

Office of Single Family Housing
Department of Housing and
Urban Development
Room 9282
Washington, DC 20410
(202) 708-3175

Office of Urban Rehabilitation
Department of Housing and
Urban Development
Room 7168
Washington, DC 20410
(202) 708-2685

Title I Insurance Division
Department of Housing and
Urban Development
Room 9156
Washington, DC 20410
(202) 708-1590

Department of the Interior

Bureau of Indian Affairs
Department of the Interior
Washington, DC 20240
(202) 208-4190

Bureau of Land Management
Department of the Interior
Washington, DC 20240
(202) 208-5717

Consumer Affairs Administrator
Office of the Secretary
Department of the Interior
Washington, DC 20240
(202) 208-5521

National Park Service
Department of the Interior
Washington, DC 20240
(202) 208-4917

**United States Fish and
Wildlife Service**
Department of the Interior
Washington, DC 20240
(703) 358-2156

United States Geological Survey
Department of the Interior
12201 Sunrise Valley Drive
Reston, VA 22092
(703) 648-4427

Department of Justice

Antitrust Division
Department of Justice
Washington, DC 20530
(202) 514-2401

Civil Rights Division
Look in your telephone directory
under "U.S. Government, Justice
Department, Civil Rights Division."
If it does not appear, call the
appropriate FIC number (see
page 253) or contact:
Civil Rights Division
Department of Justice
Washington, DC 20530
(202) 514-2151
(202) 514-0716 (TDD)

Drug Enforcement Administration
(DEA) Look in your telephone direc-
tory under "U.S. Government, Justice
Department, Drug Enforcement
Administration." If it does not appear,
call the appropriate FIC number (see
page 253) or contact:
Drug Enforcement Administration
Department of Justice
Washington, DC 20537
(202) 307-8000

**Federal Bureau of Investigation
(FBI)**
Look inside the front cover of your
telephone directory for the number
of the nearest FBI office. If it does not
appear, look under "U.S. Government,
Justice Department, Federal Bureau of
Investigation." You may also contact:
Federal Bureau of Investigation
Department of Justice
Washington, DC 20535
(202) 324-3000

Immigration and Naturalization Service (INS)
Look in your telephone directory under "U.S. Government, Justice Department, Immigration and Naturalization Service." If it does not appear, call the appropriate FIC number (see page 253) or contact:
Immigration and Naturalization Service
Department of Justice
425 I Street NW
Washington, DC 20536
(202) 514-4316

Department of Labor

Bureau of Labor-Management Relations and Cooperative Programs
Department of Labor
Washington, DC 20210
(202) 523-6098

Coordinator of Consumer Affairs
Department of Labor
Washington, DC 20210
(202) 523-6060 (general inquiries)

Employment and Training Administration
Look in your telephone directory under "U.S. Government, Labor Department, Employment and Training Administration." If it does not appear, call the appropriate FIC number (see page 253) or contact:
Employment and Training Administration
Director, Office of Public Affairs
Department of Labor
Washington, DC 20210
(202) 523-6871

Employment Standards Administration
Office of Public Affairs
Department of Labor
Washington, DC 20210
(202) 523-8743

Mine Safety and Health Administration
Office of Information and Public Affairs
Department of Labor
Ballston Towers #3
Arlington, VA 22203
(703) 235-1452

Occupational Safety and Health Administration (OSHA)
Look in your telephone directory under "U.S. Government, Labor Department, Occupational Safety and Health Administration." If it does not appear, call the appropriate FIC number (see page 253) or contact:
Occupational Safety and Health Administration
Office of Information and Consumer Affairs
Department of Labor
Washington, DC 20210
(202) 523-8151

Office of the Assistant Secretary for Veterans' Employment and Training
Department of Labor
Washington, DC 20210
(202) 523-9116
1 (800) 442-2VET
(toll free—Veterans' Job Rights Hotline)

Office of Labor-Management Standards
Department of Labor
Washington, DC 20210
(202) 523-7343

Pension and Welfare Benefits Administration
Office of Program Services
Department of Labor
Washington, DC 20210
(202) 523-8776

**Women's Bureau
The Work and Family
Clearinghouse**
Department of Labor
Washington, DC 20210
1 (800) 827-5335 (toll free)
Employers may contact this office for
information about dependent care
(child and/or elder care) policies.

**Women's Bureau
The Workforce Quality
Clearinghouse**
Department of Labor
Washington, DC 20210
1 (800) 523-0525
(toll free outside DC)
Employers may contact this office for
information about workplace quality
resources, e.g., employee training and
skills development.

Department of State

Overseas Citizen Services
Department of State
Washington, DC 20520
(202) 647-3666 (non-emergencies)
(202) 647-5225 (emergencies)

**Passport Services
Washington Passport Agency**
1425 K Street NW
Washington, DC 20524
(202) 647-0518

Visa Services
Department of State
Washington, DC 20520
(202) 647-0510

**Department of Transportation
(DOT)**

Air Safety:
**Federal Aviation Administration
(FAA)**
Community and Consumer Liaison
Division
FAA (APA–200)
Washington, DC 20591
(202) 267-3479, 8592
1 (800) FAA-SURE
(toll free outside DC)

Airline Service Complaints:
**Office of Intergovernmental and
Consumer Affairs (I-25)**
Department of Transportation
Washington, DC 20590
(202) 366-2220

Auto Safety Hotline:
**National Highway Traffic Safety
Administration (NHTSA)
(NEF-11)**
Department of Transportation
Washington, DC 20690
(202) 366-0123
(202) 755-8919 (TDD)
1 (800) 424-9153
(toll free TDD outside DC)

Boating Safety Classes:
**United States Coast Guard Office
of Boating, Public and Consumer
Affairs (G-NAB-5)**
Department of Transportation
Washington, DC 20593
(202) 267-0972

Boating Safety Hotline:
United States Coast Guard
Department of Transportation
Washington, DC 20593
(202) 267-0780
1 (800) 368-5647 (toll free)

Oil and Chemical Spills:
National Response Center
United States Coast Guard
Headquarters, G-TGC-2
Department of Transportation
Washington, DC 20593
(202) 267-2675
1 (800) 424-8802
(toll free outside DC)

Railway Safety:
Federal Railroad Administration
Office of Safety (RRS-20)
Department of Transportation
Washington, DC 20590
(202) 366-0522

Department of the Treasury

Bureau of Alcohol, Tobacco and Firearms
Look in your telephone directory under "U.S. Government, Treasury Department, Bureau of Alcohol, Tobacco and Firearms." If it does not appear, call the appropriate FIC number (see page 253) or contact:
Bureau of Alcohol, Tobacco and Firearms
Department of the Treasury
Room 5500
650 Massachusetts Avenue NW
Washington, DC 20226
(202) 535-6379

To report lost or stolen explosives, or to report explosive incidents or bombings, call:
(202) 566-7777
1 (800) 424-9555
(toll free outside DC)
(202) 789-3000

Bureau of Engraving and Printing
Congressional and Media
Affairs Division
Department of the Treasury
14th and C Streets SW, Room 533M
Washington, DC 20228
(202) 447-0193

Bureau of the Public Debt
Public Affairs Officer
Office of the Commissioner
Department of the Treasury
999 E Street NW, Room 553
Washington, DC 20239-0001
(202) 376-4302

Comptroller of the Currency
The Comptroller of the Currency handles complaints about national banks, i.e., banks that have the word "National" in their names or the initials "N.A." after their names. For assistance, look in your telephone directory under "U.S. Government, Treasury Department, Comptroller of the Currency." If it does not appear, call the appropriate FIC number (see page 253) or contact:
Comptroller of the Currency
Director, Compliance Policy
Department of the Treasury
250 E Street SW
Washington, DC 20219
(202) 874-4820

Financial Management Service
Office of Legislative and Public Affairs
Department of the Treasury
401 14th Street SW
Room 555
Washington, DC 20227
(202) 287-0669

Internal Revenue Service (IRS)
Look in your telephone directory under "U.S. Government, Treasury Department, Internal Revenue Service." If it does not appear, call the appropriate FIC number (see page 253).

Office of Thrift Supervision
(formerly Federal Home Loan
Bank Board)
The Office of Thrift Supervision
handles complaints about savings
and loan associations and savings
banks. For assistance contact:
Office of Thrift Supervision
Consumer Affairs
1700 G Street NW
Washington, DC 20552
(202) 906-6237
1 (800) 842-6929
(toll free outside DC)

United States Customs Service
Look in your telephone directory
under "U.S. Government, Treasury
Department, U.S. Customs Service."
If it does not appear, call the appro-
priate FIC number (see page 253).

To report fraudulent import practices, call U.S. Customs Service's
Fraud Hotline:
1 (800) USA-FAKE (toll free)

To report drug smuggling activity,
call U.S. Customs Service's
Narcotics Hotline:
1 (800) BE-ALERT (toll free)

United States Mint
Customer Relations Division
Department of the Treasury
10001 Aerospace Road
Lanham, MD 20706
(301) 436-7400

**United States Savings Bonds
Division**
Office of Public Affairs
Department of the Treasury
Washington, DC 20220
(202) 634-5389
1 (800) US-BONDS
(toll-free recording)

**Department of Veterans Affairs
(VA)**

For information about VA medical care
or benefits, write, call, or visit your
nearest VA facility. Your telephone
directory will list a VA medical center
or regional office under "U.S.
Government, Department of Veterans
Affairs," or under "U.S. Government,
Veterans Administration." You may
also contact the offices listed below.

For information about benefits:
**Veterans Benefits Administration
(27)**
Department of Veterans Affairs
810 Vermont Avenue NW
Washington, DC 20420
(202) 233-2576

For information about medical care:
**Veterans Health Administration
(184C)**
810 Vermont Avenue NW
Washington, DC 20420
(202) 535-7208

For information about burials, head-
stones, or markers, and presidential
memorial certificates:
National Cemetery System (40H)
Department of Veterans Affairs
810 Vermont Avenue NW
Washington, DC 20420
(202) 535-7856

For consumer information or
general assistance:
Consumer Affairs Service
Department of Veterans Affairs
810 Vermont Avenue NW
Washington, DC 20420
(202) 535-8962

Environmental Protection Agency (EPA)

Asbestos Action Program
(202) 382-3949

Emergency Planning and Community Right-to-Know Information Hotline
Environmental Protection Agency
Washington, DC 20460
(202) 479-2449
1 (800) 535-0202
(toll free outside AK and DC)

Inspector General's Whistle Blower Hotline
(202) 382-4977
1 (800) 424-4000
(toll free outside DC)

National Pesticides Telecommunications Network (NPTN)
(806) 743-3091
1 (800) 858-PEST
(toll free outside TX)

Office of External Relations
Environmental Protection Agency
Washington, DC 20460
(202) 382-4454

Public Information Center
PIC (PM-211B)
Environmental Protection Agency
Washington, DC 20460
(202) 382-2080 (general information)

Resource Conservation and Recovery Act
RCRA/Superfund Hotline
Environmental Protection Agency
Washington, DC 20460
(703) 920-9810
1 (800) 424-9346
(toll free outside DC)

Safe Drinking Water Hotline
(202) 382-5533
1 (800) 426-4791
(toll free outside DC)

Toxic Substances Control Act Assistance Information Service
Environmental Protection Agency
Washington, DC 20024
(202) 554-1404

Equal Employment Opportunity Commission

Look in your telephone directory under "U.S. Government, Equal Employment Opportunity Commission." If it does not appear, call the appropriate FIC number (see page 253) or contact:
Office of Communications and Legislative Affairs
Equal Employment Opportunity Commission
1801 L Street NW
Washington, DC 20507
(202) 663-4900
(202) 663-4494 (TDD)
1 (800) USA-EEOC (toll free)
1 (800) 800-3302 (toll free TDD)

Federal Communications Commission (FCC)

Complaints about telephone systems:
Common Carrier Bureau
Informal Complaints Branch
Federal Communications Commission
2025 M Street NW
Room 6202
Washington, DC 20554
(202) 632-7553
(202) 634-1855 (TDD)

General Information:
Consumer Assistance and Small Business Office
Federal Communications Commission
1919 M Street N.W.
Room 254
Washington, DC 20554
(202) 632-7000
(202) 632-6999 (TDD)

Complaints about radio or television:
Mass Media Bureau
Complaints and Investigations
Federal Communications Commission
2025 M Street NW
Room 8210
Washington, DC 20554
(202) 632-7048

Federal Deposit Insurance Corporation (FDIC)

FDIC handles questions about deposit insurance coverage and complaints about FDIC-insured state banks which are not members of the Federal Reserve System. For assistance, look in your telephone directory under "U.S. Government, Federal Deposit Insurance Corporation." If it does not appear, call the appropriate FIC number (see page 253) or contact:
Office of Consumer Affairs
Federal Deposit Insurance
Corporation
550 17th Street NW
Washington, DC 20429
(202) 898-3536
(202) 898-3535 (voice/TDD)
1 (800) 424-5488
(toll free outside DC)

Federal Emergency Management Agency
Look in your telephone directory under "U.S. Government, Federal Emergency Management Agency." If it does not appear, call the appropriate FIC number (see page 253) or contact:
Emergency Preparedness and Response
Office of the External
Affairs Directorate
Federal Emergency
Management Agency
Washington, DC 20472
(202) 646-4000

Federal Insurance Administration
Federal Emergency
Management Agency
Washington, DC 20472
(202) 646-2781
1 (800) 638-6620 (toll free)

Office of Disaster Assistance Programs
Federal Emergency
Management Agency
Washington, DC 20472
(202) 646-3615

U.S. Fire Administration
Federal Emergency Management
Agency NETC
16825 South Seton Avenue
Emmitsburg, MD 21727
(301) 447-1080
(202) 646-2449

Federal Maritime Commission

Office of Informal Inquiries and Complaints
1100 L Street NW
Washington, DC 20573
(202) 523-5807

Federal Reserve System

The Board of Governors handles consumer complaints about state-chartered banks and trust companies which are members of the Federal Reserve System. For assistance, look in your telephone directory under "U.S. Government, Federal Reserve System, Board of Governors," or "Federal Reserve Bank." If neither appears, call the appropriate FIC number (see page 253) or contact:
Board of Governors of the Federal Reserve System
Division of Consumer and
Community Affairs
Washington, DC 20551
(202) 452-3946
(202) 452-3544 (TDD)

Federal Trade Commission (FTC)

Look in your telephone directory under "U.S. Government, Federal Trade Commission." If it does not appear, call the appropriate FIC number (see page 253) or contact:
Correspondence Branch
Federal Trade Commission
Washington, DC 20580
(written complaints only)

Public Reference Section
Federal Trade Commission
6th & Pennsylvania Ave. NW
Room 130
Washington, DC 20580
(202) 326-2222 (publications)

General Services Administration (GSA)

Business Service Centers
Look in your telephone directory under "U.S. Government, General Services Administration." If this does not appear, call the appropriate FIC number (see page 253).

Federal Information Center
(see page 253)

Federal Information Relay Service
7th & D Streets SW
Room 6040
Washington, DC 20407
(202) 708-9300 (TDD)
1 (800) 877-8339
(toll free voice/TDD outside DC)

Surplus Federal Property Sales
Look in your telephone directory under "U.S. Government, General Services Administration." If it does not appear, call the appropriate FIC number (see page 253).

Government Printing Office (GPO)

Government Publications:
Publications Service Section
Government Printing Office
Washington, DC 20402
(202) 275-3050

Subscriptions to Government Periodicals:
Subscription Research Section
Government Printing Office
Washington, DC 20402
(202) 275-3054

Interstate Commerce Commission (ICC)

Office of Compliance and Consumer Assistance
Washington, DC 20423
(202) 275-7148

National Archives and Records Administration

Reference Services Branch
National Archives and Records Administration
Washington, DC 20408
(202) 501-5400
(202) 501-5404 (TDD)

Federal Register
National Archives and Records Administration
Washington, DC 20408
(202) 523-5240
(202) 523-5229 (TDD)

Publications Services
National Archives and Records Administration
Washington, DC 20408
(202) 501-5240
(202) 501-5404 (TDD)

National Credit Union Administration

Look in your telephone directory under "U.S. Government, National Credit Union Administration." If it does not appear, call the appropriate FIC number (see page 253) or contact:

National Credit Union Administration
1776 G Street NW
Washington, DC 20456
(202) 682-9640

National Labor Relations Board

Office of the Executive Secretary
1717 Pennsylvania Ave. NW
Room 701
Washington, DC 20570
(202) 254-9430

Nuclear Regulatory Commission (NRC)

Office of Governmental and Public Affairs
Washington, DC 20555
(301) 492-0240

Pension Benefit Guaranty Corporation
2020 K Street NW
Washington, DC 20006-1860
(202) 778-8800
(202) 778-8859 (TDD)

Postal Rate Commission
Office of the Consumer Advocate
Postal Rate Commission
1333 H Street NW
Suite 300
Washington, DC 20268
(202) 789-6830

President's Committee on Employment of People with Disabilities
1111 20th Street NW
Suite 636
Washington, DC 20036-3470
(202) 653-5044
(202) 653-5050 (TDD)

Railroad Retirement Board
844 Rush Street
Chicago, IL 60611
(312) 751-4500

Securities and Exchange Commission (SEC)

Office of Filings, Information, and Consumer Services
450 5th Street NW
(Mail Stop 2–6)
Washington, DC 20549
(202) 272-7440 (investor complaints)
(202) 272-7450 (filings by corporations and other regulated entities)
(202) 272-5624 (SEC Information Line—general topics and sources of assistance)

Small Business Administration (SBA)

Office of Consumer Affairs
409 Third Street SW
Washington, DC 20416
(202) 205-6948
(complaints only)
1 (800) U-ASK-SBA
(toll free—information)

Tennessee Valley Authority (TVA)

Regional Communications
400 West Summit Hill Drive
Knoxville, TN 37902
(615) 632-7196
(615) 751-8500 (TDD)

U.S. Consumer Product Safety Commission (CPSC)

To report a hazardous product or a product-related injury, or to inquire about product recalls, call or write:
Product Safety Hotline
U.S. Consumer Product Safety Commission
Washington, DC 20207
1 (800) 638-CPSC (toll free)
1 (800) 638-8270
(toll free TDD outside MD)
1 (800) 492-8104
(toll free TDD in MD)

United States Postal Service

If you experience difficulty when ordering merchandise or conducting business transactions through the mail, or suspect that you have been the victim of a mail fraud or misrepresentation scheme, contact your postmaster or local Postal Inspector. Look in your telephone directory under "U.S. Government, Postal Service U.S." for these local listings. If they do not appear, contact:
Chief Postal Inspector
United States Postal Service
Washington, DC 20260-2100
(202) 268-4267

For consumer convenience, all post offices and letter carriers have postage-free Consumer Service Cards available for reporting mail problems and submitting comments and suggestions. If the problem cannot be resolved using the Consumer Service Card or through direct contact with the local post office, write or call:
Consumer Advocate
United States Postal Service
Washington, DC 20260-6720
(202) 268-2284
(202) 268-2310 (TDD)

Index